BEACON
BIBLE
EXPOSITIONS

BEACON BIBLE EXPOSITIONS

BEACON BIBLE EXPOSITIONS

VOLUME 9

PHILIPPIANS COLOSSIANS PHILEMON

by

JOHN A. KNIGHT

Editors
WILLIAM M. GREATHOUSE
J. FRED PARKER

BEACON HILL PRESS OF KANSAS CITY
Kansas City, Missouri

Library of Congress Catalog Card No. 74-78052
ISBN: 083-410-3206

Printed in the United States of America

Permission to quote from the following Scripture versions is acknowledged with appreciation:

The Holy Bible, American Standard Version (ASV), copyright 1901 by Thomas Nelson & Sons, New York.

The Bible: A New Translation (Moffatt), copyright 1954 by James A. R. Moffatt. By permission of Harper and Row, Publishers, Inc.

The *New American Standard Bible* (NASB), © The Lockman Foundation, 1960, 1962, 1963, 1968, 1971, 1972, 1973, 1975, 1977.

The *Modern Language Bible,* the *New Berkeley Version in Modern English* (NBV), copyright © 1945, 1959, 1969 by Zondervan Publishing House.

The *New English Bible* (NEB), © The Delegates of the Oxford University Press and The Syndics of the Cambridge University Press, 1961, 1970.

The Holy Bible, New International Version (NIV), copyright © 1978 by the New York International Bible Society.

The *New Testament in Modern English* (Phillips), Revised Edition © J. B. Phillips, 1958, 1960, 1972. By permission of the Macmillan Publishing Co.

The *Revised Standard Version of the Bible* (RSV), copyrighted 1946, 1952, © 1971, 1973.

The Weymouth New Testament in Modern Speech (Weymouth), copyright 1929 by Harper and Brothers, New York.

The New Testament in the Language of the People (Williams), by Charles B. Williams. Copyright 1937 by Bruce Humphries, Inc.; assigned 1949 to Moody Bible Institute, Chicago.

10   9   8   7   6   5   4   3   2   1

Contents

Editors' Preface

No Christian preacher or teacher has been more aware of the creating and sustaining power of the Word of God than the Apostle Paul. As a stratagem of his missionary endeavors, he sought out synagogues in the major cities where he knew Jews would gather to hear the Old Testament. No doubt he calculated that he would be invited to expound the Scriptures and so he would have a golden opportunity to preach Christ. That peripatetic preacher was confident that valid Christian experience and living could not be enjoyed apart from the Word of God, whether preached or written. To the Thessalonians he wrote: "And we also thank God constantly for this, that when you received the word of God which you heard from us, you accepted it not as the word of men but as what it really is, the word of God, which is at work in you believers" (1 Thess. 2:13, RSV). Strong Christians, and more broadly, strong churches, are born of, and nurtured on, authentic and winsome exposition of the Bible.

Beacon Bible Expositions provide a systematic, devotional Bible study program for laymen and a fresh, homiletical resource for preachers. All the benefits of the best biblical scholarship are found in them, but nontechnical language is used in the composition. A determined effort is made to relate the clarified truth to life today. The writers, Wesleyan in theological perspective, seek to interpret the gospel, pointing to the Living Word, Christ, who is the primary Subject of all scripture, the Mediator of redemption, and the Norm of Christian living.

The publication of this series is a prayerful invitation to both laymen and ministers to set out on a lifelong, systematic study of the Bible. Hopefully these studies will supply the initial impetus.

—WILLIAM M. GREATHOUSE AND
J. FRED PARKER, *Editors*

The Epistle to the
PHILIPPIANS

Introduction

Authorship

There is no sufficient reason to doubt the authenticity of the Epistle to the Philippians. External evidence for Pauline authorship comes in part from Clement of Rome, Ignatius, Polycarp, and Diognetus.[1] The internal evidence places the issue almost beyond question. The teaching, language, style, and manner of thought are clearly Pauline.

The only significant argument advanced against Pauline authorship is based on the reference in 1:1 to *bishops (episkopois)* and *deacons (diakonois)*. These offices, so the theory goes, reflect a later stage in the development of the church; thus the letter could not be by Paul. This argument, however, is not convincing since we know that Paul appointed officials in every church he founded (Acts 14:23; 20:17; Titus 1:5). It is not unreasonable to assume that these titles which later became prominent in the church were used at the time of this writing, though without the later organizational significance attached to them.

Though the authorship has not been seriously questioned by reputable scholars, some have doubted the integrity of the letter, suggesting that it is a composite of two or more letters. This theory has been advanced in the light of the fact that Paul drastically changes his tone from 3:2 to 4:3. It has been said that this portion constitutes a separate and initial letter written shortly after Epaphroditus delivered the gift of the church. On this theory 1:1—3:1 and 4:4-23 were written later and carried by Epaphroditus on his return home. This suggestion seems to be supported by the fact that correspondence between Paul and the Philippians is implied (3:1; 4:15-16), and also by the specific reference in Polycarp's *Letter to the Philippians* (3:1-5) to "letters" (plural) by Paul to the church at Philippi.

Such a theory, though reasonable, is not compelling since Paul's change of tone can be adequately accounted for in a simpler manner. In a highly personal letter such as this one, the writer speaks informally and without definite plan. He moves rapidly and sometimes abruptly from one topic to another. Further, it seems likely that Paul is replying point by point to a letter or letters from the Philippians. These different letters provoked a change in mood by raising the question of the Judaizers, or perhaps the backslidings of Gentile converts (3:2). It is not difficult to infer that Paul is using this method in composing the entire letter (cf. 1:12 f.; 2:3 f., 27; 4:2, 8, 15). In addition, no argument can be made from Polycarp's reference to "letters" since the plural was sometimes used to describe a single writing. Thus Pauline authorship is virtually beyond dispute, and the evidence is insufficient to cause doubt as to the integrity of the Epistle.

Place and Date of Writing

The traditional view has been that Paul was in prison in Rome. Some have argued, however, that he was in Ephesus or Caesarea. Neither of the latter places are probable. We cannot be certain that Paul was ever in prison in Ephesus, though this might be inferred from 1 Cor. 15:30-32 and 2 Cor. 1:8-10. Even so the duration cannot have been long, and the Epistle suggests a lengthy captivity. It also implies a relationship of long standing between the Apostle and the church at Philippi. If Paul had written from Ephesus this relationship would have existed only three or four years. Further, Paul refers to the fact that of those with him only Timothy is acting unselfishly and sharing his concern (2:20). Such an event seems unlikely at Ephesus since some of Paul's close friends were there (Acts 19:31; 20:1).

Likewise, the Caesarean theory may be discounted. We know that in Caesarea Paul was not in immediate danger of his life. The Caesarean imprisonment would not justify the tone of martyrdom which characterizes Philippians. Also the letter proposes a visit to Philippi (2:24), which would hardly be likely to occur were Paul imprisoned at Caesarea.

At that time he had appealed to Caesar as a Roman citizen and knew he would be sent to Rome for trial, precluding the possibility of an immediate visit to Macedonia.

Though we cannot be absolutely certain, clearly the traditional view is best. The references to *Caesar's household* (4:22) and the "praetorium" (from Gk., 1:13), whose headquarters were in Rome, seem most natural if the author is in Rome. Also on this view the correspondence presupposed by the Epistle can be accounted for best because of the close and direct connections maintained between Rome and her colonies. If the Roman imprisonment is accepted, the letter was written about A.D. 60-61 during Paul's two-year captivity (Acts 28:16-31), which began about A.D. 59 and at the beginning of which he was permitted to live "in his own hired house" (Acts 28:30). The letter apparently was written late in the two-year imprisonment after several exchanges of correspondence passed over the 800 miles separating Paul and his readers. It was possibly after Paul's prison liberties had been sharply curtailed.[2]

Philippi: the City and the Church

The city of Philippi lay eight miles inland from the port town of Neapolis and was the first city in Europe to which Paul brought his ministry. Originally known as Krenides, or "The Little Fountains," named for the springs which abound in the area, it was conquered and renamed by King Philip of Macedon—father of Alexander—in the middle of the fourth century B.C.

It was the scene of the battle in which Brutus was defeated by Octavian, giving birth to the Roman Empire in 42 B.C. Octavian (Caesar Augustus), the head of the new state, rebuilt Philippi and filled it with his own soldiers, making it a military outpost and colony of Rome. The strategic location of Philippi made its colonization extremely advantageous. It commanded one of the principal trade routes, the Ignatian Way, between Europe and Asia. It was the "chief" city of Macedonia (Acts 16:12), evidently meaning the farthest eastward from Rome, and the "first" city after entering Macedonia from the east.

The inhabitants of the city in time were granted the "Italic Right" *(Ius Italicum).* Consequently they were Roman citizens and enjoyed special privileges associated with Italy itself, with the right of voting, governance by their own senate and magistrates rather than by the governor of the province, exemption from taxation and tribute, and permission to own land. The official language was Latin, though Greek was the common language. The colony was a miniature of the Imperial City, and its citizens were proud of their connection with Rome.

A variety of national types assembled in Philippi—Greek, Roman, Asiatic—representing different phases of philosophy, religion, and superstition. The inhabitants were religiously zealous, attested by the archaeological finds of the rocks near Philippi, which have been called a "veritable museum of mythology."[3] A famous shrine to Dionysius was on nearby Mount Pangaeus. Thus it was appropriate, and quite likely the desire of the great Apostle, that the gospel in the empire should begin in such a strategic and cosmopolitan city.

The church at Philippi was established by Paul and his companions in his second missionary journey about A.D. 52. There were only a few Jews in the city, an insufficient number to sustain a synagogue. Thus Paul, unable to follow his normal practice of reasoning in the synagogue, joined a group on the riverside where he "expected to find a place of prayer" (Acts 16:13, NIV). Lydia, the seller of purple, was converted, as was also the slave girl whose conversion brought a loss of profit to her masters, resulting in the imprisonment of Paul and Silas.

From the prison the two men prayed and sang praises to God and were set free by an earthquake. The prison keeper, seeing the power of God, was converted and baptized, with all his household (Acts 16:33).

From this simple beginning the church was constituted, composed initially of Lydia, the first European convert to

Christianity, in whose home the church met (Acts 16:40); the slave girl; the Philippian jailer and his family. The charter membership of this congregation indicates the power and universality of the gospel. Lydia, the businesswoman, was Asiatic and somewhat wealthy; the slave girl was a native Greek and represents the lower segment of society; the jailer was a Roman citizen and from the middle class.[4] In Christ Jesus there is no distinction of male or female, bond or free (Gal. 3:27-28).

After Paul's initial visit Luke may have remained at Philippi to organize the Macedonian churches. This is inferred from the fact that Luke uses the first person ("we") throughout his account of the organization of the church (Acts 16), but uses the third person ("they") in describing the events between Paul's departure from, and return to, the city (Acts 20:6).[5] Luke apparently rejoined his traveling missionary companions after that.

It seems likely that the church inherited the persecution centered around Paul (1:7, 28-30). Remaining steadfast, however, it thereby became attached to the Apostle in a personal way and was intensely loyal to him. Though the congregation apparently was poor (2 Cor. 8:1-2), it was marked by a spirit of fidelity and liberality. At least twice prior to the offering delivered by Epaphroditus (2:25, 30), the church had sent gifts to Paul to supply his needs—in Thessalonica (4:16) and Corinth (2 Cor. 11:9). No wonder Paul found genuine consolation in the Philippians and refers to them as *my joy and crown* (4:1)—his "sweetheart church" (Rees).

Character and Purpose of the Epistle

Although the Epistle to the Philippians is not constructed on a very orderly plan, it has endeared itself to Christian minds more than most of Paul's letters. It is the spontaneous and affectionate expression of one whose "whole remembrance" of the Philippians is highly cherished (1:3). It is written as friend to friend. With the possible exception of 2 Corinthians and Philemon, this is the most personal and informal of all the Apostle's writings. The personal quality of the letter is seen in the fact that Paul uses the personal pronoun approximately 100 times, in spite of the fact that Christ, rather than self, is constantly exalted. Its informal character is reflected in Paul's rapid movement from one theme to another (2:18, 19-24, 25-30; 3:1, 2, 3, 4-14, 15), and also in the absence of any reference to himself as an "apostle"—a reference which characterizes all his letters except those to the Thessalonians and to Philemon. *"Philippians* is more peaceful than *Galatians,* more personal and affectionate than *Ephesians,* less anxiously controversial than *Colossians,* more deliberate and symmetrical than *Thessalonians,* and of course larger in its applications than the personal messages to Timothy, Titus, and Philemon."[6]

The occasion for the letter is the return of Epaphroditus to Philippi. One of the leaders in the church, he had brought an offering from the Philippians to Paul in prison, with instructions to stay and assist the Apostle in Rome (2:25, 30; 4:10-18). While there he had fallen dangerously ill. The church had learned of the illness, and their concern had been communicated to Paul. Thus he writes to thank the church for her generosity (4:14-16) and to alleviate her anxieties concerning Epaphroditus' welfare. Also, because of the messenger's faithfulness, he wants to insure a good reception for him when he arrives home (2:25-30).

On the whole, a spirit of unity characterizes the Philippian church, though Paul finds it necessary to warn against a party spirit and to admonish two ladies, Euodia and Syntyche, to agree in the Lord (4:2). Consequently, the primary purpose of the letter is not ethical. Nor is it doctrinal, though the Apostle prays that they may grow in *knowledge* and *judgment* (1:9). And yet both moral and doctrinal precepts are strikingly evident and warmly intertwined. For example, it is in the context of Paul's reference to small, personal dissensions in the church that the most descriptive passage in Scripture of the Lord as servant—the classic "kenosis" passage—is written (2:3-11). He warns against the Judaizers, or perhaps Gentiles who had fallen away from the faith (3:2), and against those who place *confidence in the flesh* (3:3), that is, the notion that perfection is attainable by works (3:2). At the same time, he encourages his readers to walk worthy of their true "citizenship" which is in heaven (3:17-21, ASV) and to look to the final day of Christ as a runner keeps his eye on the goal (3:13-14). Thus he expertly weaves doctrinal and practical matters into a single and beautiful pattern.

Philippians has been called the "Epistle of Excellent Things," and is a good summary of all Paul had delivered to the churches in his earlier Epistles. He is unwavering in his faithfulness to the *gospel,* which is referred to nine times (1:5, 7, 12, 17, 27 [twice]; 2:22; 4:3, 15). The dominant theme of the letter is joy. The word *joy* in its verbal and noun forms is found 16 times in the four chapters of the Epistle. Some 20 times the author uses such terms as *rejoice, thanksgiving, content, praise*— none of which is dependent on outward circumstances.

Paul was able to rejoice under the most trying circumstances of his captivity. His life was filled with joy, and his exhortation to *rejoice in the Lord alway* (4:4) bubbled out of the crucible of his own experience. Because that joy which is the "fruit of the Spirit" (Gal. 5:22) is no mere emotional quality subject to fleeting highs and lows of the human psyche, the Apostle was never the victim of despair and depression no matter what his outward situation (4:12; see 2 Cor. 4:8-10). As he writes Paul is experiencing, in spite of his own uncertain future, the inner calm and peace which arose from his living union with Christ (1:21). In this sense the letter may be considered a kind of spiritual autobiography.

The church at Philippi had been formed by the singing of hymns in prison, and now Paul from another prison *with joy* addresses this church. No wonder G. Campbell Morgan, in his book *The Unfolding Message of the Bible,* called it a "singing letter, a love letter."

Here is a letter of faith. It embodies the Apostle's confidence that, as in the case of the faithful Philippian church which had such humble origins, small things are not to be despised (1:6). That Paul's labor of faith was rewarded is evident from Polycarp's *Letter to the Philippians* (1:2), written some 60 years after Paul's last visit there, in which we learn that the church was still standing firm.

It has been suggested that several of Paul's letters may be summarized by a single word or phrase. For example, "righteousness of God" in Romans, "fullness" in Colossians, and "the heavenly places" in Ephesians. While this may be an oversimplification of Paul's themes, if we were to identify such a word in Philippians it might well be *fellowship (koinōnia)*. It carries the meaning of participation and suggests that Christians share with one another in a common possession, such as *the gospel* (1:5) or *the Spirit* (2:1), or Christ's *suffering* (3:10). The word can also be used to denote a financial contribution (Rom. 15:26), or a partnership (Acts 2:42; Gal. 2:9).

Paul's frequent use of *koinōnia (fellowship)* in Philippians will be seen as we review the body of his Epistle, but it is worthy of note here that sin, the breaking of fellowship, is not once mentioned. The mutual bonds of love which bind Paul and this Christian community together are no mere human sentiment. He and they are knit together as common members of the Body of Christ—members who have been "partners" together in the gospel, who accept Jesus as Lord, and pattern their ministry after Him. No more beautiful picture of the relationship between genuine disciples of Christ is to be found in the New Testament than in this simple and charming letter to the Philippians.

Topical Outline of Philippians

Greeting (1:1-2)
  Partners in Service (1:1-2)

Thanksgiving and Prayer (1:3-11)
  The Fellowship of Praise (1:3-8)
  Partners in Prayer (1:9-11)

God's Action in Adversity (1:12-26)
  Uses of Adversity (1:12-18)
  Triumph over Adversity (1:19-26)

Appeal for Single-mindedness and Obedience (1:27—2:18)
  Conduct Worthy of the Gospel (1:27-30)
  Motivation to Oneness of Spirit (2:1-4)
  The Supreme Example of Christ's Humility and Obedience
    (2:5-11)
  The Admonition to Obedience (2:12-18)

Paul's Concerns and Future Plans (2:19-30)
  Concern for and Commendation of Timothy (2:19-24)
  Concern for and Commendation of Epaphroditus (2:25-30)

The Threat of Legalism (3:1-16)
  The True Israelites (3:1-3)
  Paul's Pre-Christian Pedigree (3:4-6)
  The Knowledge of Christ Jesus (3:7-10)
  Pressing Toward the Final Mark (3:11-16)

An Appeal for Purity and Unity (3:17—4:9)
  Some Personal Examples (3:17-21)
  Several Significant Exhortations (4:1-9)

Closing Word of Gratitude and Grace (4:10-23)
  Expression of Appreciation for the Philippians' Gift (4:10-20)
  Final Greetings and Benediction (4:21-23)

Greeting

Philippians 1:1-2

PHILIPPIANS 1

Partners in Service

Philippians 1:1-2

> 1 Paul and Timotheus, the servants of Jesus Christ, to all the saints in Christ Jesus which are at Philippi, with the bishops and deacons:
> 2 Grace be unto you, and peace, from God our Father, and from the Lord Jesus Christ.

In the first two verses of the letter Paul speaks three times of his Lord—*Jesus Christ, Christ Jesus,* and *the Lord Jesus Christ.* Christ is the Person, the spiritual Reality, creating and preserving the union between Paul, Timothy, and other Christian companions in the Roman prison with the faithful believers at Philippi. All are participants in the gospel and share in the fellowship of service to their common Lord.

1. *The Servants* (1*a*). This Pauline expression, *servants,* as used here, probably goes back to the Old Testament title given to Moses (Exod. 14:31; Num. 12:7; Josh. 1:2; Ps. 105:26), Joshua (Judg. 2:8), the prophets (Jer. 25:4; Dan. 9:6, 10; Amos 3:7), as well as to David (Pss. 78:70; 89:3, 20)—"the servants of God *('Ebed Yahweh').*" The term denoted God-given authority as a divinely accredited messenger. It meant to be one chosen by God. Thus, though Paul does not speak

of himself as an "apostle" here because of his special relationship to the Philippians, he obviously places himself in the succession of the prophets and thereby deftly alludes to his authority.

a. Paul and Timothy. There is no suggestion that Timothy had any part in the writing of the letter. Almost immediately, in verse 3, Paul uses the pronoun "I" rather than "we" and continues his personal references throughout the Epistle. The Apostle was grateful for the loyalty of his "son in the faith" (cf. 2:22; 1 Tim. 1:2) and includes Timothy in his greeting as an expression of esteem (see also Rom. 16:21).

It has been suggested that Timothy is mentioned here because at a point or two in the letter Paul offers a gentle rebuke and wants his readers to know that the censure has the sanction of his partner.[7] Such a sanction would hardly be necessary in writing to the Philippians. The reference to Timothy not only speaks highly of him, but also speaks volumes concerning the character of Paul. Timothy is Paul's junior in age, experience, and partnership. It is not easy for the senior member of a team to place his assistant on the same level with himself, and yet Paul had sufficient grace to do so.

Timothy was present with Paul at the founding of the church at Philippi (Acts 20:1-6). The Philippians would be glad to be remembered by Timothy, whom no doubt they had come to love for his faithful service among them. Indeed, both Paul and the Philippians regarded Timothy so highly, and he felt such a special connection with them, that Paul planned to send him back to the congregation as soon as possible (2:19-22).

b. Servants of Jesus Christ. Paul and Timothy are true fellow "bondservants" (Weymouth) and are described, literally, as the "slaves" *(douloi)* of Jesus Christ. That is, they belong to Him only and owe Him absolute obedience. Here is the Christians' true relationship to Christ. They are Christ's property, body and soul, at His complete and continuous disposal. They are not their "own" (1 Cor. 6:20) because they have been bought "with the precious blood of Christ" (1 Pet. 1:18-19). As a slave exists to do the will of his earthly master, so they exist to do the will of Christ, even as Jesus' "meat" was to do the will of His Father in heaven (John 4:34). Christ is their absolute and common Master. They are His "love slaves" (cf. Exod. 21:1-6), who have freely accepted His sovereignty. To be the slave of Christ is to be free from sin (Rom. 6:16-18, 20, 22). Paul and Timothy consequently shared in a unique fellowship. The intimacy of these servants is based not so much on their past experiences together as on their common commitment to Christ and their emancipation from unrighteousness.

2. *The Saints* (1*b*). For a fuller exposition of the meaning of *saints,* see the writer's comments on Col. 1:2 in this volume. However, several significant thoughts may be expressed here.

a. The Greek word *hagios* (saint) and its Hebrew equivalent *(kadosh)* are usually translated "holy." In Hebrew usage, things that were holy were separated *from* that which was unclean, and were set apart *for* service to God. In this sense the priests were holy (Lev. 21:6), the tithe was holy (Lev. 27:30, 32), the ark was holy (Exod. 26:33), the Jewish people were a holy nation (Exod. 19:6). An object or person by virtue of being holy was distinctive or different.

When the New Testament speaks of "saints" or "holy ones" it means they are different from other persons (Barclay). The difference, however, is not superficial but arises out of their relationship to Christ as Lord. They have become new creatures in Christ Jesus (2 Cor. 5:17) and share His resurrected life. As such they live in the atmosphere, the spirit, and the power of Christ. The Christian's calling to holiness, to a life of "sainthood," is fulfilled only *in Christ Jesus* and by continuous faith—union with Him (1 Cor. 1:30). "In Christ Jesus [the saint's] holiness is and remains" (Karl Barth).

b. Saints (hagioi) is found only in the plural in the New Testament except in 4:21, where the word refers to a group. It refers to all New Testament believers or Christians, and not to a spiritual elite. Clearly for Paul there is no individualized holiness, only "social holiness" (Wesley). While personal holiness is realized in Christ, it is never separated in spirit or fellowship from the total Body of Christ.

c. Saints in Christ Jesus ... at Philippi means the church or "true Christians" (Phillips) at Philippi. Refusing to make any distinctions, Paul addresses *all* those in the church (1:4, 7, 8, 25; cf. 4:21), indicating his love for them regardless of their deserts. *Saints* and *servants,* "bond slaves of Jesus Christ," are virtually synonymous. Thus there is a close fellowship between Paul and Timothy, the bond slaves, and the believers at Philippi.

d. The reference to *the bishops and deacons* is the first mention in order of time of these offices in the New Testament. *Bishops (episkopois),* literally "overseers," refers to spiritual leaders of the local congregation (Acts 20:28). At this stage in the development of the Church, local congregations had more than one "overseer," or pastor. The use of the term does not reflect an organizational significance which it later acquired. "Bishop" seems to be the same as "elder" or "presbyter" (Acts 20:17). Since Philippi was a Roman colony, the Jewish term "presbyter" would be unfamiliar. No doubt the church chose to call their leaders by names which would be in general use, and Paul is following their accepted practice.

The *bishops* or pastors managed primarily the internal affairs of the church, whereas the *deacons* gave attention to the external affairs. *Deacons (diakonois),* literally "those who serve," refers to persons who were apparently responsible for the temporal and material needs of the congregation (Acts 6:1-6; 1 Tim. 3:8-13). *Diakonos* (deacon) occurs at least 30 times in the New Testament, but only here and in 1 Timothy 3 does it have the technical meaning of "deacon." Elsewhere in the KJV it is translated "minister" 20 times and "servant" 7 times. Since "minister" now has an ecclesiastical connotation, "servant" is the better rendering (Ralph Earle, *Word Meanings in the New Testament,* 5:13).

It may be that Paul refers to these offices as a means of officially expressing appreciation to those responsible for the gift sent to him, or for giving to those leaders his spiritual counsel which he hopes they will carry into practical effect.[8] Whatever the reason, it is clear that the *saints* and *servants,* which include the *bishops* and *deacons,* are all partners in service.

3. *The Salutation* (2). The greeting to the Christians from Christ in this verse is the common form in Paul's earlier Epistles (Rom. 1:7; 1 Cor. 1:3; 2 Cor. 1:2; Gal. 1:3; Eph. 1:2; Col. 1:2; 1 Thess. 1:1; 2 Thess. 1:2; Philem. 3). He unites the normal Greek and Latin greeting, "joy" or "prosperity" *(charas),* with the Eastern salutation, "well-being" (Heb., *shalom;* or Gk. *eirēnē*), and transforms them into a rich Christian blessing. Here is an illustration of the fact that God makes all things new.

a. Grace be unto you, and peace. Grace (charis) expresses the free favor of God, or His undeserved inclination toward us (2 Cor. 4:15; 12:9). It is the love of God to sinful man, appearing in human experience and reaching its ultimate manifestation in "the redemption that is in Christ Jesus" (Rom. 3:24). Grace is the gift of God which justifies unto salvation (Eph. 2:8-10; Rom. 11:6). It also refers to the fruit of this divine favor—the dispositions which result from grace. Thus we are admonished to "grow in grace" (2 Pet. 3:18). Grace brings the gift of *peace,* which is both reconciliation with God and inner assurance which results from faith in Christ's atonement (Rom. 5:1, 11).[9] "Reconciliation is always at the basis of the Pauline conception of peace" (Vincent). (For further meanings of *grace* and *peace* see author's comments herein on Col. 1:2.)

b. From God our Father, and from the Lord Jesus Christ. The second *from (apo)* is not present in the Greek, suggesting the close union in Paul's mind of the Father and

Jesus Christ. God's grace comes from the Father through Christ (Rom. 3:24). *Lord (kyrios,* literally "master") was used in the Septuagint to translate the word for "Jehovah." Though the title is occasionally used in the New Testament as a title of honor ("Sir," Matt. 13:27), in the Epistles it is constantly employed of Christ. Thus *Lord* as used by Paul indicates full deity. That Jesus was divine was the faith of the New Testament Church, as expressed in its earliest Christian creed, "Jesus is Lord" (1 Cor. 12:3; cf. Phil. 2:6, 9-11).

Jesus means "Savior" (Matt. 1:21). He is the Lord, the Master of Paul and Timothy and the Philippians because He is their "Savior," or Deliverer. Contrast the experience of the damsel possessed with a "spirit of divination" at Philippi. She was the slave of those who could not be her savior, while Paul and his companions were "slaves of the Most High God" (Acts 16:16-17, C. B. Williams). *Christ (Christou)* was a proper title meaning "Anointed One," or "Messiah" (Isa. 61:1). The Anointed One was the Appointed One, God's Vice-Regent on earth, the officially accredited Messenger from heaven to earth (Matt. 17:5). When the emphasis rests on the historical Jesus, Paul puts "Jesus" first in any combination; when "Christ" takes precedence he underscores the risen Jesus, the eternal Messiah.[10]

The Holy Spirit is not mentioned because this grace and peace is the Holy Spirit himself dwelling in us, revealing to us the Father, and bringing to our remembrance the teaching of the Son from whom He comes. The meaning of the salutation is clear: "No peace without grace . . . no grace and peace but from God our Father . . . no grace and peace from God our Father, but in and through the Lord Jesus Christ."[11]

Thanksgiving and Prayer

Philippians 1:3-11

The Fellowship of Praise

Philippians 1:3-8

> 3 I thank my God upon every remembrance of you,
> 4 Always in every prayer of mine for you all making request with joy,
> 5 For your fellowship in the gospel from the first day until now;
> 6 Being confident of this very thing, that he which hath begun a good work in you will perform it until the day of Jesus Christ:
> 7 Even as it is meet for me to think this of you all, because I have you in my heart; inasmuch as both in my bonds, and in the defence and confirmation of the gospel, ye all are partakers of my grace.
> 8 For God is my record, how greatly I long after you all in the bowels of Jesus Christ.

Perhaps the most distinctive quality of this letter is its extremely personal nature, seen here in Paul's phrase *my God.* During his days of confinement he had been communing much with God, and his sense of dependence had been growing ever stronger and more personal. As his relationship to God became richer his affection for the Philippians became greater. The inseparable relation between love for God and concern for others is seen in the fact that Paul even calls God as witness to the depth of his feeling for his friends at Philippi. Fellowship with others in Christ is incomparable.

With thanksgiving and *joy* (*charas,* 4) Paul offers his praise to God for the Philippians. In the Christian life these go together, for "what we have the comfort of, God must have the glory of" (Matthew Henry). Thanksgiving and joy are qualities of the spirit and not the result of favorable circumstances. Joy is deeper than happiness, which is dependent on what "happens." Paul's circumstances are unpleasant, and yet "the joy of the Lord" is his strength (Neh. 8:10). His is the joy promised and provided by Christ (John 15:11; 17:13), the norm of the Christian life (Col. 1:11). *Joy* gives especial vitality and power to prayers.

1. *The Joy of Memory* (3). Moffatt translates *upon every remembrance of you* as "for all your remembrance of me." This rendering points to the Apostle's thanksgiving to God for the Philippians' gift of money, that is, material gifts, and also for their spiritual gifts, their *fellowship* or partnership with him *in the gospel* (5). If this translation is accurate, Paul is referring to the church's "memory" or remembrance of him.

Literally, the phrase says "on account of the whole remembrance of you." The most frequent interpretation, then, is that Paul is expressing thanks for his total past experience with the Philippians, and not merely for disconnected recollections. His overall remembrance resulted in unbroken thanksgiving and joy. If memory is the fine art of forgetting, Paul was the recipient of this noble gift. He had been granted the power to forget the harsh experiences of imprisonment and suffering at Philippi, except as they enriched his relationship to God and to the Philippians. At the same time, he remembered with gratitude their conversion (Acts 16) and subsequent thoughtfulness on several occasions, even quite recently (4:15-18).

2. *The Joy of Supplication* (4). Verse 4 is parenthetic before Paul continues his thanksgiving in verse 5. Nonetheless it is a suggestive interpolation. The word *prayer* is *deēsei* and indicates an intense request for a necessary gift (cf. James 5:16). Thus the *American Standard Version* renders verse 4 this way: "Always in every supplication of mine on behalf of you." Paul's love for the Philippians is expressed in genuine intercession to God for their welfare. He does not pray from a sense of obligation, nor out of an attempt to forget his own circumstances. His prayers are truly intercessory. The fre-

quent repetition of *you all* suggests that Paul refuses to recognize any divisions among the Philippia.. . His prayers are for *all* the congregation, the whole fellowship of believers.

3. *The Joy of Participation* (5). Here Paul takes up his thanksgiving again and expresses the ground of his gratitude. He speaks of the Philippians' *fellowship* with him *in the gospel from the first day until now* (5). Tender memories must have flooded Paul's mind as he thought of the *first day* he preached to them, and of their subsequent gifts to him in the spread of the gospel. Sharing in the work of Christ or the gospel became the basis for their mutual love and fellowship. This inward or spiritual fellowship had deepened across the years. The Philippians had first given themselves (2 Cor. 8:5); then they wanted to see the gospel succeed though it meant suffering and sacrifice. Consequently, they gave of their possessions, becoming bound together with Paul in the trials of captivity and the toils of Christian witnessing and teaching for the sake of the gospel. They understood the nature of the church as being a "workshop, not a dormitory" (Maclaren). Thus Paul refers to them as members of a new community, "fellow partakers" (*sugkoinōnous,* 7) of his grace.

Koinōnia (*fellowship,* 5) literally indicates "participation." It has at least three meanings: *(a)* the fellowship of Christians with one another; *(b)* the fellowship of Christians with Christ or the Holy Spirit; *(c)* the sharing of possessions (Acts 2:42; Rom. 15:26; 2 Cor. 8:4; 9:13; Philem. 6; Heb. 13:16).[12] Paul evidently had all three meanings in mind. The word speaks of the vital, living relationship of the Apostle and the Philippians to Christ, and thus to each other—a relationship that had found expression and enrichment in their offerings to him at various times.

A sign of one's professed love for the gospel seems to be the measure of sacrifice one is prepared to make in order to assist in its progress. Only this kind of self-giving has a future return. Because the Philippians had shared in the *fellowship* "in furtherance of the gospel" (ASV), they will participate in the rewards with Paul also. Even in the secular contests, "the crown is not only for him that striveth, but for the trainer, and the attendant, and all that help to prepare the athlete. For they that strengthen him, may fairly participate in his victory."[13]

4. *The Joy of Assurance* (6). Paul is filled with joy because of his confidence in the purpose and power of God. He was convinced of God's sovereign control, and this confidence grew out of his experience with God. The One who had begun *a good work* in the Philippians *will perform it,* literally, "will go on completing" it. Since the chief reference is to the divine work of salvation, and there is no definite article in the Greek, "the" *good work*—as in the *New English Bible*— is a better rendering.

A variety of views have been advanced as to the nature of this *good work.* It could be the Philippians' participation with the Apostle in the gospel; it could be a reference to the planting of the church in Philippi; it could suggest "growth in grace"; or it could mean the Christian life as a whole. These are not mutually exclusive, but the latter may be preferable in the light of the technical words that are used for *begun* and *perform. Enarksamenos* (began) is used in Gal. 3:3 to attribute the beginnings of the Christian life in the Galatian Christians to God the Holy Spirit (cf. also 2 Cor. 8:6). In classical Greek it is a word of ritual. The verb from which it comes is *enarchestlai,* and was used to describe the ritual at the beginning of a Greek sacrifice. The verb used for completing the sacrifice was *epitelein* (to perfect or consummate). Paul seems to be suggesting that the Christian life is a continuous sacrifice to Christ (Rom. 12:1).[14]

Whatever the precise meaning, it is God who has begun this *good work,* and He will *perform it until the day of Jesus Christ,* the final day when the Lord returns. The phrase carries the idea of a day of testing. Old Testament prophets spoke of the "day of the Lord" as a time of judgment as well as redemption. Paul is confident that God will advance the Philippians in grace, so that they may be constantly prepared to meet the day of trial.[15] For all those in Christ it will be a day of light and victory (1 Thess. 1:10).

The emphasis of verse 6 is both the sovereign initiative of God in salvation (see Acts 16:14), and the sovereign faithfulness of God in Christ. He begins, not that He may conduct an experiment, but that He may perform a design. Paul's confidence was no doubt buttressed and confirmed by his past experience. But it was born of and sustained by a personal relationship to God, on whose character and work the persuasion rested. The biblical doctrine of "perseverance" is a confidence in God. The continuing work of the Spirit is the divine guarantee of the preservation of the saints. "He is able to guard until that Day what I have entrusted to him" (2 Tim. 1:12, RSV margin). Because God completes what He begins, man's possibility is always greater than his ability (Robert R. Wicks, exposition, *Interpreter's Bible*).

However, one must not draw any hard and fast doctrine of "eternal security" from this verse. God preserves; the believer perseveres. Therefore, Paul admonishes the Philippians to stand firm (1:27) lest his work among them be "in vain" (2:14-16; cf. also Col. 1:19-23). Yet God will "perfect" (NASB) or bring to "completion" (NIV) the work He has initiated by His Spirit. He will "evermore put His finishing touches to it" (Moule). Both the beginning and the ending are His work. He is both the Author and Finisher of our faith (Heb. 12:2).

> *And every virtue we possess,*
> *And every victory won,*
> *And every thought of holiness,*
> *Are His alone.*
>
> —HARRIET AUBER

5. *The Joy of Christlike Affection* (7-8). "Open my heart," wrote Robert Browning, "and you will see graven on it, 'Italy.'" Such human affection characterized Paul and the Philippians. Because Paul carried the Philippians in his

heart, it was "right" *(meet)* for him to care for or *think* of them. *Phronein (to think)* is more than a mental exercise. A favorite expression of Paul in this letter (see 2:2, 5; 3:15-16, 19; 4:2, 10—translated in KJV "one mind," "mind," "minded," or "care"), it involves action of the heart at the level of motives and denotes a deep concern and empathetic interest. The closeness of feeling arose out of the common participation *(koinōnia)* in the grace of God. This sense of oneness continued even when the Apostle and the church at Philippi were separated by distance.

Paul and his friends not only shared a common grace, but they shared in suffering and conflict as well. Paul was a prisoner for Christ's sake and the gospel's and suffered on behalf of the churches (Eph. 3:13; Col. 1:24; 2 Tim. 2:10). In turn, the church at Philippi suffered with Paul by entering into the afflictions of his apostleship (4:14-15), by their gifts and prayers, and by their devotion to Christ in the face of common enemies (1:28-30—"the same conflict").

If the reference to the *defence and confirmation of the gospel* (7) refers to Paul's preaching ministry, it means removing prejudice, overpowering objections to the gospel, and declaring the truth. If, however, it points to Paul's imprisonment, it suggests his impending trial before the imperial court (see 2 Tim. 4:16) or the provincial judges. Evidently the Apostle is setting forth a contrasting possibility —whether he is in prison or whether he is arraigned for the sake of the gospel, the Philippians share with him in the grace of his God-given commission.[16]

Paul was not on trial; the gospel was on trial. His bonds *(desmois)* were a defense and confirmation of the "glad tidings." His faithfulness in suffering was evidence that the gospel was a noble and divine cause. *Confirmation (bebaiōsei)* was the obligation under which the seller came to the buyer to guarantee against all claims his right to what he had purchased.[17] Paul's defense then was a guarantee of the gospel, and the Philippians were "fellow partakers" *(sugkoinōnous)* of grace and of this confirmation.

Verse 8 probably means more than a mere intense desire

to see the Philippians. Paul says, *How greatly I long after you all in the bowels of Jesus Christ* (the oldest manuscripts read "Christ Jesus"). *Splanchnois (bowels)* refers to the upper intestine, liver, or lungs. These, so the Greeks believed, were the seat of the emotions and affections. Thus the "bowels of Christ Jesus" indicates the "affection of Christ Jesus." This is a powerful metaphor describing perfect union with Christ. The genuine human affection toward the Philippians (7) is wrapped around with divine love. Christ is the life of Paul's life, the heart of his love. Christ's heart has become his so that he can love the Philippians with the very love of Christ. "The believer has no yearnings apart from his Lord; his pulse beats with the pulse of Christ; his heart throbs with the heart of Christ" (Lightfoot). (Compare 2:5-8 and Rom. 12:10.) Could the transforming power of the gospel be more strikingly revealed than in the union or fellowship of these two unlikely parties—a former devotee of Pharisaism on the one hand, and on the other, a group whose total life had been formed by the proud atmosphere of a Roman colony!

Partners in Prayer

Philippians 1:9-11

9   And this I pray, that your love may abound yet more and more in knowledge and in all judgment;
10   That ye may approve things that are excellent; that ye may be sincere and without offence till the day of Christ;
11   Being filled with the fruits of righteousness, which are by Jesus Christ, unto the glory and praise of God.

The fellowship or partnership Paul shares with the Philippians has been expressed in his prayers of thanksgiving and praise (3-4). But his prayers also include specific requests in their behalf. Here is one of the most outstanding prayers of the Apostle for his churches.

1. *The Substance of the Petition* (9-10)

   a. *A prayer for progress in love—that your love may abound yet more and more* (9). The English word *love* has been stripped of its power by its denotation of sexual passion and romantic feeling. Even in the Greek language the words for erotic attraction *(eros)* and fraternal and family affection *(philia)* were translated "love." Paul's word in this verse is *agapē*, divine love, demonstrated in God's spontaneous and undeserved action in Jesus Christ for rebellious and sinful man. "Herein is love, not that we loved God, but that he loved us, and sent his Son to be the propitiation [or 'atoning sacrifice,' NBV] for our sins" (1 John 4:10; also 3:1). This love has been shed abroad in the hearts of believers (Rom. 5:5). Thus when Paul says *your love* he clearly means "God's love in you."

Since those in whom the love of God dwells love those whom God loves (1 John 4:20-21), this is an admonition to love one another. In the light of the tendency among some to disunity and faultfinding (4:1-2), Paul makes this a matter of prayer before proceeding to admonition and attempts to correction. If we can remember that love is a possibility only because God "first loved us" (1 John 4:19), we may learn that the most effective way to help a brother is to pray for him. If "a word of rebuke or correction has to be spoken, let it be prayed over first, and then spoken in love" (R. P. Martin)—a valuable lesson for those in the Church of Jesus Christ.

The love of God in us is for the sake of others (see 1 Corinthians 13), so Paul prays that it may *abound (perisseuē)*. The word is present tense, expressing continuous growth and advancement. It can be rendered "may keep on overflowing." Thus Paul is praying "that your love for one another will never be doled out in parsimonious pinches, but will rather tumble forth like some magnificent cascade."[18] To underscore his meaning, he adds the superlatives "more and more." "The spiritual prosperity of believers should be measured not so much by the point they have reached, but by the fact and measure of the progress they are making" (Rainy).

b. A prayer for light in making moral choices—in knowledge and in all judgment. Phillips' paraphrase of verse 9 is illuminating: "My prayer for you is that you may have still more love—a love that is full of knowledge and every wise insight." Love may be "blind," but only if we refer to our sentimental moods and sensual infatuations. God's love which is ours through Christ is not an undisciplined emotion nor an unenlightened mysticism. It calls for and seeks after truth or knowledge. Thus growth and progress in love are not the Apostle's only concern. Love must grow in *knowledge* and *judgment* if the Christian is to be well-rounded and symmetrical.

Epignōsis (knowledge) generally conveys the idea of a mental grasp of spiritual truth, a thorough, full understanding of general moral principles. The main reference here, however, is to the biblical sense of knowing God in a personal and intimate way, that knowledge which comes in conversion to Christ and the Christian faith. The better the Philippians' *knowledge* of God, the clearer their understanding of their mutual responsibilities and relationships as fellow believers. *Aisthēsei (judgment* or "discernment" [ASV]) is used only here in the New Testament (though cognates of it are found in Luke 9:45 and Heb. 5:14). It refers to the practical ability to make moral choices in particular situations, to distinguish the authentic and the superficial. It is a spiritual and moral sense or feeling, an insightful intuition or gift that has been cultivated and disciplined. Hence, Paul prays "that ye may not only *know* but *feel* that you are of God, by the Spirit which he has given you; and that your feeling may become more exercised in Divine things, so that it may be increasingly sensible and refined" (Adam Clarke).

All (pasē) judgment probably means "all kinds of" discernment. The genuine spirit of love of some at Philippi may have lacked discernment, so that they had misunderstandings over insignificant matters (see 4:2). The more love grows, the more sensitive the moral sense becomes. It has been said that Venus glass would sliver into fragments if poison were poured into the cup. Likewise, the growth of the love of God within the Christian makes him increasingly sensitive to all forms of evil. Informed love is the only basis for discrimination. But love, if it is to have "tact," must be nourished by truth. This is why Jesus rebuked Peter who forbade the Master to die (Matt. 16:21-23). His love was unenlightened.

c. *A prayer for proper priorities—that ye may approve things that are excellent,* and also *be sincere and without offence. Approve* (10, *dokimazein*) is the verb used for assaying metals to detect any flaw or alloy.[19] It was often used to denote the testing of coins to determine the genuineness of currency. In Luke 14:19 it describes examination—proof or testing—of cattle. The object of the verb here *(diapheronta)* may be rendered "things that differ" (Weymouth) or "which excel." In Rom. 2:18 the exact phrase is found and seems to mean "the things which really matter." Translated *excellent* in this verse, it indicates that which is superior, the best among things that are good, of which only those of more advanced spiritual maturity are able to detect the superiority. Thus Moffatt translates the clause, "enabling you to have a sense of what is vital."

The prayer is for the spiritual ability not only to distinguish between good and evil, but between good and better, between better and best. Maxie D. Dunnam in his comments in *The Communicator's Commentary* series suggests that the "categories of good and evil, decent and indecent are too broad. The opportunity of the Christian to impact [his environment] with transforming power . . . comes at this very point—being confronted with a choice between the decent and the excellent, the good and the best. . . . Our culture is so far down the path of sexual promiscuity, selfish indulgence, moral indifference, flabby thinking that only those who consistently choose the superlatively good can make a difference."

Sincere and *without offence* (10) correspond to *knowledge* and *judgment* in verse 9. *Sincere* in its derivation points to honey without wax, implying unmixed motives or single-mindedness (James 1:8). *Eilikrineis* (*sincere* or "pure," RSV, found only in this verse and in 2 Pet. 3:1) comes from *eile* (the splendor of the sun) and *krinō* (I judge). That which is *sincere* is that which may be examined in the clearest and strongest light, without a single flaw or imperfection being revealed. Paul's language here comes from the practice of holding up cloth or pottery against the sun to see if there be any fault. Moffatt translates it "transparent." "Sincerity" is perfect openness to God and is thus as strong a word as "perfection" itself. "The soul that is sincere is the soul that is without sin" (Adam Clarke).

Eilikrineis may have also been derived from *eilein,* which means to "shake back and forth" until all foreign substance is extracted and the remaining portion is pure. The word also means to test "by rolling and rocking." This may imply conflict, suffering, and challenge. If so, it suggests that in times of difficulty the faithful discover the reason for their life and faith.

Without offence ("void of offense," ASV) describes the character of the man who walks without stumbling or perhaps without causing others to stumble; who overcomes obstacles, though unexpected. It is the image of the traveler who, in spite of hindrances, arrives in good time at his journey's end.[20] Such a one will be ready "for" *(eis,* not *till)* the day of Christ (cf. Eph. 5:27; Jude 24). The emphasis here seems to be on the readiness for this day, whereas verse 6 *(until, achri)* stresses God's continuous work in achieving this state of preparedness.

2. *The Ultimate Aim of the Petition—being filled with the fruits of righteousness, which are by Jesus Christ, unto the glory and praise of God* (11). The oldest and best manuscripts read *fruit (karpon) of righteousness* (cf. Gal. 5:22; Eph. 5:9; James 3:18; Heb. 12:11; Rom. 6:22). The phrase can mean the fruit which is being right with God or the evidence of such a relationship by the display of the ethical characteristics mentioned in Gal. 5:22—love, joy, peace, and so on. These are complementary, but in the light of the clause *which are by Jesus Christ,* the first interpretation seems primary. In either case, the righteousness here pictured is that which is by Christ, in contrast to the righteousness which is by the law (3:9).

Without this righteousness which is in Christ, no fruit

is possible (cf. John 15:4). But the pure and discerning character for which the Apostle prays and which is possible in Christ will express itself in deeds of love and service to *the glory and praise of God. Glory (doxan)* is the manifestation of God's power and grace; *praise (epainon)* is the recognition by men of these divine attributes. As a tree filled with fruit honors the gardener, so a person with the fruit of righteousness brings *glory and praise* to God—the ultimate aim of the believer's life.

God's Action in Adversity

Philippians 1:12-26

Uses of Adversity

Philippians 1:12-18

12 But I would ye should understand, brethren, that the things which happened unto me have fallen out rather unto the furtherance of the gospel;
13 So that my bonds in Christ are manifest in all the palace, and in all other places;
14 And many of the brethren in the Lord, waxing confident by my bonds, are much more bold to speak the word without fear.
15 Some indeed preach Christ even of envy and strife; and some also of good will:
16 The one preach Christ of contention, not sincerely, supposing to add affliction to my bonds:
17 But the other of love, knowing that I am set for the defence of the gospel.
18 What then? notwithstanding, every way, whether in pretence, or in truth, Christ is preached; and I therein do rejoice, yea, and will rejoice.

These verses appear to be a reply to an inquiry of the Philippians concerning Paul's situation in prison. From the declaration *I would ye should understand* (12), we may infer that they had written or sent a message by Epaphroditus

(2:25) expressing their concern for his welfare. They want to know of his situation (12-18), of the possibility of his visiting them (25-26), and of the condition of Epaphroditus (2:26). They have suffered with him for the sake of the gospel in a common fellowship of adversity (1:7, 28, 30), and are anxious to learn of his personal situation and of the state of the gospel in Rome. The Apostle attempts to dissolve their anxieties concerning him, and assures them that God is bringing good out of evil, glorifying himself, and turning events to the favor of His servants who love Him. Frustrations are being transformed into fulfillments. Liabilities are being converted into assets. Troubles which they might expect would hinder the gospel have been captured and made to serve the gospel (Rees).

1. *The Advance of the Gospel* (12-13). Paul's commitment is so complete that he cannot explain how it is with him without stating how it is with the gospel—*the things which happened unto me have fallen out rather unto the furtherance of the gospel.* He has been guarded constantly but allowed to live in his own hired house, to receive those who come to visit him, and to declare to them the good news of the kingdom of God (Acts 28:16, 30-31). But his imprisonment has not been a restriction of the gospel; *rather (mallon)* it has become an occasion for its advancement.

The emphatic term *rather* suggests the Philippians may have been expecting bad news. Some have thought it points to a change in Paul's circumstances, particularly when considered in the light of the reference to his defense (*apologia,* 7). Thus it has been suggested that Paul has been transferred from his hired lodging (Acts 28:30) into the prison where those on trial are held. The Philippians would consequently expect that this stricter custody would mean greater hardships. So the Apostle removes the supposition.[21] *Prokopēn* ("progress," ASV), found also in verse 25, was used to describe pioneers preparing for an army or group. It comes from the verb *prokoptein,* meaning to cut away trees and undergrowth. Thus Paul's captivity, instead of hindering the progress of the gospel, has actually served to clear away obstacles and to increase its propagation (cf. 1 Tim. 4:15).[22] This is what Paul supremely wants, no matter what happens to him personally.

The way the gospel was being advanced was by means of his *bonds in Christ* (13). Paul was a prisoner not because he was a violator of the law, but because of his Christian faith. *In Christ* may refer to Paul's way of suffering, that is, without complaint and with joy because of his union with Christ, which gave attraction and power to his witness. Verse 13 may be better rendered, "My bonds became manifest in Christ," that is, for Christ's sake, "throughout the whole praetorian guard" (ASV).

Praitōriō has been given four leading interpretations: *(a)* the praetorian guard, meaning soldiers; *(b)* the emperor's palace; *(c)* the barracks of the praetorian guard; *(d)* the judicial authorities, or those who hear the prisoners' cases. The last interpretation, if accepted, would square with the reference to *defence* in verse 7, and is a reasonable possibility.[23] Lightfoot has shown fairly conclusively that *praitōriō* cannot be applied to the *palace* (as in the KJV), nor to the soldiers' barracks or the whole praetorian camp. Instead, it refers to a band of men, a guard, or body of soldiers. Though the last interpretation above *(d)* cannot be excluded, the first *(a)* seems to be the best. We know that Augustus had 10,000 such men. This interpretation is congruent with Luke's statement that Paul dwelt for a time in his own hired house (Acts 28:30-31).

In Eph. 6:20, written from the same prison shortly before Philippians, Paul speaks of being an ambassador in a "chain" (*halusei;* cf. also Acts 28:20). This refers to the chain coupling the guard and the prisoner together. Day after day, week after week, soldiers were assigned to guard duty in Paul's house. With every change of guards Paul was given a new opportunity to witness for Christ. In his two-year imprisonment scores of guards would have heard the gospel from Paul. He had witnessed in the Philippian prison (Acts 16:25-32); now he witnesses still (4:22). In addition to this personal witnessing, it is possible that Paul has already officially defended himself and the gospel once (1:7).

The Word of God is not bound (2 Tim. 2:9), so that he can say the gospel is presented throughout the "whole praetorian guard." *And in all other places* (13) is clearly inaccurate. Better to read, "and to all the rest" (ASV), or "and to everyone else" (NIV). This phrase substantiates the conclusion that Paul is not referring to a *palace,* but to a group; probably to those who visited him and to others to whom the Word of the Lord would be subsequently related. His imprisonment then has afforded a fresh opportunity to witness for Christ to those *outside* the Christian community.

2. *Encouragement of the Christians in Rome* (14). A further consequence of Paul's captivity was a positive effect on his fellow believers in the local congregation—those *within* the Christian community—*and many of the brethren in the Lord, waxing confident by my bonds, are much more bold to speak the word without fear* (14). The RSV rendering is more accurate: "Most of the brethren have been made confident in the Lord because of my imprisonment." "Most" *(pleionas)* of the brethren indicates that some are not thus affected by his bonds, although the majority of the Romans have become "more abundantly bold" (ASV) to speak the "word." The full phrase "the word of God" (ASV) or "Word of the Lord" is strongly attested, but the KJV probably preserves the primitive technical formula for Christian preaching.

Lalein (to speak) denotes the fact, rather than the substance, of speaking.[24] That is, their tendency to silence is actually overcome. Not that they have not been speaking, but they are given new and greater boldness to declare God's Word without fear. Their conquest of fear is not based on the probability of Paul's release, for this is by no means certain; but on his triumphant spirit and his evident success in witnessing. It is his courage that has given new heart to the timid Romans who, possibly through persecutions, have grown discouraged.

One of the fruits of proclaiming the gospel, aside from

bringing persons to Christ, is the encouragement it gives others to be bold in their witnessing and their daily Christian living (Dunnam).

3. *Proclamation of Christ* (15-18). Some were preaching Christ whose motives were less than pure—*some indeed preach Christ even of envy and strife* (15), *of contention, not sincerely* (16). Who were these persons? A variety of responses has been given: unbelievers who wanted to intensify the hatred of Paul's foes; Jews who wanted to refute and discredit the gospel; Judaizing Christians who mixed law and grace in ways contrary to Paul's views; or disgruntled or rigid Christians who were jealous of the Apostle and desired to undermine his influence.

It may be that all of these kinds of persons were involved, since Paul says their motives were mixed. However, in other places Paul has no tolerance for the Judaizers who he thinks subvert the gospel, and his acceptance here would seem to eliminate them as a possibility.[25] In any case the Apostle seems to be saying that of those who have become more bold to declare the Word of the Lord, some are doing so out of a spirit of *strife (erin)*, or partisanship. Their aim, unlike the Apostle's, is not primarily to exalt Christ, but to advance their own particular interests.

The word translated *contention* is *eritheias,* which may be rendered "rivalry" or "out of faction." It originally meant working for pay. In time it came to describe a careerist, one who magnifies himself or canvasses for office. These proclaimers of Christ then are self-promoters and self-seekers.[26] They are not preaching *sincerely,* that is, not "purely" or "chastely." They are not speaking the whole truth, but only that which serves their purpose. Their motives are mixed, corrupted with selfishness (cf. James 3:14). These, therefore, are not preaching in the truest sense. Consequently, Paul uses *kataggellousin,* "to announce," which is a different word from that normally used to describe preaching. They are making known the facts of the gospel, perhaps of Jesus' life, death, and resurrection, but they are doing so out of jealousy or other unworthy motives. They are orthodox but have no heart.

The aim of these persons was not to exalt Christ but to injure Paul—*supposing to add affliction to my bonds* (16). They think they are, literally, "raising up friction" for Paul in his bonds. They are seeking to make his imprisonment a "galling" experience, possibly by arousing his enemies against him, thus putting his life in greater peril, or at least by troubling him in spirit. These persons apparently are the insincere ones in 2:21, who are looking "after their own interests, not those of Jesus Christ" (RSV; cf. Matt. 23:15). Some have suggested that they are old teachers of the Church who are envious of the wide popularity of Paul.[27] Whether that be true or not, it is a characteristic of human nature that jealousy usually arises within one's own class or profession: doctors are jealous of doctors, ministers of ministers, and so on. In any case, their actions stem from something personal against Paul. Their preaching, so they assume, will make Paul's imprisonment unbearable.

Others are preaching Christ for the right reasons—*of love, knowing that I am set for the defence of the gospel* (17). These, in spite of personal misunderstandings, preach (*kē-russousin*, "proclaim," 15) out of the highest motives of love *(agapē),* not out of partisan and factious ambition (cf. 1 Corinthians 13). Their aim is the same as that of Paul, who is *set (keimai),* appointed, like a soldier posted on guard by his captain, for the *defence (apologian)* of the gospel. "Defence" includes all his witnessing and propagandizing for Christ. This seems not to refer primarily to his defense in his own personal trial. However, if it is in his thinking at all, these— the personal defense and the defense of the gospel—are equated in the Apostle's mind.[28] He is enduring "hardness, as a good soldier of Jesus Christ" (2 Tim. 2:3-4). He views himself as much "on duty" as the guards are who are posted to watch over him (R. P. Martin).

Paul's positive evaluation—*What then? notwithstanding, every way, whether in pretence, or in truth, Christ is preached* (18). *Notwithstanding (plēn hoti)* is better rendered "only that" (ASV). This is in fact the only way Paul feels about the matter (cf. 1 Cor. 1:17). Those who are preaching out of *pretence* (*prophasei*, literally, "pretext") are those who are speaking *not sincerely* (16). Their purpose in preaching, though not the substance of their message, is different from that of Paul. Not necessarily their message, but their spirit is faulty—devoid of reality. Again Paul, as in verse 16, uses the word *kataggelletai*, that is, at least Christ is "announced," if not genuinely "proclaimed."

Paul seems to subdue all personal annoyance over the situation, and expresses in rather abrupt language a decisive act of the will: *and I therein do rejoice, yea, and will rejoice* (18). He will not allow any private grievance to cool his love for the gospel and its advance. The all-absorbing passion of his life is the *furtherance of the gospel* (12). Consequently, he dwells on the good that is being accomplished—Christ is being announced—not on the bad motives of the partisans (4:8). Attention to essentials spares him from any bitterness of soul. The truth of the gospel has captured his love, thus he will catch any blow to himself, rather than allow it to hinder the gospel. In this sense he glories in his tribulations (Rom. 5:3).

Triumph over Adversity

Philippians 1:19-26

> 19 For I know that this shall turn to my salvation through your prayer, and the supply of the Spirit of Jesus Christ,
> 20 According to my earnest expectation and my hope, that in nothing I shall be ashamed, but that with all boldness, as always, so now also Christ shall be magnified in my body, whether it be by life, or by death.
> 21 For to me to live is Christ, and to die is gain.
> 22 But if I live in the flesh, this is the fruit of my labour: yet what I shall choose I wot not.
> 23 For I am in a strait betwixt two, having a desire to depart, and to be with Christ; which is far better:
> 24 Nevertheless to abide in the flesh is more needful for you.
> 25 And having this confidence, I know that I shall abide and continue with you all for your furtherance and joy of faith;
> 26 That your rejoicing may be more abundant in Jesus Christ for me by my coming to you again.

1. *The Basis of the Triumph* (19). The set of circumstances

from which Paul expects deliverance may mean his personal, final salvation (cf. Rom. 5:9 for the future tense of *salvation*), the personal antagonisms of his adversaries who are preaching with impure motives, or his ultimate vindication in court. Probably all are included. These things *shall turn*, literally, "shall come off," or "eventuate to" his *salvation*, that is, his spiritual development and truest welfare in the long run. *Salvation (sōtērian)* cannot mean his release from prison, for this is uncertain, and further, to him personally it matters not whether he lives or dies (20).

Sōtēria was used by prophets and psalmists in the Old Testament to indicate victory in a contest for the right. Paul evidently pictures himself as in a battle, wrestling "not against flesh and blood, but against principalities, against powers" (Eph. 6:12), over which the ultimate issue will be victory (cf. 1:27-30). Furthermore, his imprisonment will perfect his character to the glory of Christ. He is certain that "all things work together for good to them that love God, to them who are the called according to his purpose" (Rom. 8:28), and that his striving in this situation will be his witness in the day of judgment. Paul's confidence rests on God's faithfulness to His servants in similar circumstances in times past.

The first part of verse 19 is a quotation from Job 13:16 (Septuagint), to which Paul's wording is identical. He is certain that whether he is acquitted or not, his stand for Christ will be vindicated. This was the expectation of Job who said, "I know that I shall be vindicated" (Job 13:18, RSV). Paul seems to be comparing himself with this ancient overcomer. Verses 12-15 of chapter 2 are very close to the final injunctions of Moses to the Israelites (cf. Deuteronomy 31), and may indicate a comparison with Moses also. It would appear that Paul is encouraging himself in the Lord (cf. 1 Sam. 30:6) by considering the similar lot of the saints of whom he has read in the Old Testament Scriptures.[29] In so doing, he is reminded of God's faithfulness and is enabled to see the uses of adversity. Paul's confidence also is based on the divine aid available through Christ and on the continued prayer support of his friends at Philippi.

The fellowship that Paul and the Philippians enjoy makes him constantly aware of the need for the *prayer* (literally, "supplication," cf. comment on v. 4) of his "fellow" Christians in order to appropriate *the supply of the Spirit of Jesus Christ. Epichorēgias* implies "bountiful supply" (Gal. 3:5) and means help which undergirds and strengthens the object (as in Eph. 4:16: "a ligament which acts as a support"). The word comes from *chorus,* which describes those who were employed as a background in Greek tragedies. The expense of the chorus was to be borne by a person selected by the state, who defrayed expenses both of training and maintenance. Also the word was used to describe the beneficences of wealthy citizens who, giving a banquet, furnished food, and *in addition,* entertainment for the evening.[30] Thus Paul's experiences will be made to eventuate into his salvation by the "resources of the Spirit" (Phillips), who will "furnish all that is necessary" (Adam Clarke). He will not only initially supply grace but will continue to dispense sufficient grace as the need arises.

The Spirit of Jesus is found only here in the New Testament. Similar expressions make it clear that the reference is to the Holy Spirit (Acts 5:9; 16:7, RSV; Rom. 8:9; 1 Cor. 12:4; 2 Cor. 3:17; Gal. 4:6). Whether the Spirit *is* the supply or *brings* the supply makes little difference. Lightfoot is probably right in saying, "The Spirit of Jesus is both the Giver and Gift." Paul knows he can count on the strength of the Spirit whom the Lord promised to His disciples in the day of their arraignment before tribunals and magistrates (Mark 13:11; Luke 12:11-12) and for all the demands of his life. He desires the church's prayer for this enablement.

The basis of the Apostle's triumph over adversity is *through* the *prayers* of the Philippians *and the supply of the Spirit of Jesus Christ.* Both are necessary. There is only one preposition here *(dia, through),* tying together *prayer* and *supply.* As their prayers ascend, the supply of the Spirit descends. Their prayers and God's grace are like "two buckets in a well; while one ascends the other descends."

2. *The Hope of the Triumph* (20-24)

a. *The supreme aim and hope of Paul's life.* Paul's *earnest expectation and . . . hope* is that in the present or future testing he will not have reason to *be ashamed.* Rather, he desires that whatever the outcome of his trial, he will act and speak with courage so that Christ will be honored in his *body, whether it be by life, or by death. Earnest expectation* is a single word in the Greek *(apokaradokian)* and suggests the intense turning away of one's vision from everything to fix on the object of its desire. Literally it means "stretching out the head" to see something in the distance, which in the case of Paul, meant the day of Christ. The Apostle's aim is at all cost to avoid, both *now* and *always,* bringing reproach on the cause of Christ. The thought is made lucid by the NEB translation: "that . . . the greatness of Christ will shine out clearly in my person, whether through my life or through my death." Here is the challenge of every Christian—to communicate the gospel through one's person.

Paul had not been "put to shame" (ASV) in defending the gospel before coming to Rome (Rom. 1:14-16), and it is his determined hope that he will not now lack *boldness,* literally, "openness in speaking" (cf. Acts 14:13). Rather, he desires that *Christ shall be magnified in my body, whether it be by life, or by death* (20). *Christ* is the subject of this clause, which is cast in the passive voice. Meyer suggests the passive is used because the Apostle feels he is the organ of God's working.[31] Thus Paul does not say, "I shall magnify Christ," but "Christ shall be magnified in my body." His body will be the "theater in which Christ's glory is displayed" (cf. Rom. 12:1; 6:13).[32]

b. *The joy and goodness of life in Christ—for to me to live is Christ* (21). Beginning at verse 21 Paul seems to be musing to himself, "working out his feelings as he shares his unedited thoughts" (Dunnam). Some have thought that the broken sequence of the words, particularly verses 21-24, suggest the verses have been tampered with by a later scribe. However, we should not expect lucid prose from one who is confronted with the issues of life and death. Paul is being drawn by two strong desires and two significant truths: (1) the joy and goodness of life, and (2) the possibility and gain of death. Literally, "the living is Christ." Because "to live" is the subject of the sentence, Lightfoot translates: "To me life is Christ." Or it has been rendered, "Living, I shall live Christ." *To me* does not mean "in my opinion." It is more emphatic and is tantamount to saying, "The commitment of my life is to Christ." Christ is the Object of Paul's natural life. He is the Beginning and End. In the light of the reference to the *body* (20) Paul evidently is speaking of his total physical and practical life of service (cf. Rom. 6:16). That which makes this earthly life meaningful and fruitful is Christ.

Such a life is not a human possibility. It is a divine work. Consequently, the reference presupposes the deep and inward life of God in the soul. Thus Paul declares: "I [have been] crucified with Christ: nevertheless I live; yet not I, but Christ liveth in me: and the life which I now live in the flesh I live by the faith of the Son of God, who loved me, and gave himself for me" (Gal. 2:20). Paul has completely yielded himself to Christ, who lives in him and for him (cf. 2 Cor. 4:10, 16; 5:15, 17; Col. 3:3). He is "constrained" by a new force—love (2 Cor. 5:14). For him life is lived to the full only in Christ, for "this is life eternal," to "know thee the only true God, and Jesus Christ whom thou hast sent" (John 17:3). He seems to be saying: "The presence of Christ is the cheer of my life, the spirit of Christ the life of my life, the love of Christ the power of my life, the will of Christ the law of my life; and the glory of Christ the end of my life."[33]

c. *The possibility and gain of death*—*to die is gain,* that is, to die would be gain. The form of the words *to die* denotes the act of dying, not the process (cf. 1 Cor. 15:31; 2 Cor. 5:12), nor the style, of death (Moule). Clearly, then, Paul has in mind his possible martyrdom. The Greek tense indicates not that death itself is gain, but the state after death, or resulting from Paul's death, is gain.

Kerdos (gain) was used to describe interest on money. Thus to die is to cash in both principal and interest and to have more of Christ than when living.[34] Paul's concept of *gain* is quite in contrast to the selfish motive of material gain which characterized the merchants of Philippi, and which first awakened hostility to the preaching of the gospel there (Acts 16:19). J. W. C. Wand translates this: "To me indeed life means Christ, and death would be an added advantage."[35]

The gain consists not only in the Apostle's being ushered into the immediate presence of the Lord (23; also 2 Cor. 5:8) and receiving his heavenly reward, but primarily in the promotion of the gospel by the witness which his martyrdom for Christ will produce. Since Paul's aim is to magnify Christ, and his death will accomplish this, his death will be a gain for the proclamation of the gospel and for him personally. He wants his life to be spent in the service of Christ, and death for him will be the crowning service. Wesley has captured Paul's spirit and thought in one of his hymns of consecration:

> *Ready for all Thy perfect will,*
> *My acts of faith and love repeat,*
> *Till death Thy endless mercies seal,*
> *And make the sacrifice complete.*

Paul was not claiming, nor does Christian faith claim, that this bodily life is something from which death provides a welcome escape. When the supreme purpose of one's life is Christ, death neither takes from nor adds to that glorious fact. Christ transforms both life and death, making life good and death a means to a greater end.

Hamlet, in his famous "To be, or not to be" soliloquy, debates whether "'tis best to live and suffer the arrows of fortune or die and risk the chance of accusing dreams." Neither prospect is pleasant. He "regards both life and death as evils, and does not know which is the lesser; St. Paul regards both as blessings and knows not which to prefer."[36] The unbeliever, represented by Hamlet, is obsessed by the evils and frustrations of life. The Christian, as illustrated by Paul, majors on the goodness of life and the opportunities it affords. The Apostle was "not found trying to weigh two sets of bitters against one another, but two sets of sweets. Life here, this side of death, is good; life there, on the other side of death, is better" (Paul Rees).

For 30 years Paul has lived, not for self, material things, or personal advancement—but for Christ. He is prepared to die because he is prepared to live. Right living ensures right dying: "To be all for Christ while I live, to find at length He is all for me when I die."[37] The entire verse might be rendered: "To me, living and dying, Christ is gain." Maclaren comments beautifully on this passage: "It matters very little to the servant whether he is out in the cold and wet 'ploughing and tending cattle,' or whether he is waiting on his master at the table. It is service all the same, only it is warmer and lighter in the house than in the field, and it is promotion to be made *an indoor servant*."[38]

d. *The dilemma of the committed—if I live in the flesh, this is the fruit of my labour: yet what I shall choose I wot not* (22). The brokenness of the grammar indicates the Apostle's quandary. His choice is between continuing his work (assuming a favorable verdict at court) and sealing his testimony by his death. To *live in the flesh* refers to Paul's earthly life and ministry, and obviously not to "life in sin" which the term normally suggests (as in Rom. 7:5, 18). Christ is the fruit of Paul's labor (Rom. 1:13; 1 Cor. 3:6). Grotius explains *fruit of my labour* as an idiom for "worthwhile." Thus "if I live in the flesh, glorifying Christ, this is worth my while."[39] Wand's translation is illuminating: "So long as physical existence gives an opportunity of fruitful work, I hardly know which to prefer." According to Barth's rendering, to live "means to me reaping harvest." When the alternative is brought to Paul's mind he knows not which to choose. Moffatt renders *I wot not* (*wot*, the old English word for "know") as "I cannot tell." However, some think *gnōrizō (wot)* means "declare." If so, then the idea is thus: If it is better for the church that I live, then I will not declare my personal choice.

Paul's state of indecision resulted from the pressure of opposite forces—*I am in a strait betwixt two* (23). Literally, "I am pressed." *Sunechomai* carries the idea of violence and external control (cf. Luke 12:50; Acts 18:5; 2 Cor. 5:14). It describes a traveler in a narrow pass, walled in on either side, able to go only straight ahead. Thus Moffatt translates this: "I am in a dilemma." If he could follow his human desire, Paul would choose to die *and to be with Christ.* This is evidently his dominant inclination since *having a desire to depart* literally reads, "the" desire, suggesting that this is not just one among many desires. *Epithumia (desire)* normally is used in the New Testament in referring to evil desire or lust. Here, however, it refers to normal, natural desire, from which we may infer that these too—even strong spiritual impulses—must be as subject to God's will as the desires of the sinful flesh (cf. Gal. 5:16, 24).

Analusai (depart) is a metaphor drawn from the loosing of tent stakes and ropes for breaking camp (cf. 2 Tim. 4:6; 2 Cor. 5:1). As a euphemism for death it provides an appropriate way for Paul, a tentmaker by trade, to describe the departure from this life. Sometimes it was used to describe the pulling up of anchors and setting sail. Adam Clarke suggests that it was a metaphor drawn from the commander of a vessel in a foreign port who wants to set sail for his own country but has not yet had orders from his owner. Barclay points out that it is also the word used for solving problems. The state that follows death will bring solutions to life's deep riddles (1 Cor. 13:12).

It is the destination made possible by death, namely being *with Christ,* and not death itself, which fuels Paul's yearning *to depart.* While logically those two are to be distinguished, chronologically they go together. To depart and to be with Christ are simultaneous. That is, the dead come immediately into the presence of the Lord. For the Christian, to be absent from the body is to be present with the Lord (2 Cor. 5:8; also John 14:3). This experience of being with Christ Paul describes in superlative terms which are partially obscured by translation. *Pollō-mallon kreisson* literally means, in rather poor English grammar, "more better by far."

Yet Paul is willing, if God wills, to make his personal longing to see Christ subordinate to his pastoral responsibility to his fellow believers at Philippi (24).

Here is the other side of Paul's dilemma. On the one hand he desires to be with Christ; on the other is the recognition of his duty toward the church. Between these alternatives he maintains a "holy equilibrium." The will of God must be done regardless of his own desire. *To abide in the flesh,* literally, "to remain by the flesh" *(epimenein),* means "to stand fast by" as a soldier refusing to leave his post (cf. v. 17).

No man lives to himself. Thus Paul must think of the welfare of his friends at Philippi. He is willing to forgo eternal bliss for earthly service. Is not this the "mind of Christ" which he desires so much for the Philippians (2:5-8), and which has characterized the life of the great Apostle (1 Cor. 10:33; Rom. 9:3)? No truer picture of the Christian's understanding of the relation of this world to the "other world," of "reward" and "service," could be drawn. Paul's longing is not for death but for Christ. Death will simply be a doorway into a fuller relationship with Him. In no sense does he consider it release from the responsibilities of this temporal existence. The charge that the Christian is so "other-worldly" as to be concerned only with "pie in the sky by and by" is a caricature based on a misunderstanding of the Christian faith. The good of the "other" must always come first ahead of any personal desires. Consequently, Paul is willing to continue his service that the Philippians might be "more strengthened, like young fowls, who need their mother until their feathers are set."[40]

3. *The Result of the Triumph* (25-26). The tone of these verses, which are free from the heavy overtones of imminent martyrdom found in verses 20 and 23, has led scholars to

speculate that there may have been reasons for Paul to expect a release from prison. Whether the apparent expectation that he would see the Philippians again was fulfilled remains uncertain. Of this, however, we can be sure— whatever occurred, God would make it work together for His glory and their good.

The beginning of verse 25 should be read with verse 24. That is, Paul is confident that his life is advantageous to the Philippians; thus, he is expressing a personal perspective (2:24) rather than a prophecy. He is simply stating his persuasion that God will permit what is best. *Abide and continue* are a play on words. *Menō* (*I shall abide,* or "remain" [RSV]) with the prefix *para* ("beside") becomes *paramenō* ("I shall continue"). The meaning of Paul, then, is "I shall remain with you all, and I shall remain ready to stand beside and help you all." Such help will contribute to the Philippians' "progress" (*furtherance, prokopēn;* cf. comment on v. 12) and "joy in the faith" (ASV).

Paul's coming to them again would be an answer to prayer, confirming their faith and promoting their joy. The word *rejoicing* in verse 26 fails to capture the mood of the Philippians if Paul were restored to them. The Greek word is *kauchēma* and means "glorying" (ASV), "exultation," or "boasting." Literally, the verse says, "that your boasting may abound in Christ Jesus in me through my presence again with you." *Kauchaomai,* "to glory," may be used in both a false and a legitimate sense (cf. Rom. 15:17; Eph. 2:9). Thus the Philippians' "boasting" *(kauchēma)* must be in Christ; though the occasion for it would be Paul's restoration from prison. His return to Philippi would be cause for giving glory to God. *Parousia (coming)* is the word used in profane Greek describing the ceremonious entry of a king or governor into a city, with all the manifestations of joy which attended it. Paul is assured that if he is permitted to see the Philippians again, their mutual fellowship will cause them to give him a royal welcome.

Appeal for Single-mindedness and Obedience
Philippians 1:27—2:18

This entire section must be understood as a unit, the artificial chapter division after 1:30 notwithstanding. It is a sustained appeal for unity of heart and mind and for obedience to Christ. Paul's appeal is based on the Philippians' respect for the Apostle, the impression they make on unbelievers, the gratitude for being Christians, and primarily the example of Christ (2:5-11). Here is a view of what Christ, through His Apostle, expects of the Church which bears His name.

Paul has relieved the Philippians by discussing his personal situation and that of the gospel in Rome. Now he shifts attention from himself to his readers. Though the affectionate tone remains at least until verse 30, the Apostle now turns to exhortation. A clue to the interpretation of this passage may be found in Paul's references to obedience—both Christ's obedience (2:8) and that of the Philippians (2:12). A leading virtue of "servants" and "saints" is obedience, in which Paul and his readers share a common fellowship. The counsel which is here offered presupposes a spirit of obedience. Paul expects the Philippians to follow him as he follows Christ.

Conduct Worthy of the Gospel
Philippians 1:27-30

27 Only let your conversation be as it becometh the gospel of Christ: that whether I come and see you, or else be absent, I may hear of your affairs, that ye stand fast in one spirit, with one mind striving together for the faith of the gospel;

28 And in nothing terrified by your adversaries: which is to them an evident
token of perdition, but to you of salvation, and that of God.
29 For unto you it is given in the behalf of Christ, not only to believe on him,
but also to suffer for his sake;
30 Having the same conflict which ye saw in me, and now hear to be in me.

1. *Our Heavenly Citizenship* (27). With skill Paul joins the inner state of the church, which needs some improvement in love and brotherly acceptance, with its outward impact on the surrounding pagan environment—*only let your conversation be as it becometh the gospel of Christ.* The word *only (monon)* means "above all, at all costs" (cf. Gal. 3:2). The Apostle has great expectations of this congregation and wants to avoid being disappointed in them. With appropriate tact he encourages and admonishes the Philippians before addressing some obvious faults mentioned later.

Conversation in current usage is too limited in meaning to be an accurate translation. It comes from the Latin word *conversari,* meaning "to conduct oneself." At the time of the King James translation (1611), *conversation* referred to the total life and conduct of an individual, not merely to his manner of speaking. Thus the *American Standard Version* translates the verse this way: "Only let your manner of life be worthy of the gospel of Christ." The gospel is not only a message to bring deliverance, but also a guide to be followed.

However, even this clarification does not bring out the full meaning of the Apostle. The word he uses is *politeuesthe,* which comes from *politēs,* "citizen." Its original meaning was for one to be guided by certain regulations and laws. Philippi was a Roman colony, which meant that some of her inhabitants were "citizens" of Rome. They were thereby entitled to all the privileges of such citizenship (cf. Introduction). But this also involved them in certain obligations. A Roman colony was a bit of Rome on foreign soil. Her citizens were subject to her laws, not those of the provincial authorities. Though they may never have seen Rome, their first allegiance was to the imperial city. Literally, Paul is saying to the Philippian Christians, "Conduct yourself worthily as citizens of the glad tidings of Christ," as well as of the city of Rome. The thought is amplified in 3:20 where Paul states, "For our conversation is in heaven." Moffatt's well-known translation of this verse reads, "But we are a colony of heaven." "As Philippi was to Rome, so is earth to heaven, the colony on the outskirts of the empire, ringed round by boundaries, and separated by sounding seas, but keeping open its communications, and one in citizenship" (Maclaren). Thus Paul is declaring, "By all means let attention to your heavenly citizenship be supreme, no matter what."

This appeal for a consistent Christian life is placed in the context of a reminder that his visit to them is still uncertain. They are not to count on his coming to them again. Whether or not he is able to come, they should begin to act immediately. Secondary motives would be insufficient to produce in them a lasting steadfastness and acceptable conduct. They must stand firm because of the character of God and the quality of their devotion, and not because of a desire to produce a good impression on a man, even Paul. In their own particular set of circumstances they are to perform their spiritual duties and not wait for a more expedient time.

Paul hopes to hear that the Philippians are standing *fast in one spirit, with one mind striving together for the faith of the gospel. Stēkete (stand)* may be a military metaphor meaning to stand firm, to refuse to retreat in spite of enemy onslaughts (cf. 2 Thess. 2:15; John 8:44). Or the metaphor may be drawn from the spectacles of the Roman amphitheater. *Pneumati (spirit)* has been interpreted as the Holy Spirit by some, and as the human spirit by others. The Holy Spirit appears preferable since the exact expression *(en heni pneumati)* is used in 1 Cor. 12:13 and Eph. 2:18, where the references are unquestionably to the Holy Spirit. If the human spirit is referred to, it means that quality in man which makes fellowship with God a possibility. Even if this interpretation be adopted, it is clear in Paul that a genuine "common spirit" is not a possibility apart from the Holy Spirit.[41]

One mind is, literally, "one soul" *(psychē). Psychē* is the seat of the affections, desires, and passions. These must be brought under the control of the Holy Spirit (Rom. 8:4-5). "One soul" seems to be an athletic metaphor indicating teamwork and synchronization. Here it signifies a deep inward unity of purpose that is possible only in the Holy Spirit (cf. Acts 4:32). Paul's concern is that the strife characteristic of the church at Rome will not be manifest among the Philippians. They must strive *together,* not in opposition to each other but in a common cause. They have entered the Kingdom violently, and they must continue to protect and extend it violently (Matt. 11:12). The Roman colonies were sometimes expected to extend their frontiers by aggressive warfare. In the same way the "colony of heaven" which is at Philippi is to "fight the good fight of faith" (1 Tim. 6:12), thereby enlarging itself.

The Philippians' struggle, and that of all Christians, is a dual one—against their foes (28) and positively *for the faith of the gospel.* However, *faith* is not here to be personified as though one were to strive either "with" or "for" it in an objective sense. Nor does it mean merely a body of teaching, although this may be included (cf. 1 Tim. 6:20; 2 Tim. 1:14; Jude 3). Rather, it refers to the trust and commitment which comes as a result of hearing the gospel. The entire expression suggests the maintenance of a right relationship to the gospel and thus to Christ, and could also well include the winning of converts to the gospel. The Philippians are to keep themselves in such a spirit of love as to be able to fight "side by side like one man for the faith of the gospel" (Moffatt).

2. *The Divine Enablement* (28-30). Paul is concerned with the spiritual progress of the Philippians. He knows that timidity and fear are an impediment to advancement. Fear, particularly, may arise from lack of trust in God. Thus the Apostle in these verses points to a reservoir of divine strength—*of God* (28)—which will enable them to overcome all opposition and to accept the creative aspects of suffering for Christ's sake.

   a. *Power to overcome opposition—in nothing terrified*

by your adversaries. Pturomenoi (terrified) originally applied to a frightened animal, particularly a shying horse, or the uncontrollable stampede of a startled herd. This onslaught of fear had been brought on by the opposition of the Philippians' *adversaries (antikeimenōn).* The word in the New Testament is used to denote the enemies of Jesus (Luke 13:17), the opponents of the Apostle at Ephesus (1 Cor. 16:9), the Antichrist (2 Thess. 2:4), and Satan, the adversary of God and man (1 Tim. 5:14-15). In the light of the remaining portion of the verse, "opponents" here does not refer to Jewish subverters of the gospel but to pagans. It is likely a reference to mob violence, the hatred of the Philippian populace who felt threatened and rebuked by the purity of life of the believers. From verse 30 it appears Paul may have in mind the opposition which he himself earlier encountered in Philippi.

Whoever the enemies are, the Philippians need not be intimidated. The phrase is paraphrased by Phillips thus: "not caring two straws for your enemies." If Paul is comparing himself to Moses giving final injunctions to the Israelites recorded in the last chapters of Deuteronomy (cf. comment on 1:19), he may well be using Moses' language: "Do not fear or be in dread of them" (Deut. 31:6, RSV).

Both the opposition against the church, and the believers' endurance certify two things: the *perdition* of the opponents and the *salvation* of the faithful—*which is to them an evident token of perdition, but to you of salvation, and that of God* (28). Literally it means, "seeing it is a clear demonstration to them of destruction, but of your *[humōn]* salvation." Both *sōtērias (salvation)* and *apōleias (perdition)* refer to final destiny. Courage, steadfastness, and fidelity point to a source of divine strength and evidence the reality of one's salvation. They also betoken the destruction and ruin and waste (cf. 2 Thess. 2:3) which await all the enemies of God.

These startling results of faithfulness are clearly a divine work, that is, "from God" (ASV). Lightfoot thinks this expression "from God" suggests a practice of the gladiators whose destiny depended upon the participators who by a signal indicated whether they were to live or die. Thus the gladiators closely watched the sign from the grandstands. But the "Christian gladiator does not anxiously await the signal of life or death from the fickle crowd." He gets his signal "from God," who gives him a surer sign of deliverance. Such poise on the part of the Christian indicates that God is working in him, and becomes a sign to the opponents of their ruin. They witness a superhuman work in the faithful and thus feel despair: "If God is against us, who can be for us?"[42]

Is Paul thinking of this way in which God dealt with him as a persecutor of the Church, particularly as he witnessed the triumphant death of the first Christian martyr, Stephen (Acts 7:59-60; 9:5)? The Philippians also know a classic example of this way of God with men. One of their number, the former Philippian jailer, had been convicted and converted by seeing the power of God manifest in the lives of Paul and Silas (Acts 16:27-34).

b. Power to suffer gracefully. Suffering for the sake of Christ is both a trust and a privilege. While it is not to be sought, if it comes for the sake of Christ, it is to be joyfully accepted as an opportunity for faithful stewardship and accountability. In such case it is granted in and by the grace of God—*for unto you it is given in the behalf of Christ, not only to believe on him, but also to suffer for his sake* (29). Literally it says, "Because to you it was granted." Note that *echaristhē (given)* is formed on the stem of the noun *charis,* meaning "grace" or "favor." Thus even as belief in Christ, or absolute saving trust, is a gift of God, so also is suffering for the sake of Christ (cf. Matt. 5:11-12; 2 Tim. 2:12; Eph. 2:8; John 1:12-13).

In fact, believing and suffering seem to go together. To believe means, not primarily to consent to a body of propositional truth, but to entrust oneself to what the gospel proclaims. To believe on Christ is to commit oneself to Him fully and to seek to bring glory to Him by one's life as a citizen of His kingdom. Those who believe are given the opportunity of being conformed to Christ through suffering.

To Ananias God said regarding Saul, later Paul, at his conversion: "I will show him how much he must suffer for my name" (Acts 9:15-16, NIV).

Suffering is not a mark of God's anger (Acts 5:41; Col. 1:24; 1 Pet. 4:13). To the Philippians, it was the "marriage gift when they were espoused to Christ: the bounty when they enlisted in his service. Becoming one with him they entered into the fellowship of his suffering" (3:10).[43] They are to take heart because their suffering is for "Christ's sake" (2 Cor. 8:2).

Paul refers to his own case and assures the Philippians that their experience is one with his—*having the same conflict which ye saw in me, and now hear to be in me.* The Philippians had seen Paul's conflicts with enemies on his first visit to them (Acts 16:12, 19; 1 Thess. 2:2), and now they have heard that he is engaged in similar conflict. *Conflict (agōna)* seems to be an allusion to the familiar athletic contests. Paul pictures the Christians as athletes in the arena, engaged in a wrestling match against their pagan opponents (Eph. 6:12). The Philippians and Paul, as are all Christians, are in the same conflict. Consequently, they are striving together in a fellowship of obedience and suffering, assured that the same grace of Christ will make them more than conquerors through Him that loved them (1:7; Rom. 8:37).

PHILIPPIANS 2

Motivation to Oneness of Spirit

Philippians 2:1-4

> 1 If there be therefore any consolation in Christ, if any comfort of love, if any fellowship of the Spirit, if any bowels and mercies,
> 2 Fulfil ye my joy, that ye be likeminded, having the same love, being of one accord, of one mind.

3 Let nothing be done through strife or vainglory; but in lowliness of mind let each esteem other better than themselves.
4 Look not every man on his own things, but every man also on the things of others.

1. *Christ Supports Spiritual Unity* (1-2). The danger of disunity seems to have been the only factor threatening the Philippian congregation at this time. This may be a perennial danger whenever believers are serious about their faith and commitment to Christ. To avoid this peril and to preserve spiritual oneness the Philippians are to recall the participation *(fellowship)* in the Spirit by whom they were baptized into the Body (1 Cor. 12:13) and by whom they have access to the Father (Eph. 2:18). Since there is "one Spirit" they are to keep the unity of the Spirit in the bond of peace (Eph. 4:3). Here is the source of spiritual oneness and the theological foundation of all Christian unity.

It should be noted that *therefore* evidently refers back to 1:27. Further, Paul's use of *if* is used rhetorically to "get a grip on their attention" (Robertson) and in no way expresses doubt. It might be better rendered "since." The Apostle's appeal to unity is fivefold:

a. He appeals to the authority of Christ—*if there be . . . any consolation in Christ. Paraklēsis (consolation)* may be translated "exhortation," for Paul often used the cognate verb in the sense of "I exhort" or, as in the following, "I beseech" (see Rom. 12:1; 15:30; 16:17; 1 Cor. 1:10; 4:16; 16:15; Eph. 4:1; Phil. 4:2).[44] The phrase *in Christ* thus appears to be a kind of apostolic authorization—Paul's authority is from the Lord, or it may be a subtle reminder that no one can live in unity with Christ and at the same time have broken fellowship with others. It may be observed that the related word, *Paraclete,* has been rendered as the "Advocate," "Comforter," or "One who strengthens." The "strength" to which Paul here refers has its source in Christ (cf. the meaning of "in Christ," 1:1).

b. He appeals to the power of love—*any comfort of love;* literally, "consolation" or "incentive." *Paramuthion (comfort)* has the force of constraint or motivation. Christ's love for His Church (2 Cor. 5:14; Eph. 5:25), Paul's love for the Philippians, and their love for one another should motivate them to settle their differences.

c. He appeals to their common life in the Holy Spirit—*any fellowship of the Spirit.* For the meaning of *fellowship (koinōnia),* see 1:5. There is no article before Spirit, but it is presupposed that this fellowship of spirit is a gift of the Holy Spirit. When one lives in spiritual discord with another, one gives evidence that the life of the Spirit is not present.

d. He appeals to their "affectionate sympathy" (Dibelius, see Col. 3:12) and compassion—*any bowels and mercies.* The Greek word *splanchna* refers to the inward parts, but Paul uses it to mean the heart and lungs. The Hebrews used a comparable metaphor for feelings, which meant bowels. Thus Paul is referring to the seat of the emotions, "the abode of tender feelings" (Lightfoot). *Mercies* translates *oiktirmoi,* which signifies the active and outward manifestations of the deepest and tenderest of feelings for one another.

Clearly Paul is not giving a word of superficial advice, but he is turning their minds to the lofty aims of the Lord's will that they be one. He further seeks to persuade them to unity by the constraining power of love, their joint participation in the Spirit, and the guidelines of human affection which believers should feel for, and demonstrate to, their brothers in the faith.

e. He appeals to the Philippians to live in unity to complete his joy—*fulfil ye my joy* (2) or, as Lightfoot puts it, "Fill my cup of gladness to overflowing." This fervent appeal by the Apostle has been called a "tautology of earnestness."[45] But it is no selfish plea. Paul loves the Philippians as with the love of Christ (cf. 1:7-8). They share with him in a mutual fellowship. Thus what would complete his joy and love, would also be for their good (1:3-4). They are his "joy and crown" (4:1), and yet he will rejoice in them even more if they will acknowledge the source of their spiritual unity and live in peace.

The meaning of the verse seems clear: If there is any divine strength or "support" available "to those who are in Christ Jesus" as you are (and there is); if there is any consolation or incentive which springs from your love (and Paul is confident there is); if participation in the Holy Spirit means anything (and it does); if there be in you any affectionate tenderness (and Paul is sure there is); [46] then dwell in harmony. In so doing you will complete your fellowship and also my joy. If Paul's appeal is followed, a fourfold result will follow. The Philippians will be *likeminded, having the same love,* literally, "having the same mind and the same love." Further, they will be *of one accord, of one mind,* literally, "sharing the same soul" and "minding the one thing." The Philippians are to act "together as if but one soul activated them."[47] The reinforcement given by these expressions to the appeal to spiritual oneness is intentional. With all the intensity he can gather, Paul is calling not for a unity of judgment, but for a moral unanimity—a oneness of disposition.

2. *The Submission of Spiritual Unity* (3-4). William Barclay has distilled the meaning of verses 3 and 4 by stating that Paul is addressing the three great causes of discord and disunity, namely, selfish ambition, the desire for personal prestige, and concentration on self.

The clause *Let nothing be done through strife or vainglory* (3*a*) is incomplete, for "let" and "be done" are not in the Greek. In the light of the word *phronountes* (*of one mind,* "minding" or "considering") of the previous verse, the ellipsis might be better supplied, "thinking nothing in the way of strife."[48] *Strife (eritheian),* "rivalry" (NEB, Phillips), "faction" (ASV) is the same word as is rendered *contention* in 1:16, where it is used to describe Paul's enemies. Here it seems to denote party squabbles, petty and self-seeking conceits producing a spirit of quarrelsomeness. The submission of spiritual unity will not countenance anything that is done "according to faction" or "groundless conceit" *(vainglory, kenodoxian).*

But in lowliness of mind let each esteem other better than themselves (3b). This is no plea for an abject servility which is often the mask of a false humility. Rather, it is a call for genuine self-appraisal which acknowledges that one has shortcomings unknown to others; and that others possess obvious virtues which one himself does not demonstrate. True humility grows out of a clear recognition of one's dependence upon God.

Look not every man on his own things, but every man also on the things of others (4). The verse is an imperative. One is not to fix his eye merely on his own interests, as a runner fixes his eye on the goal alone and nothing else (cf. Rom. 12:10). This may be more than a simple admonition to consider the interests of others. It may mean to fix one's attention upon the gifts, the spiritual endowments, the good qualities in fellow Christians. The phrase "every man" is used twice. Probably in the first usage, and certainly in the second, the Greek is plural. It may then be rendered by "each circle" or "each set."[49] The church at Philippi has not been affected by heresy. Rather, there is a threat to the fellowship on account of the self-preoccupation of certain individuals who have formed cliques or parties within the church.

A genuine humility will prevent any from insisting even on what he considers to be his own rights (see 1 Cor. 6:7),[50] or his group's rights. The Spirit of Him who was "meek and lowly in heart" (Matt. 11:29) will safeguard against pride in one's own spiritual attainments, on the one hand, and merciless and destructive criticism of the faults of others, on the other hand. Lest the Philippians have not yet caught what Paul is saying, the Apostle turns to the supreme example of the incarnate Lord.

The Supreme Example of Christ's Humility and Obedience

Philippians 2:5-11

5 Let this mind be in you, which was also in Christ Jesus:
6 Who, being in the form of God, thought it not robbery to be equal with God:

7 But made himself of no reputation, and took upon him the form of a servant, and was made in the likeness of men:
8 And being found in fashion as a man, he humbled himself, and became obedient unto death, even the death of the cross.
9 Wherefore God also hath highly exalted him, and given him a name which is above every name:
10 That at the name of Jesus every knee should bow, of things in heaven, and things in earth, and things under the earth;
11 And that every tongue should confess that Jesus Christ is Lord, to the glory of God the Father.

Here is one of the most majestic and profound Christological passages in all of Holy Writ. No man could presume to scale the mountain peaks of revelation in these verses. On reading them one is more inclined to praise than to analyze or theologize about them. Indeed, considering the careful construction and balance of clauses, it may well be that they are a poem or hymn used in worship by the Early Church. But one cannot avoid interpretation, and historically these verses have given rise to numerous and sometimes opposing viewpoints. Whatever particular nuances of meaning one may find here, Paul's essential message (identical with the thought expressed in 2 Cor. 8:9) is not difficult to discover if it be remembered that his primary purpose is practical in nature. He is dealing with a problem which threatens to dissolve the unity of the believers at Philippi. Over against the spirit of some to assert themselves selfishly, Paul sets the spirit of Christ as the supreme example of obedience.

1. *The Reason for Obedience* (5-6). The Philippians are to maintain unity and humility because of Christ's example of humility and obedience. Thus, says the Apostle, *let this mind be in you, which was also in Christ Jesus* (5); literally, "Think *[phroneite]* this in yourselves" (Vincent). "Think" is also used in 1:7 and 2:2. However, as has been seen, it connotes more than mere thought. It refers primarily to disposition. *Was* is not in the original text. Perhaps "is" could be better supplied. Moffatt translates the verse: "Treat one another with the same spirit as you experience in Christ Jesus." Or it has been rendered: "Have this mind within your community which ye have also in Christ Jesus." This way of

putting it is consistent with the admonition that the Philippians work out their own salvation (12), and serves also as a legitimate warning against the erroneous divorce which some professed Christians make between their strictly Christian life and their ordinary social relationships with their fellows. Here is set forth the absolute impossibility of loving God without at the same time loving one's fellowmen.

Who, being in the form of God (6a). The Greeks had two separate words for "form." One of them referred to mere external shape or appearance, as when a mirage takes the form of water. In such case there is no true equivalence between the appearance and that which it appears to be. The other Greek word suggests that the appearance or form of the object is the true revelation or expression of the object itself. That is, the form participates in the reality; thus the reality discloses itself in the form.[51] It is the second word *(morphē)* which Paul here employs (cf. also Mark 16:12). However, here it seems to have the same general meaning as "nature." Thus the phrase has been rendered: "The divine nature was his from the first" (NEB). Christ is the *morphē theou (form of God),* that is, the true and full expression or revelation of God. This revelation cannot be explained by any human categories. It is wholly inexplicable aside from the assertion that the absolute source of the revelation is God himself. Thus Paul speaks of Christ Jesus as being, or "subsisting" *(huparchōn,* and not the simple *einai,* "to be") in the form of God. To put it differently, that which is revealed, namely God, is prior to, or precedes, the form or the revelation itself. But the Revelation, or Christ the Revealer, is One with the Revealed, or God. Because this is so, the revelation of God in Christ is true. Consequently, Paul is proclaiming kerygmatically and didactically what the Church later maintained theologically—that God and Jesus Christ are *homoousias,* "of one substance," of one nature.

Thought it not robbery to be equal with God (6b). *Harpagmon (robbery)* comes from a verb meaning to "snatch," "clutch," or "seize violently." Thus the RSV translates the clause: "did not count equality with God a thing to be grasped." "Equality" seems not to refer to *nature* so much as to *relationship* (Rees). Thus Christ did not give up His equality with God when He became man. Rather, He refused to grasp or "clutch" at equality by self-assertion, or to exploit it to His own profit. As Vincent has put it, "He was not unable to assert equality with God. He was able not to assert it." Being the Revelation of God, it seems reasonable to assume that Christ might have claimed His right to be recognized as equal with God. But contrary to the accusation of His enemies (John 5:17-18), this is precisely what He refused to do—insist upon His own rights or usurp the place of God. He refused to seek self-enrichment or self-gratification. Paul may have in mind the contrast between the first Adam, who selfishly desired to be "as gods" (Gen. 3:5), and Christ, the second Adam, who unselfishly looked on the *things of others* (4).

2. *The Requirement of Obedience* (7-8). Christ willingly accepted the consequences of His self-denial, and *made himself of no reputation* (7a), literally, "emptied himself" *(heauton ekenōsen)*. Here is the well-known "kenosis" passage which has been used variously as the basis for tedious, speculative theories that have obscured the real meaning more often than they have illuminated it. A. B. Bruce has observed, in his book *The Humiliation of Christ,* that the "diversity of opinion prevailing among interpreters in regard to the meaning of [this] passage is enough to fill the student with despair, and to afflict him with intellectual paralysis." The practical setting should point in this case to the principle that the simplest interpretation is the best. It seems unnecessary to ask as many have done, Of what did Christ empty himself? His deity? His nature? His divine prerogatives? His equality? Paul simply says that Christ emptied himself. *Ekenōsen* means "pour out" with Christ *himself* as the object. Thus Christ emptied himself of himself.

The "kenosis" is Christ's act of self-abnegation in which His original native glory which He had enjoyed from eternity was hidden in His becoming man (John 17:5, 24). At no time did He allow selfish considerations to dominate His spotless life. Verses 7 and 8 have been compared with Isa. 53:12, which says, "He poured out his soul to death" (RSV). However, this refers to the giving up of His life on the Cross and not to the kenosis of the Incarnation. Nonetheless, this comparison is particularly striking in the light of the reference in verse 8 to death, and in the light of the assertion *and took upon him the form of a servant* (7), literally, "having taken the form of a slave." *Labōn (took)* is an aorist participle, indicating simultaneous action.[52]

The implication is that "subsisting" in the *form (morphē)* of God, and "having taken" the *form (morphē)* of a servant are simultaneous and not incompatible. The latter is the revelation of the former, and the former is the "explanation" of the latter. Christ's servitude was no playacting. By taking the form of a servant, He revealed the true meaning of servitude. He did not become an actual "slave" of any single man—though His servitude was expressed to individual men (Luke 22:27)—but was the actual "slave" of mankind.[53] This divine action tells us what God is like.

And was made in the likeness of men (7), or "he became *[genomenos]* like men" (plural). The reference is to the humanity of Jesus which had a beginning in time, and should be taken in the sense of Gal. 4:4: "God sent forth his Son, born of a woman" (ASV; see also Rom. 8:3). Donald Baillie, in *God Was in Christ,* has pointed out perceptively: "The Church has never taught that the human element in Jesus, His manhood, is consubstantial or co-eternal with God, but that it is consubstantial with ourselves and belongs to the order of created things." *Likeness (homoiōmati),* however, cannot be taken to be anything less than man as though Christ's humanity were only a mask or disguise. He was "really *like* men, as He truly *was* man"; but "He was also *more than man, other than men,* without which fact there would be not resemblance but *mere identity*" (Moule). Jesus Christ was truly Man, but it was in and through Him that the revelation of God came, which at the same time made Him unique and distinct from man—"very man" and "very God."

The only way Paul can express this truth is to speak of His likeness to man. Christ "is the Son of man now as well as the Son of God which He was before" (Robertson). Thus the Church's faith declares that our Lord's humanity was permanently added to His divinity.

And being found in fashion as a man (8). *Schēma (fashion)* denotes the way Christ appeared in men's eyes, as distinct from His essential nature. Thus Barth translates: "Being found in his being as a man." His contemporaries saw Him as they saw other men, subject to human drives and suffering (Heb. 4:15). Compare Isa. 53:2: "He had no form or comeliness that we should look at him, and no beauty that we should desire him" (RSV). A divine miracle is required to see God in this "servant." Faith that He is the full and true Revelation of God comes "not of blood, nor of the will of the flesh, nor of the will of man, but of God" (John 1:13). The confession that He is the Christ springs from a revelation not of "flesh and blood," but of the "Father which is in heaven" (Matt. 16:16-17). Or as Paul puts it, "No one can say 'Jesus is Lord' except by the Holy Spirit" (1 Cor. 12:3, RSV).

He humbled himself, and became obedient unto death (8). Christ's entire life on earth in its devotion to the Father and the acceptance of our human lot is intended by the phrase *he humbled himself.* However, the climax of His life, namely, His humiliation in the suffering and death on Calvary, is most prominently in view. It is this spirit of humility and obedience, as supremely illustrated in Christ, which is urged on the Philippians (v. 3).

The significance of the obedience of Christ is amplified in Heb. 5:8-10 (see also Rom. 5:12-19). His obedience is a sign of His deity and authority, for He accepted death *as obedience,* whereas ordinary men view it as a necessity.

It is not stated explicitly to whom Christ's obedience was rendered. Although the phrase *unto death* means "to the extent of death," there is reason to maintain that Christ rendered obedience to the power of the elemental spirits, that is, to death itself.[54] (This idea is reflected in Acts 2:27, 31; Rom. 10:6-8; Eph. 4:8-10; and 1 Pet. 3:19). This He did "that through death he might destroy him [who has] the power of death, that is, the devil; and deliver them who through fear of death were all their lifetime subject to bondage" (Heb. 2:14-15). However, it must be emphasized that Christ's acts of self-humiliation and obedience to death were voluntary, for of himself He laid down His life (John 10:17-18). The death of the Cross indicates the climax of Christ's self-abasement, for it was the most ignominious of all the modes of death known in Paul's day. The law of Moses had spoken a curse against it (Deut. 21:23), and the Gentiles reserved it for their most hated and common criminals. Thus the Cross was surrounded by the deepest of shame (Heb. 12:2). But by His obedience even unto the death of the Cross, Christ has "abolished death" and "brought life and immortality to light through the gospel" (2 Tim. 1:10). Consequently, "the cross of Christ has come to be his crown of glory"[55] (cf. Rom. 5:19).

3. *The Reward of Obedience* (9-11). At this point in the thought of Paul attention is changed from the humiliation and obedience of the Son of God, to God who takes the initiative. The obedience of Christ is rewarded or crowned by the act of exaltation in which the Father raised the Son from the dead and elevated Him to the place of honor. Jesus' resurrection and glorification are the Father's response to the obedience which led Him to the Cross, "the Father's 'Amen' to the Son's 'It is finished'" (R. P. Martin).

Wherefore (dio), or in consequence of His obedience, *God also hath highly exalted him* (9), literally, "superexalted Him." Jesus not only taught that exaltation follows self-humiliation, He also demonstrated it (see Matt. 18:4; 23:12; Luke 14:11; 18:14*b*). The exaltation of Christ includes His resurrection and ascension. He is lifted up to the enjoyment of that dignity of equality with God which was His by right, but which He did not grasp for as His personal possession for His own self-exploitation. Further, the Father has *given him a name* (9*b*), "freely bestowed upon Him a name." Some manuscripts read *"the* name," clearly distinguishing it from every other name (Eph. 1:20-21). Lightfoot suggests that "Jesus" is not here referred to, as many have shared that name, but the "name of Jesus." If a specific name is intended as supreme, it is probably "Lord" (cf. 11; also Acts 2:26), particularly in the light of verse 11. In the days of Paul, a soldier took his oath in the name of Caesar, indicating Caesar's authority.[56] In similar fashion, the new name of Jesus, that is, "Lord," indicates His absolute sovereignty or rulership based on absolute power. The meaning seems to be that Jesus is installed in the place which properly belongs to God himself.

That at the name of Jesus every knee should bow (10; also cf. Isa. 45:23); better, "in the name of Jesus" (ASV), or following Moffatt, "before the Name of Jesus." This does not suggest that every knee should or will bow when the actual name of Jesus is mentioned, but that Jesus is given the honor appropriate only to God, since Jesus bears "the name above all names" (v. 9, NEB), that is, the name of God himself. The Jews avoided pronouncing the divine name, but in Christ Jesus there is One who can be precisely named, through whom God can be known and worshiped. The verse may mean that in this name every prayer of man shall be offered (cf. John 14:13-14; also Eph. 2:18; 3:14; 5:20; Acts 3:6), but the allusion to things or beings in heaven, in earth, and under the earth no doubt includes the whole of creation (see Rom. 8:22; 1 Cor. 15:24-28; Eph. 1:20-22). All things, both animate and inanimate, cannot now avoid or gainsay His Lordship.

That every tongue should confess that Jesus Christ is Lord (11). The latter part of this clause seems to have been the earliest creed of the Church (see Rom. 10:9; 1 Cor. 12:3; 8:6). *Confess* encompasses the idea of thanksgiving, or joyful acknowledgment (Vincent; see Matt. 11:25; Luke 10:21). By an alternate reading of one letter, which is supported by some manuscripts, *exomologēsētai* may be rendered "shall confess," making it to be a prophetic utterance.[57] The meaning in this case would be that though all do not now personally accept the Lordship of Christ, at the final day, because

He will be their Judge, they will be unable to deny that He is also Lord, *to the glory of God the Father* (cf. Rev. 5:13). Thus Christ's self-surrender continues even in His exaltation (cf. 1 Cor. 15:28). His throne is no rival to that of His Father (Rev. 3:21). His Lordship is grounded in the Father's sovereignty and His intention to "gather together in one all things in Christ" (Eph. 1:10; also 1:20-23), so that ultimately "God may be all in all" (1 Cor. 15:28).

According to Paul, then, it is the "servant" who has become the "Lord." The practical application which the Apostle has in mind for the Philippians is expressed in the words of Jesus: "Whosoever will be chief among you, let him be your servant" (Matt. 20:27). Thomas A. Langford, in his book *Christian Wholeness,* beautifully summarizes this section, verses 5-11: "Jesus is the Lord Who is servant, and Jesus is the servant Who is Lord. As the Lord Who is servant, Jesus identifies with human life so as to establish a redemptive relationship. As servant Who is Lord, Jesus calls us to acknowledge his lordship through our servanthood."

The Admonition to Obedience
Philippians 2:12-18

> 12 Wherefore, my beloved, as ye have always obeyed, not as in my presence only, but now much more in my absence, work out your own salvation with fear and trembling.
> 13 For it is God which worketh in you both to will and to do of his good pleasure.
> 14 Do all things without murmurings and disputings:
> 15 That ye may be blameless and harmless, the sons of God, without rebuke, in the midst of a crooked and perverse nation, among whom ye shine as lights in the world;
> 16 Holding forth the word of life; that I may rejoice in the day of Christ, that I have not run in vain, neither laboured in vain.
> 17 Yea, and if I be offered upon the sacrifice and service of your faith, I joy, and rejoice with you all.
> 18 For the same cause also do ye joy, and rejoice with me.

The main point in the hymn concerning Christ in the previous section is Christ's obedience (2:8; cf. Heb. 5:8). Paul now applies this example of the obedient Lord to the Philippians. *Wherefore* is the connecting link between example and application. The Apostle admonishes that, as Christ obeyed, so should they. The admonition, however, is tempered by love. With pastoral concern he tenderly addresses the Philippians as *my beloved* (found twice in 4:1). Because of the mutual fellowship which they enjoy with him, they have always obeyed (12). That is, since he is their spiritual father, they have from the beginning of this relationship recognized his authority over them as coming from God.

1. *The Practicality of Obedience* (12). In view of their past obedience, Paul admonishes them, *Work out your own salvation* (12*b*). The structure of the sentence indicates that the phrases *not as in my presence only, but now much more in my absence* are to be connected with *work out,* and not with *obeyed.* Paul's use of *now (nun)* suggests that his absence means more than his bodily separation from them. He has been present to them until now by letter even when he could not give them a spoken message. *My absence* evidently refers to the ominous possibility of his death, following which the Philippians will not have his guiding admonitions. Consequently, they must begin to act for themselves, or work out their own salvation. This "working at" (cf. Moffatt) the continuous task of following Christ's example of obedience, of growing into the full stature of Christ, is to be *with fear and trembling,* that is, in the spirit of vigilance, humility, and dependence upon God (see 1 Cor. 2:3; Eph. 6:5), as one would hold something exceedingly precious and rare. It includes the fear of disappointing God. The identical phrase is used in 2 Cor. 7:15 and Eph. 6:5, where it is the attitude to others which is described. It thus denotes the spirit which should characterize the mutual relationships of the Philippians.

Here is no denial of justification by faith, for it is "saints," not "unbelievers," who are being addressed. *Salvation (sōtērian)* is something they already possess. The word which Paul uses for *work out* has the idea of bringing to completion (Barclay). The word can have the meaning of preservation and also health as in Acts 27:34. It is instructive to know that *salvation* comes from the same Latin word as *salve,* an ointment for healing. To be saved is to be made whole. In some measure this spiritual health is being threatened at Philippi. The Philippians are to *work out* as a community in their social relationships what God has "worked in" by faith.

The Philippians have been urged to fix their eyes on the interests of others (2:4) and not to be preoccupied with their own concerns. This reference to *salvation* seems to look back to 1:28 where the salvation of the Christian community as a whole is in view. Thus Paul seems to have in mind the corporate life of the Philippian church, and not merely the personal well-being or *salvation* of the individual believers. They are encouraged to reform the quality of their church life, working at this matter until the spiritual health of the community, diseased by the beginnings of strife and bad feelings, is restored.

The Philippians must be obedient to the pattern of Christian life modeled in the humility and exaltation of Christ; but even more importantly, the church itself must *work out* its own version of that pattern in dealing with its particular set of problems. In view of verses 14 and 15 (as well as chapter 3), it is possible that there is in the beginning stages at Philippi the spirit of self-righteousness, which threatens the unity of the fellowship. Thus each factious group is to *work out* its own salvation and stop comparing selfishly its own spiritual progress with the other groups. This interpretation is valid if Paul, as seems likely, is comparing himself to Moses, who gave his parting injunctions to Israel as a body (Deut. 31:27).

2. *The Promise of Obedience* (13). The working may be done with assurance, *for it is God which worketh in you both to will and to do of his good pleasure* (13); (also cf. 2 Pet. 1:10). *Worketh (energōn)* and *to do (energein)* are from the same verb. It is always used of God's action and of effective action. Thus Lightfoot translates it, God "works mightily" in you. Salvation is all of God, both the "willing" and the "doing," from start to finish. He creates both the will to change the

situation of His people and also accomplishes the desired state of harmony among them. In no way does this undercut man's part, which has been clearly affirmed in the previous verse. As Paul Rees puts it, "Grace and free-will, for all their interlocking mystery, are not ultimately contradictory." Paul is suggesting that the genuine Christian attitude is that of giving God all the glory. This some of the Philippians obviously were slow to do. The context indicates that "among you, in your midst," may be better than *in you*, particularly since *of his good pleasure* (*his* is not in the original) means literally "for the sake of the goodwill" (see 1:15 where the same word, *eudokian*, is used). Paul is confident that God is working, and will continue to work even after his own death, to promote goodwill at Philippi. If Paul is still comparing himself to Moses, he intends this verse as a promise (cf. Deut. 31:8).

3. *The Purpose of Obedience* (14-18). It is unnecessary to determine whether *murmurings and disputings* (14) are directed against one another or against God. Probably it is the former. Clearly, however, each involves the other. *Goggusmōn (murmurings)* indicates a spirit of discontent and stubbornness, the sins which stained the shield of the people of God in the wilderness (cf. Exod. 16:7; Num. 11:1; 16; 1 Cor. 10:10). *Dialogismōn (disputings)* suggests ill-natured controversies, dissensions, even litigation. It is possible that the plague of settling quarrels at pagan law courts had developed at Philippi as at Corinth (see 1 Cor. 6:1-11). The word translated *disputings* also means "questionings" (ASV) or "doubtings" (cf. Rom. 14:1). *Murmurings and disputings* are put in the order in which they normally develop. Quite often, though not always, intellectual doubt follows moral revolt against God and broken relationships with our fellows. The Christian must remember that "explanations, if they come at all, come after obedience, not before"[58] (cf. John 7:17).

The Philippians are called upon to make adjustments in their community of believers so that God's intention for them as a witnessing community may be fulfilled. Paul clearly sets forth in the following verses the purpose of obedience.

a. *That ye may be blameless and harmless* (15); better, that ye may "become" (*genēsthe;* ASV) or "show yourselves to be what you profess." *Blameless (amemptoi)* in the eyes of men means an irreproachable life toward which no criticism may be justifiably directed. *Harmless (akeraioi),* used by Jesus in His phrase "harmless as doves" (Matt. 10:16), denotes sincerity, purity, and that which is unmixed. The word was used of wine that is unmixed with water; or of metal that contains no alloy. Thus it has been rendered "guileless" or "innocent" (Moffatt).

This kind of life characterizes *the sons of God, without rebuke.* "Children of God" (ASV) is more adequate because it points to the character of God's family, and thus to a family likeness (John 1:12). *Amōmēta* [various readings] (*without rebuke,* or "without blemish" [ASV]) alludes to Momus, a carping deity among the Greeks, who did nothing worthwhile himself but found fault with everybody and everything. The Christian is to walk so circumspectly that even a Momus himself, or the most severe critic, may discover no occasion to find fault with him (Matthew Henry). The word *amōmos* is related to sacrifices, implying a sacrifice that is fit to be offered to God. Barclay has suggested that the words translated *blameless, harmless,* and *without rebuke* have to do with the Christian's relation to the world, to himself, and to God.

Deut. 32:5 is the inspiration for Paul's description of the calling and purpose of the Church. In the Old Testament reference, the Israelites were a "perverse and wicked generation" who failed to carry themselves as children of God. Paul applies this term to a hostile world which surrounds the church. He is hopeful that the Philippians *in the midst* of a "society morally warped, spiritually persecuted" (A. S. Way) will be as a faithful and sound witness. The vocation of believers is to be fulfilled *in the midst (meson)* of such a *crooked and perverse* society. It is true that believers are redeemed out of the values of this present evil world (Gal. 1:4);

they do not belong to the world nor share its spirit (1 John 2:15-17). Nonetheless, they are still in the world (John 17:15) and must not withdraw into safe and comfortable seclusion, thereby abdicating their commission to go into the world with the gospel (John 17:18; Mark 16:15). The Lord's people are to bear their witness *in the midst* of the world.

Paul describes the Church's influence by the metaphor of light in a dark place (cf. 2 Pet. 1:19). Believers are to be qualitatively different from the surrounding darkened society so that they will *shine as lights in the world* (15*b;* cf. Dan. 12:3). *Phōstēres* (*lights,* or "luminaries" [ASV margin]) refers to the heavenly bodies—sun, moon, and stars. As these provide light for the physical world, so the light of the Christian is to be poured out on the darkness of the moral and spiritual world. The image may also be that of lighthouses on a seacoast. In either case the Christian is to be a "light-bearer" (see Matt. 5:14-16), reflecting the glory of God like the light of a jewel (cf. Rev. 21:11).

Though his light is reflected from that "Light, which lighteth every man that cometh into the world" (John 1:9; cf. 8:12), he is to be an active "light-giver" since he is a "child of light" (1 Thess. 5:5), "holding fast" (RSV) and *holding forth the word of life* (16*a*). As Christ's "light-bearers" (Williams) and light-givers the Philippians are by their testimony and example to portray the *word of life. Epechontes (holding forth)* means both "holding firmly" or "holding out" (Weymouth; cf. NIV) in the sense of "offering" or "presenting." The latter meaning is illustrated by the word's use in classical Greek to offer wine to a guest (Vincent). The Philippians, as all Christians, are to hold fast against all "adversaries" (1:28) the truth of the gospel as a torchbearer securely clutches the light he carries; and also to offer the *word of life* to a world in the darkness of sin's grave.

Word of life, consistent with the biblical usage, must not only refer to a stated message, but to Jesus Christ, the Living Word, who is himself both Light and Life (John 1:4; 8:12; 1 John 1:1). This Word of Life frees from sin and death (Rom. 8:2). It is Christ himself, the Bread of Life, whom the

Christian offers to a hungry world. When he does so, Christ's servant becomes to those who partake the "savour of life unto life" (2 Cor. 2:16).

b. But, further, Paul has in mind a personal purpose for the obedience of the Philippians, namely, *that I may rejoice in the day of Christ, that I have not run in vain, neither laboured in vain* (16b). Increasingly the great Apostle is thinking of the final day of Christ (cf. 1:6, 10), the day of judgment and rewards, usually expressed in Scripture as "the day of the Lord." Paul speaks as if he were already looking back on his life, as though his labors on behalf of the Philippians were completed. He hopes for some cause to *rejoice* (*kauchēma;* literally, "boast") among those at Philippi when he comes to give a final account of his stewardship to God. If they failed then, he would have *run in vain* and *laboured in vain* (cf. Gal. 2:2). The imagery is of the runner in the stadium who learns upon completing his course that he has been disqualified and therefore has wasted his energies. *In vain (eis kenon)* was sometimes used of water running to waste, or of the training which appeared fruitless to a defeated athlete, or of a weaver of tent cloth who received no wages because a width of cloth was rejected as badly woven.[59] These images reflect the thought which seems to plague the Apostle regarding his apostolic ministry (1 Cor. 9:27; see also Gal. 2:2).

Almost abruptly Paul introduces another metaphor— that of sacrifice and ritual. In perhaps the most somber personal reference of the entire letter, the Apostle views the prospect of his execution for Christ as a very live possibility, if not probability. Yet his spirit is overcome with joy based on his faith that God's will for his life is best. He invites the Philippians to share his rejoicing and victory.

His personal hope that he will not have run in vain is not a selfish one, as verse 17 indicates: *Yea, and if I be offered upon the sacrifice and service of your faith, I joy, and rejoice with you all* (17). Literally, "If I am being poured out as a libation" (cf. RSV), suggesting, in sacrificial terms, that Paul has in mind a violent, even a bloody death. *Spendomai (offered)* was sometimes used to denote the fact that when an animal was about to be slain in sacrifice, wine was poured on it as a solemn act of devoting it to God (cf. Num. 15:5; 28:14).[60] Thus, if Paul's dying will in any way complete or perfect the sacrifice of the Philippians' faith, or their deeds of service, including their gifts to him (4:14; also see 2 Cor. 8:2; Heb. 13:16), he will gladly do it (cf. 2 Cor. 12:15; 2 Tim. 4:6). Moule frames Paul's thoughts thus: "Labored for you, did I say? Nay, if I have to say also *died, poured out my heart's blood,* it is only joy to me." His martyrdom and the Philippians' life (cf. Rom. 12:1) would together constitute a single mutual offering to God.

For the same cause (or "likewise in the same way") *also do ye joy, and rejoice with me* (18). Here is an invitation for the Philippians to receive with joy the news he has just conveyed, and to share his joy and triumph. Paul's words are a loving imperative, similar to those of the brave Athenian (mentioned by Plutarch) who returned to Athens from the victorious battle of Marathon, bleeding to death with the wounds he had received in the action. Coming directly to the house where the magistrates were assembled, he uttered only, "Take your share of our joy," and immediately dropped dead at their feet.[61]

Here is a challenge to believers to pour out their lives in total abandon, "as a drink offering" (ASV margin), as a sacrifice, for the sake of others—and to do it with joy.

Paul's Concerns and Future Plans

Philippians 2:19-30

At this point the subject matter of the letter changes, and Paul expresses his hopes for the future and his intention to send Timothy on a goodwill mission to Philippi. These verses give insight into the depth of feeling and character of the imprisoned Apostle. The mood seems extremely personal. It is indeed remarkable to find within a single chapter one of the most profound Christological passages in all the New Testament, and perhaps the deepest human sentiments reflected in any of Paul's writings. Such was the character of the Apostle that he saw no dichotomy between the spiritual and secular, doctrine and discipleship, commitment to God and concern for man.

But in verse 19 is to be connected with verse 12. Paul has already alluded to his unavoidable absence occasioned by his captivity. But he is concerned about the Philippians. He knows they are anxious about his welfare, and to relieve their anxiety, he is dispatching Epaphroditus to them, even before the outcome of his trial is known. Further, he is deeply interested in their spiritual progress, which is being threatened, and promises soon to send Timothy, whose visit will be a significant follow-up to the appeals for unity and steadfastness which are the heart of this letter. From his young associate the Apostle will also, in turn, receive a report from Philippi. It is this mutual fellowship of concern that provides the background for these verses.

Concern for and Commendation of Timothy

Philippians 2:19-24

19 But I trust in the Lord Jesus to send Timotheus shortly unto you, that I also may be of good comfort, when I know your state.
20 For I have no man likeminded, who will naturally care for your state.
21 For all seek their own, not the things which are Jesus Christ's.
22 But ye know the proof of him, that, as a son with the father, he hath served with me in the gospel.
23 Him therefore I hope to send presently, so soon as I shall see how it will go with me.
24 But I trust in the Lord that I also myself shall come shortly.

Paul had a shepherd's heart which would not permit him to suppose that his responsibility was discharged as soon as he won new converts to Christ. He continued to share in the concern for their growth and development in the faith. Since he cannot go himself to Philippi, he hopes *in the Lord Jesus to send Timotheus shortly* (19a). The expression *in the Lord Jesus* is no idle cliché with the Apostle. It is not by accident that in no other references to his proposed journeys does Paul use this phrase (cf. Rom. 15:24; 1 Cor. 16:7; 2 Cor. 13:1; 1 Tim. 3:14; Philem. 22). Not knowing what a day may bring, he can make his plans only as the Lord wills (see 1 Cor. 4:19). In fact, his whole life from center to circumference is under the control of Jesus Christ (cf. 1:8, 14, 21; 2:24; Rom. 9:1). All his actions are subject to his Master. Thus if the Lord approves his plans—and evidently only divine intervention will permit Paul to escape death—he will send Timothy (cf. James 4:15).

Apparently Paul not only has confidence in Timothy's ability to ascertain the situation at Philippi, but also feels that he can press home the appeals of this letter, thereby helping to improve the situation as well. Consequently, Timothy will come so that he *also may be of good comfort* (literally, "strengthened"), *when I know your state* (19b). The word translated by the phrase *may be of good comfort (eupsuchō)* was used in classical and Hellenistic Greek as a sepulchral inscription to mean, "Farewell, may it be well with your soul." It is then possible that Paul may have his own approaching death in view. He may be saying that once he has a good report through Timothy concerning the Philippians he will be ready to depart this life.

In any case, Paul is delighted to send him because he has no (other) man *likeminded* (20a). Only here in the New Testament is the word *isopsuchon* (literally, "one-souled," or "equal-souled") used. One wonders where the other friends of Paul's imprisonment were—Luke, Aristarchus, Tychicus, Onesimus, Epaphras, and John Mark. Perhaps they had not yet reached the city or had been sent on another mission which involved Paul's "care of all the churches" (2 Cor. 11:28). The meaning could be that there is no other like Timothy, but more likely that no one else aside from Timothy sees things as Paul does or shares his concerns. He was associated with Paul in the writing of 1 and 2 Thessalonians; 2 Corinthians; and now Philippians; Colossians; and Philemon. He is mentioned in 1 Corinthians and Romans, and two of Paul's pastoral letters are addressed to him. Three characteristics of Timothy are given which qualify him for this assignment. Paul Rees has put them in a charming alliteration: (1) He is *sympathetic;* (2) he is *selfless;* and (3) he is *seasoned.*

The Philippians were assured, Timothy *will naturally care for your state* (20*b*). *Gnēsiōs (naturally),* "truly" or "genuinely" (ASV margin), implies kinship and may be understood as "like a brother."[62] The word translated *care* suggests in the original a mindfulness or earnestness of thought.

Further, Timothy will not make the journey for any personal honor it may bring him, but only because of a sincere concern for those to whom he is sent. *All* [others] *seek their own, not the things which are Jesus Christ's* (21). *Hoi pantes,* literally, "one and all," or "all without exception," cannot refer to those faithful persons with right motives mentioned in 1:14, 17. No doubt some in Rome are willing to go to Philippi but are unable or unqualified, lacking the proper qualities and disposition. However, of those who can go and are competent, Timothy is the only one who is willing to undertake the task.

The assignment of resolving personal quarrels in the Philippian church would require tact, wisdom, and patience. Though Timothy was a young man (1 Tim. 4:12), physically weak (1 Tim. 5:23), and temperamentally reserved (2 Tim. 1:6-7; 1 Cor. 16:10), he was anxious to help, and Paul says of him: *Finally, ye know the proof of him, that, as a son with the father, he hath served with me in the gospel* (22). *Dokimē (proof)* was used of gold and silver which had been tested and could be accepted as current coin. It indicates not only that which is revealed by testing but also that which results from testing. Timothy's record is known to all as one of sterling character and absolute faithfulness. He stood by Paul in Philippi (Acts 16), in Thessalonica and Berea (Acts 17:1-14), in Corinth and Ephesus (Acts 18:5; 19:21-22), and even now is with Paul in Rome (Phil. 1:1). He had even been sent earlier as a delegate to Jerusalem (Acts 20:4). In it all he had served cooperatively with Paul for "the furtherance of the gospel" (NASB), even when it meant occupying a secondary place to the great Apostle. Furthermore, his companionship with Paul in the work of the gospel is couched in the intimate terms of the parent-child relationship.

Though Paul still has hope that the Lord may allow him to come to Philippi himself (24), he will send presently this young man, *so soon as I shall see how it will go with me* (23). The oldest manuscripts use a word from the verb *aphidein (see),* meaning to see something from a distance. Thus as soon as Paul can see the final outcome of his trial a little more clearly, he will send Timothy with the news. Until then he can't spare him, but in his place he will immediately send another.

Concern for and Commendation of Epaphroditus

Philippians 2:25-30

> 25 Yet I supposed it necessary to send to you Epaphroditus, my brother, and companion in labour, and fellowsoldier, but your messenger, and he that ministered to my wants.
> 26 For he longed after you all, and was full of heaviness, because that ye had heard that he had been sick.
> 27 For indeed he was sick nigh unto death: but God had mercy on him; and not on him only, but on me also, lest I should have sorrow upon sorrow.
> 28 I sent him therefore the more carefully, that, when ye see him again, ye may rejoice, and that I may be the less sorrowful.
> 29 Receive him therefore in the Lord with all gladness; and hold such in reputation:
> 30 Because for the work of Christ he was nigh unto death, not regarding his life, to supply your lack of service toward me.

For the moment the Apostle leaves his more distant plans in favor of the immediate present, which includes commending Epaphroditus to the Philippian church. Whether he is still with Paul as he writes or already has begun his journey back to Philippi is uncertain. Most interpreters accept the former view and describe him as the bearer of the letter.

The name *Epaphroditus* means "charming." This is the man, mentioned only here in the New Testament (probably he is not the same as the Epaphras of Col. 1:7 and 4:12), who had conveyed a gift of money from the Philippian congregation (4:18) as an expression of its partnership in the gospel (1:5). Thus Paul speaks of him as *your messenger, and he that ministered to my wants* (25*b*). The word for *messenger* is *apostolos,* that is, one sent on an errand. In Christian usage it had come to refer to those closest to Christ. Within this special circle Paul places Epaphroditus. Barclay notes that the word translated "minister" is *leitourgos,* which in ancient Greece referred to outstanding philanthropists who of their resources assumed certain civic responsibilities (cf. also 4:18-19). However, as though this tribute to Epaphroditus were insufficient, Paul refers to him as *my brother, and companion in labour, and fellowsoldier* (25). Together they have shared in a common will, a common work, and a common warfare.

It seems probable that it was the intention of the Philippians that Epaphroditus should remain indefinitely as companion to Paul. However, their plans did not materialize. Unhappily, he had become ill, even *nigh unto death* (27). After the Philippians were informed of his sickness, he became *full of heaviness* (26) or "sore troubled" (ASV) lest they should worry about him. The term translated *heaviness (adēmonōn)* is used to describe the Lord's agony in Gethsemane (Matt. 26:37; Mark 14:33) and denotes enormous mental and spiritual disturbance. In this frame of mind *he longed after you all.* If Epaphroditus were in any way involved in the factions at Philippi, this clause may have been inserted to indicate his impartial affection for them (Moule). If his illness had been accompanied by homesickness, which is likely, Paul finds reasons to excuse it; or perhaps his maturer years have made him more charitable than when, long before, he refused to tolerate John Mark's similar plight (Acts 15:38). Nonetheless, *God had mercy on him,* and on Paul also, *lest I should have sorrow upon sorrow* (27). Had Epaphroditus died, the loneliness of bereavement would have been added to the misery of the Apostle's imprisonment. Consequently, Paul is "very eagerly" *(more care-*

fully) sending him back that, *when ye see him again, ye may rejoice, and that I may be the less sorrowful* (28).

Here Paul is accepting full responsibility for the decision that Epaphroditus should return (vv. 25, 28). None should feel that his mission had failed or that he was deserting the Apostle in his hour of great need. Not only should there be no faultfinding, the Philippians should be joyful that his health had been restored and he is to be with them once again. Should they label Epaphroditus as a deserter or a weakling, Paul's anxiety or sorrow will only be increased. Accepting his return as a providential ordering and a divine overruling of their plans is the proper response to Epaphroditus' return. Genuine Christian love is slow to prejudge motives and "always eager to believe the best" (1 Cor. 13:7, Moffatt).

The Philippians were gracious enough to send him to Paul in time of need; and now exercising a reciprocal concern, Paul seeks to relieve the Philippians. *Receive him therefore in the Lord with all gladness; and hold such in reputation* (29), literally, "hold such men as valuable"; *because for the work of Christ he was nigh unto death, not regarding his life, to supply your lack of service toward me* (30). Some texts say simply, "the work," indicating that the work of Christ was being given a technical meaning, as "the Way," or "the name" (Acts 15:38). *Parabouleusamenos* (some readings) ("having disregarded" or "exposing") is from a verb meaning "to venture." It is a word used by gamblers, who staked everything on a turn of the dice. Epaphroditus, for the sake of Christ, had been willing to risk his life by becoming associated with a man who was being tried by the government. The early Christians called those who hazarded their lives for Christ *parabolani,* or "the riskers," as Aquila and Priscilla risked their lives for Paul (Rom. 16:4).[63] By so doing, Epaphroditus had been able to supply or complete in person what the Philippians themselves, because of distance, are unable to do (cf. Col. 1:24).

The examples of Timothy and Epaphroditus, the one being willing to accept a difficult assignment and risking failure in handling disruption in fellowship, the other giving little thought to personal conflict and hazarding his life for *the work of Christ,* challenge any easygoing Christianity which softens the stern demands of commitment and exacts only limited self-denial and little, if any, self-effacing sacrifice.

The Threat of Legalism

Philippians 3:1-16

Paul's commendation of his friends, Timothy and Epaphroditus, is followed by a scathing denunciation of his foes. Expressions of affectionate intimacy in the first two chapters give way to a solemn warning against those who distort the gospel and pride themselves in being "the circumcision." Probably he has in mind the Judaizers, whom he referred to as "deceitful workers" in 2 Cor. 11:13. They insisted that the rite of circumcision must be enforced on Gentile Christians in order to make them "full" or "bona fide" Christians (Acts 15:1). His warning of the threat of legalism includes a highly personal statement of his own religious journey, and an exaltation of that *righteousness which is of God by faith* in Christ (9).

This dramatic change in the mood of the Apostle has led some to conclude that virtually all of chapter 3 does not belong to the present letter, but is part of Paul's correspondence with the church on another occasion. This conclusion, however, need not be drawn, since there are abrupt breaks in other Pauline letters (e.g., 1 Cor. 15:58; Gal. 6:10). Further, the change in tone is not sustained throughout the chapter, and we have no reason to believe from external sources that Paul's attitude changes in the course of his writing the letter. Nor does the word *finally* suggest that the Apostle is about to finish his writing, making the succeeding verses to be extraneous or from another source. The word *to loipon (finally)* was used elsewhere in Paul's Epistles before the close of his writing was in sight (cf. 1 Thess. 4:1), and literally means "as for the rest."

Certainly Paul was capable of communicating with both warm affection and challenging exhortation. We assume, then, that these verses are a part of the author's design and that, having spoken to the church about its inner tensions, he now turns to the things he wants to say about dangers and pressures from outside. With strong language the Apostle addresses a crucial problem which threatens the unity of the church at Philippi, that is, the problem of works righteousness. He cautions: *My brethren* (encompassing all parties within the church), "let your rejoicing be in the Lord and not in any work of the flesh" (cf. Luke 10:20). In this passage Paul issues a severe attack against the legalists who would pervert and minimize the gospel. The only safeguard against their impersonal, lifeless brand of religion is a genuine knowledge of Christ which shares His resurrection power and participates in the fellowship of His sufferings (10).

The True Israelites

Philippians 3:1-3

> 1 Finally, my brethren, rejoice in the Lord. To write the same things to you, to me indeed is not grievous, but for you it is safe.
> 2 Beware of dogs, beware of evil workers, beware of the concision.
> 3 For we are the circumcision, which worship God in the spirit, and rejoice in Christ Jesus, and have no confidence in the flesh.

1. *A Threefold Warning* (1-2). Three times Paul warns, *Beware of* (literally, "have your eye on," "look out for" [NBV, RSV, Williams], "be warned against") *dogs, evil workers,* and *the concision* (2). "The" precedes each of these appellations.

Some interpreters feel these terms describe three different classes: Gentiles *(dogs)*, self-appointed, self-seeking teachers *(evil workers)*, and unbelieving Jews *(the concision)*. Most expositors, however, feel Paul is describing not three classes, but one—the Judaizers—described by words indicating their character, conduct, and creed.[64] Against the interpretation that the reference is to unbelieving Jews, the context seems to favor the view that these are converted Jews who are attempting to turn Christianity back to Judaism. These Judaizers infuriated Paul by their insistence that salvation comes by the work of the law. Against such a false doctrine and conception of circumcision he writes trenchantly to the Galatians (5:2-6). While the Jews troubled him, the Judaizers evoked anger and disrespect from the Apostle. He describes them as dogs, a term which the Jews applied to the Gentiles (Matt. 15:26-27). Thus he reverses the metaphor. Everywhere in Scripture "dog" is used as a word of contempt, reproach, or dread. The writer may have in mind the pariah dogs of the East, which, half-wild, feed on leftover garbage. Like them these Judaizers are feeding on the garbage of Jewish and fleshly rites. They are *evil workers,* or "deceitful workers," men who work ostensibly for the gospel but actually are working for evil (2 Cor. 11:13).[65] They are "work-heroes,"[66] who are constantly harping, even yelping in doglike fashion (Ps. 59:6, 14), on the necessity of works to secure salvation. *Katatomē (concision)* refers to the mere cutting off or mutilation of the flesh. Thus, these persons are "the incision-party" (Moffatt), who, by placing confidence in the flesh, insist on an empty symbol apart from faith.

Paul speaks of writing *the same things to you* (1). This may refer to another letter, to his warnings in the previous chapter against dissension, to those things which he had spoken earlier to them orally (Paul had visited Philippi after founding the church there), or to that which immediately follows. Probably a combination of these possibilities is more accurate. In any case, his repetition is *not grievous* (literally, "irksome" [ASV]) to him, and to the Philippians it is *safe,* or perhaps "certain" (as in Acts 22:30; 25:26). That is, his repeated admonition will make his views certain to them.

2. *A Threefold Identification* (3). Over against the formalism of the Judaizers, who made outward forms essential to salvation, Paul declares that those who trust Christ alone for salvation form the true Israel of God (cf. Rom. 2:25-29; 9:24-26; Col. 2:11; 1 Pet. 2:9-10). Not an external sign but a cleansing of the heart is the genuine evidence of a right relationship to God, the word *peritomē (circumcision)* being reserved for the genuine believers in Christ, the spiritual circumcision (Eph. 2:11). Three affirmations or evidences are given to identify genuine Christian status and privilege.

a. *True Israelites "worship by the Spirit of God."* True worship is "in spirit and in truth" (John 4:24) and requires the "broken and contrite heart" (Ps. 51:17) of the individual worshiper. These are the indispensable elements of worship, whereas outward forms and observances are merely tools or occasions for worship. True devotion and sincerity of the heart are inspired by the Holy Spirit of God alone.

b. *True Israelites rejoice* (literally, "boast" or "glory" [ASV]) *in Christ Jesus. Rejoice (kauchōmenoi)* is better rendered "exult" (cf. 1:26; 2:16; Rom. 5:2; 1 Cor. 1:31; 2 Cor. 10:17). This is clearly one of Paul's favorite words, occurring some 35 times in his writings and only twice elsewhere in the New Testament. The Christian does not consider circumcision as having value in itself, nor make it something other than a mere sign. His faith and hope are in Christ. The believer does not "boast" in legal observances, external ceremonies, or his own good works as grounds for acceptance with God. Such boasting is the essence of sin. Rather, he exalts the sovereign grace of God and His matchless gifts on which he has no claim. "The only pride of the Christian is that he is a man for whom Christ died" (Barclay). His only glory is the Cross.

In the cross of Christ I glory,
Towering o'er the wrecks of time;
All the light of sacred story
Gathers round its head sublime.

—JOHN BOWRING

c. True Israelites have no confidence in the flesh. Flesh
denotes all that man is, or thinks he is, and achieves aside
from the Spirit of God. It expresses the innate tendency of
sinful man to achieve standing before God and to secure, by
his own effort, acceptance with Him. To place one's confidence, one's trust, in anything or anyone other than Christ
is to have *confidence in the flesh.* The Apostle rejects with
horror such an attitude of self-dependence and evokes a full
exposure and listing of those things in which he formerly,
and futilely, trusted.

Paul's Pre-Christian Pedigree

Philippians 3:4-6

> 4 Though I might also have confidence in the flesh. If any other man thinketh
> that he hath whereof he might trust in the flesh, I more:
> 5 Circumcised the eighth day, of the stock of Israel, of the tribe of Benjamin,
> an Hebrew of the Hebrews; as touching the law, a Pharisee;
> 6 Concerning zeal, persecuting the church; touching the righteousness
> which is in the law, blameless.

Personal experience is cited by Paul to enforce his
warning against the false teachers who have troubled all the
churches he has founded, and now are endangering the
peace of the Christians at Philippi. He allows the Philippians to view his pre-Christian life so they may better understand why he is warning them in such unequivocal terms.

Putting himself in the place of the Judaizers for a moment, Paul argues that if the external privileges of the flesh
have merit of themselves, he would have *more* in which to
place his trust than all the rest (4) (cf. Gal. 1:14). And, indeed, he once trusted passionately in them.

There follows a descriptive list of the Apostle's qualifications to speak as a full-blooded Jew. Seven advantages

are detailed as though Paul were numbering them on the fingers of his hands (Bengel). He catalogs them in two categories: privileges by birth and privileges by attainment.

1. *Virtues Inherited by Birth* (4-5a). Paul lists four:

a. He had been *circumcised the eighth day,* according to the Law (Gen. 17:12; Lev. 12:3; Luke 1:59). Consequently, he is no proselyte to Judaism, for in the case of proselytes, circumcision was not performed until adult age (Acts 16:3). Paul could claim to be a true-blooded Jew from the cradle, and nursed in the ancestral faith.

b. He is *of the stock of Israel,* that is, descended directly from the patriarch Jacob. Even the Ishmaelites could hark back to Abraham, and the Edomites could claim Isaac as their father; but only the Israelite could trace his descent to Jacob.

c. Paul is *of the tribe of Benjamin,* from which had come Israel's first king, and which faithfully refused to revolt from Rehoboam (1 Kings 12:21).

d. He is *an Hebrew of the Hebrews,* of Hebrew parents, and one who unlike many Hebrews still can speak the Hebrew language (Acts 21:40).

Ability to speak Hebrew and Aramaic was a mark of faithfulness to the old culture and traditions and was retained at times only with great effort and discipline. Paul still knew the languages though he was born and reared in the Gentile city of Tarsus (see Acts 22:2 which tells of Paul addressing the crowd in Aramaic).

2. *Virtues Acquired by Choice and Conviction* (5b-6). The Apostle now lists the three privileges he could boast of by personal attainment.

a. *As touching the law,* he formerly was a Pharisee (5), one who meticulously observed the whole Mosaic law (Acts 23:6; 2 Cor. 11:22). The Pharisees were the strictest sect of the Hebrew religion, the most ardent expositors and defenders of the Law.

b. Concerning zeal, one of the notable Jewish virtues, he had been found *persecuting the church* (Acts 8:1-4; 9:1-6, 13-14; Rom. 10:23). Paul seems never to forget his persecution of the early Christians, the Nazarenes, at Jerusalem and Damascus, based on his misdirected *zeal* for God (Acts 22:3; cf. Rom. 10:2). He uses the present participle of the word, *diōkōn, persecuting,* as if the action were still before his eyes. While the memory remained, he knew the mercy of God in forgiveness and conversion (1 Tim. 1:12-13) and the power of God who turned the arch-persecutor into the faithful Apostle and fearless missionary.

c. Touching the righteousness which is in the law, he had omitted nothing and was *blameless,* or "found blameless" (6, ASV). The criterion is carefully worded. It is only by reference to this law, which included the moral requirements, that he can be judged as *blameless.* As viewed by men, and in accordance with external standards, he measured up. But his life did not yet correspond to the divine standard of inner righteousness.

In these seven things (5-6) Paul had at one time trusted. This trust has been described as confidence in a rite, confidence in one's race, confidence in one's religion, confidence in one's record, and confidence in personal righteousness.[67] But from bitter experience the Apostle testifies that they failed to bring him to a personal knowledge of God, for indeed the law as such is impersonal. These and all like things of the flesh are the bleak alternative to the life-giving participation in the sufferings of Christ. To trust in these can only lead to a pseudoworship of God and an illegitimate confidence in self (3). Six times in this Epistle Paul uses *pepoitha (confidence).* He knows in whom he believes, and this knowledge is the basis of his joy.[68] Thus the one-time proud Pharisee turns to his conversion, which brought about for him a "transvaluation of all values."

The Knowledge of Christ Jesus

Philippians 3:7-10

> 7 But what things were gain to me, those I counted loss for Christ.
> 8 Yea doubtless, and I count all things but loss for the excellency of the knowledge of Christ Jesus my Lord: for whom I have suffered the loss of all things, and do count them but dung, that I may win Christ,
> 9 And be found in him, not having mine own righteousness, which is of the law, but that which is through the faith of Christ, the righteousness which is of God by faith:
> 10 That I may know him, and the power of his resurrection, and the fellowship of his sufferings, being made conformable unto his death;

Probably no other passage of Paul's writings delineates so clearly as this paragraph the meaning of *the knowledge of Christ*. The Apostle is still dealing with how one can stand in right relationship to God or receive that righteousness which is acceptable to Him. His Pharisaic piety could not guarantee this and in fact is a barrier to it, since it leads to pride and self-commendation. It is, therefore, renounced and replaced by *the knowledge of Christ Jesus my Lord*. Obviously, Paul's understanding of *righteousness* has been profoundly altered.

1. *A Different Perspective* (7-8). Paul is using the commercial language of profit and loss. Prior to his conversion, he had placed the supposed advantages just recited in verses 5 and 6 on the credit side of the ledger, considering each as having value in itself. Note that *gain (kerdē)* (7) is plural. It is as though he had often reminded God of these "virtues" one at a time. Here is the essence of man's sin. He trusts his intellectual acumen, his humanistic ideals, his personal virtues, his disciplined life, his honesty, even his religious exercises—and presents them to God as though they merited salvation.

Repentance is to become horrified at one's past; and Paul, on the Damascus Road, saw that this native trust in his own achievements was more of a hindrance than a help, more of a bane than a blessing. Thus he transferred them from the credit side of the ledger to the debit side, considering all of them together (*zēmian, loss*, is singular) as one great loss (Matt. 16:26). It is "on account of Christ" that Paul is willing to collect all his former virtues, put them in one parcel, as it were, and write that bundle off as *loss*. He does not merely dismiss them, he "counts" them as liabilities.

The progression and power of the Apostle's thought is marked by five strong particles of the original *(alla men oun ge kai),* translated *yea, doubtless* (8). They may be rendered better, "but, yea, indeed, rather, also" (indicating the most fervent emotion) *I count* (present tense) *all things but loss for the excellency of the knowledge of Christ Jesus my Lord.* Not only the religious advantages of the earlier verses but *all things,* or anything, which might be reckoned as meritorious and claimed as acceptable to God by the natural man, are dispensable in gaining Christ. Christ has become Paul's own personal Lord, and in relation to the "incomparableness" *(huperechon, excellency) of the knowledge of Christ,* all other things are as nothing. Such knowledge so far outstrips the privileges of Judaism and man-made religion that it can only be considered in a class by itself. When compared with this Highest Good all relative "goods" are not worthy of the name (cf. Eph. 3:19).

For whom I have suffered the loss of all things. The verb might be rendered, "I was mulcted" (of all my possessions). The aorist tense points to a definite time when Paul was transformed, undoubtedly his Damascus Road experience. However, the Apostle also may be thinking of the treatment which he received at the hands of the Jewish authorities. He may have been excommunicated by the Jews, disowned by his family, or had his property confiscated. More likely he is thinking of the fundamental fact that allegiance to Christ meant the renunciation of all that he had come to prize (cf. Gal. 6:14). *And do count them but dung.* The present tense is used, indicating Paul's attitude at the moment. *Skubalon (dung)* appears nowhere else in the New Testament. It means "dregs," "chaff," "excrement," or "refuse" (ASV) that is rejected from tables and left to dogs. The word is much stronger than mere *loss,* for it suggests that which is never to be touched again. Such is God's estimate of all religious observance and practice which is not rooted in Christ and His atoning merit.

2. *A Personal Possession* (8b-10). The goal of Paul's reevaluation is the supreme one of gaining Christ. In contrast to the seven things specifically mentioned as *loss*, Paul lists seven things to be gained (8-11), all of which center around the person of Christ.

a. *That I may win Christ* (8b), literally, "gain" Christ (ASV). This involves more than finding Christ, or being found by Him, as was the case at Paul's conversion. The "gain" includes the continuous compounding of value that one discovers in Him and receives from Him throughout the Christian pilgrimage. "Life with Him is cumulative in value. It mounts in richness. . . . He is to us a greater and greater Christ as we live in His love and are nourished by His mind" (Paul Rees).

The tense indicates both the present and the future. Paul is never satisfied with his knowledge of Christ but is constantly longing for a deeper fellowship with Him. He has gained Christ but has not exhausted the unsearchable riches in Christ (Eph. 3:8; Col. 2:2-3).

b. *And be found in him* (9a). A use of this verb from Epictetus refers to death, suggesting that Paul desires to be "found in Christ at death," and before Him at the Judgment (cf. 2 Pet. 3:14).[69] However, Paul also has in mind a present experience, which is to mature until its completion at the return of Christ. He wants this vital union with Christ to be actual now. He desires to be discovered now in Christ, as the manslayer was found in the city of refuge where he was safe from the avenger of blood (Num. 35:25).

c. *Not having mine own righteousness, which is of the law, but that which is through the faith of Christ, the righteousness which is of God by faith* (9b). Better, "not having any righteousness which can be called mine" (Vincent). Each of these "gains" relates to and clarifies the others, but this one specifically provides the meaning of the previous one. To be "found in Christ" is nothing else than having the righteousness which comes from God. Here is Paul's doctrine of justification by faith which he elaborated upon in Romans and Galatians (Rom. 1:17; 3:24; 4:5; 10:3). *Righteousness* means both a right relationship to God and also union with God. The only "righteousness" which has value is that which comes "from God" (ASV) through *faith* (self-surrender or trust) in Christ. Several elemental truths are being advanced here: (1) That righteousness which is acceptable to God cannot be acquired by human effort on the basis of the law; (2) It is a gift of God in Christ; (3) The means through which divine righteousness comes to men is faith, a trusting response to God's initiative.

d. That I may know Him (10a). The grammatical construction is such that several variations of interpretation are possible, though the fundamental meaning is clear. It may express purpose—"in order that I may know Him"; or it may point to the result—"so that I may know Him"; or that God's righteousness received by faith makes it possible for the believer to know Christ and His saving benefits. Certainly it is consistent with Paul's teaching to claim that it is only by having the righteousness of God that one may know Him.

The knowledge here spoken of is not that of mutual comprehension (1 Thess. 1:4), or that which comes by mere familiarity (Acts 10:28); or insight which results from a logical analysis of the facts (Eph. 5:17). It is not merely a knowledge about Christ, but a personal, experiential knowledge of Christ.

The Pauline expression "to know Christ" suggests the warmth of a close and direct relationship and is tantamount to "fellowship with Christ." The phrase "in Christ" (cf. 2 Cor. 5:17) describes the same moral and spiritual union between Christ and the believer. The Old Testament uses the verb "to know" of sexual intercourse (Heb. *yada;* Gk. *ginōskein*), indicating the most intimate knowledge possible between persons. To know Christ in an intimate way is Paul's supreme desire.

e. And the power of his resurrection, and the fellowship of his sufferings (10*b*). There is only one article in the Greek, which suggests that the ideas expressed are to be taken as one. Paul is clarifying what he means by "knowing Christ." He wants to know Him "in" the *power of his resurrection.* It is his desire that the power which raised Jesus from the dead shall operate in his life also, not just initially, but moment by moment raising him from the death of sin into the newness of life in Christ (Rom. 6:4; 8:11; Eph. 1:12, 20; 2:5-6; Col. 2:12; 3:1; 2 Cor. 4:10; 12:10). It is not accidental that the power of the Resurrection is mentioned first, and then Christ's sufferings. Only if one knows *the power of* Christ's *resurrection* can he then share in *the fellowship of his sufferings* and live a life that is permeated with a redemptive quality (Col. 1:24). Paul regarded his own apostolic sufferings as an extension of the "dying of Jesus" borne in his body (2 Cor. 4:10; cf. Rom. 8:36). The phrase gives a clue as to the significance which Paul gives to his own sufferings. They were for Christ's sake and therefore not merely bearable but to be received with joy.

f. Being made conformable unto his death (10*c*). Paul means more than a willingness to die as Christ died—on a cross. He has in mind our death and resurrection in Christ, but this requires the outworking described in Rom. 6:11. Paul is calling for a death to self in order to live unto God (Gal. 2:20). Self is to be dethroned, crucified (Gal. 5:24; 6:14) so that Christ might be enthroned as supreme Lord. Thus Moffatt translates, "with my nature transformed to die as he died." The reference is clearly to an inward transformation, a conformity to the spirit of Christ. Wesley, in his *Notes upon the New Testament,* caught the meaning and stated it thus: "So as to be dead to all things here below" (cf. Gal. 4:19).

Pressing Toward the Final Mark

Philippians 3:11-16

11 If by any means I might attain unto the resurrection of the dead.
12 Not as though I had already attained, either were already perfect: but I

follow after, if that I may apprehend that for which also I am apprehended of Christ Jesus.

13 Brethren, I count not myself to have apprehended: but this one thing I do, forgetting those things which are behind, and reaching forth unto those things which are before,

14 I press toward the mark for the prize of the high calling of God in Christ Jesus.

15 Let us therefore, as many as be perfect, be thus minded: and if in any thing ye be otherwise minded, God shall reveal even this unto you.

16 Nevertheless, whereto we have already attained, let us walk by the same rule, let us mind the same thing.

1. *Reaching for Ultimate Completion in Christ* (11-14). *If by any means I might attain unto the resurrection of the dead* (11). The Apostle has a vision, though its lines are not yet fully discernible, of the ultimate completion of the work of Christ in his life. He is risen with Christ spiritually and is living in the power of His victorious life; but he still cherishes the prospect of a consummation which will occur in and following *the resurrection of the dead.* The word Paul normally uses for *resurrection* of all persons both good and bad is *anastasis* (cf. Acts 17:32; 26:6-8; 1 Cor. 15:42). Here, however, he employs a word rarely used in the New Testament (Acts 4:2; 1 Pet. 1:3), *exanastasin,* literally, "resurrection . . . from among the dead" (Williams). Some have thought this word is used to refute the idea, as at Corinth, that the only resurrection hope of the believer had already been fulfilled in the experience of the new birth (1 Cor. 15:12; cf. 2 Tim. 2:18; and Polycarp's *Letter to the Philippians,* 7:1).

However this may be, Paul is thinking about the resurrection of the righteous and the quality of life which will accompany those who are raised in Christ. He wants to attain or "arrive at" (NBV, NEB; *katantēsō eis)* the "perfection" (cf. 12) which is appropriate to resurrected believers. *If by any means* reflects the uncertainty of his immediate future, expressed in 1:22-23, and which hangs in the balance. However, there is no lack of certainty about his salvation and ultimate triumph, for he knows that nothing can separate him from the love of God (Rom. 8:38-39). *If* expresses the spirit of humility and not of doubt, for the power of Christ's resurrection working in him is the earnest and guarantee of this prospect. But steady progress toward the goal is necessary.

Paul makes it clear that the completion of the divine work of grace within him awaits this resurrection of believers—*not as though I had already attained, either were already perfect* (12). *Elabon (attained)* is not the same word translated *attained* in verse 11. There it presents the figure of a pilgrimage—arriving at the journey's end. Here it means "to receive" a prize (cf. 1 Cor. 9:24). Paul is denying that he at once obtained the prize in the moment of conversion. He must continuously put forth effort to receive it. He has won the prize in Christ but has not as yet fully received it. *Perfect* must be the same as that which is to be *attained,* or "received." These are a kind of parallelism. Thus *perfect* here has the sense of "perfected" (Clarke). Paul has not completed his Christian course and thus has not yet arrived at the goal so as to receive the prize.

Nonetheless he declares: *but I follow after, if that I may apprehend that for which also I am apprehended of Christ Jesus* (12b). Verse 12 and the verses which follow (possibly through 16) reveal the tension between Paul's present attainment and his aspiration for the future. The key word in understanding this creative tension seems to be *apprehend,* which means "to seize." "Apprehending" is done when one is in full possession (cf. Mark 9:18; John 8:34; 12:35; 1 Thess. 5:4) (Bengel). Paul is saying then, "I am pursuing the prize, namely Christ, in order that I may lay hold on Him, or fully possess Him, and thus fulfil His purposes in my life, for He first laid hold on me, and possessed me." Hence, his whole life is a constant "passionate longing after Christ" (Weiss). Such an aim is appropriate for every believer—"We love him, because he first loved us" (1 John 4:19).

Whether the final goal Paul has in mind refers to the knowledge of Christ (v. 10) or to the participation in the resurrection of believers with its consummating blessedness or "finishedness"—and competent New Testament scholars can be cited in support of either view—matters little. In either case, the Apostle refuses to claim that his Christian character is complete or his Christian course finished.

Though final perfection must necessarily await the *resurrection*, and Paul humbly confesses he has "not yet" *apprehended* it, there is room for progress in God's pilgrim people. Thus forgetting others, and even his own spiritual accomplishments or failures, Paul determines *this one thing I do, forgetting those things which are behind, and reaching forth unto those things which are before* (13).

One thing evidently refers to both *forgetting* and *reaching forth*. The former must include the Apostle's past life—his Jewish prerogatives (vv. 7-9), his past experiences of suffering as a Christian, his successes and failures, his triumphs and miseries. "To forget" in the biblical sense is not merely to obliterate from the mind—which is probably not possible. Rather, it is the opposite of "remembering" *(anamnēsis)*, which is recalling from the past into the present "an action which lies buried in history, in such a way that the result of the past action is made potently present" (R. P. Martin).

Although a certain kind of remembering in order to praise God for His past blessings is wholesome (Eph. 2:11), forgetting must be continuous in the life of the Christian. Only thus can there be spiritual progress (2 Pet. 3:18; 1 Thess. 4:10).

Reaching forth unto those things which are before is an allusion to the Grecian games, as are verses 11 through 17. For Paul, his conversion was the beginning, not the end of the race. The picture is that of a runner leaning or throwing himself forward, stretching himself out with all his energies. The runner does not look back nor compare himself with the relative position of others on the track. Chrysostom commented: "The runner reckons not up how many circuits he hath finished, but how many are left."

Paul obviously has in mind the last day, resurrection, the Judgment, and the distribution of rewards to the faithful (1 Cor. 3:14; 9:25; 2 Tim. 4:8). The prospects of the finish line and the prize of victory motivate him to "finish [his] course with joy" (Acts 20:24).

Knowing there is yet ground to be traversed, and a reward to be received, Paul continues, *I press toward the mark for the prize of the high calling of God in Christ Jesus* (14). *Press* is the same word as in 12 *(I follow after),* and in 6, where it is translated *persecuting.* Paul is pursuing the prize in Christ with the same singleness of purpose, freedom from encumbering weights, and ceaseless exertion with which he had earlier pursued or persecuted the Church. He will not run off on side issues as a dog that jumps every trail and holds to none; he will not encumber his spiritual progress by the load of legalism and external rites; he will not allow himself to become complacent as a result of thinking himself to have attained final perfection. *Skopon (mark;* the cognate verb *skopein,* "to watch," "to look" is used in 2:4) may indicate the goal toward which the runner proceeds, or the definite aim with which he runs. According to the latter interpretation, the runner was expected to follow a white mark from the starting place to the goal. If he went beyond the line, he did not run lawfully and thus was not crowned though he arrived first. Paul seems to allude to this regulation in 1 Cor. 9:26, where he states he must "run without swerving" (Moffatt).

Prize and *high calling* have been viewed by interpreters both as the same and as distinct. The latter seems preferable to this writer, though obviously they are intrinsically bound together. The *high calling* comes to the believer in order that he may enter the race and attain the *prize* which suggests the crown or trophy (1 Cor. 9:24; 2 Tim. 4:8). In Paul's case, he heard and answered the call at his conversion—beckoning him from his sin and into fellowship with Christ. The Christian is summoned from above (Heb. 12:2). His *high* or "upward" (RSV, NASB) *calling* is *of God in Christ Jesus,* who will say to the faithful at the end of the race, "Well done, good and faithful servant" (Matt. 25:23, cf. 21). The prize is "promised when the call is issued, and given when the call is fulfilled" (Vincent). And insofar as the promise is certain, one already has the prize, and yet he pursues it.

Because Christ is the One through whom this summons is addressed, He evidently is the Prize. If the Christian life is a progressive discovery of what it means to have been grasped by Christ, as Paul has been saying, its goal or *prize,* therefore, is nothing else than Christ himself. Progress in the life of the Christian is as though one were moving toward a light at the end of a long tunnel. He never has the full light till he has arrived there, but he has ever increasing light in proportion as he goes forward (Prov. 4:18).[70]

2. *The Call to Continuous Consistent Conduct* (15-16). We may infer from verse 15 that the preceding declarations dealing with a form of Christian perfection were evoked because of controversy. Some in the Philippian church tended to be *otherwise minded.* The word *phroneite (minded)* indicates more than an intellectual difference; it reveals a different outlook and a consequent different conduct. Evidently there were some who were teaching that it is possible to be "perfect" in a final sense here and now. They may have professed a spiritual superiority to that of their fellow believers toward whom they had a condescending or judgmental attitude, as the Gnostics looked down on those who could never attain the rank of the *teleioi* (the "perfect"). At the opposite extreme it appears that an antinomian party may have been present in the church, not only denying "perfection" but giving no attention to ethical conduct. For them the grace of God made both Christian discipline and further effort superfluous. Paul seems to be addressing them with his portrayal of the runner going hard for the tape.

Because the Church seems perennially plagued by those who make claims regarding perfection in some extreme form on the one hand, and those who deny any kind of "perfection" in Christian experience, the response of the Apostle is highly significant. He advocates a specific, though relative and progressive, "perfection" which he expects of every Christian, and denies the impossible claim of absolute perfection which must ever be future in this life. A careful look at the words and thoughts of Paul should make clear his understanding, which must be viewed in the context of daily conduct.

Telos, from which the adjective *teleios* comes, literally means "end." To the Greek mind it suggested, on the one hand, that which is last, final, or complete; and on the other, that which is accomplishing its purpose or function, mature or full-grown. Both senses are seen in various forms of the word throughout the New Testament. Thus it is used in the sense of "fulfilled" (Luke 22:37; John 19:28), "perfect" or "perfected" (Luke 13:32; John 17:23; 2 Cor. 12:9; Phil. 3:12; Heb. 2:10; 5:9; 7:19; 9:9; 10:1, 14; 11:40; 12:23; James 2:22; 1 John 2:5; 4:12, 17-18), "finish" and "finished" (John 5:36; Acts 20:24), and "consecrated" (Heb. 7:28). The adjective *teleios* occurs 19 times in the New Testament, all of which are translated "perfect" in the Authorized Version, except in 1 Cor. 14:20 where it is rendered "men," in contrast to "children," and in Heb. 5:14, "of full age," in contradistinction to a "babe."

Unless Paul was manifestly contradicting himself—an accusation which even from a literary standpoint would be grossly unfair—it must be asserted that the perfection which he disclaims in 12 (verb *teleioō*) is different from that which he now claims in 15, *Let us therefore, as many as be perfect* (adjective *teleios*). The difference in meaning corresponds to the above understanding of the Greeks. The *perfect* here are those who are functioning as Christians in accordance with God's purposes and *high calling.*

In Acts 20:24 the verb is used to allude to a "race" or a "course." The Apostle seems to have a similar picture in mind here, where the word means "fit for the race, strong in faith" (Wesley, *Notes upon the New Testament*). To change the metaphor, Paul's reference is to those who are thoroughly instructed and "mature" (RSV, etc.; cf. 1 Cor. 14:20; 2:6; Eph. 4:13; Heb. 5:14), who possess a perfection which belongs to the true Christian who has advanced by faith beyond the stage of the novitiate. This Christian perfection must not be understood to have accrued merely by a passage of time, or by the keeping of the law, or by some vague maturation process. Paul does envision those who *are* "mature," who are "spiritual" (cf. 1 Cor. 2:15; 3:1). Rather, it is a distinct work of God, a "by grace through faith" perfection. Thus the writer of the Epistle to the Hebrews exhorts his readers to allow themselves to be "borne on to perfection" (Heb. 6:1).

The *perfect* in this verse are described as those who wisely *worship God in the Spirit . . . and have no confidence in the flesh* (3). It points to those who "have entered fully into the spirit and design of the Gospel" (Clarke). The *perfect* Christian believer is one "who, by the grace of God, has in fact entered that spiritual adulthood in which with single-mindedness he moves from one degree of progress and perfection to another" (Rees). This is possible only for those "that are alive from the dead" and have yielded their "members as instruments of righteousness unto God" (Rom. 6:13, see also 19).

Thus minded, literally, "of this mind," evidently points back to the single-mindedness expressed in 13. Thus this realized (Christian) perfection is equated with wholeness and self-unity, and may be considered as being synonymous with the theological term "entire sanctification" (1 Thess. 5:23; contrast James 1:8). The single-minded, the *perfect,* will prove themselves so by a "holy discontent" with their spiritual progress, judged in the light of the ultimate goal (Rom. 8:29). Augustine stated that one may be an increasingly "perfect pilgrim," though not yet a "perfect possessor,"[71] in the sense of having received the final prize. Similarly, J. Paul Taylor has observed that Paul "denied perfection as a winner (12), but professed perfection as a runner and included others in that classification (15). The perfection of heart here fits us for the perfection of heaven hereafter."[72]

So confident apparently is Paul of the truth he has affirmed regarding true Christian perfection that he believes God will illuminate the minds and correct the behavior of those who are *otherwise minded—God shall reveal even this unto you.* The church at Philippi had the beginnings of the same spirit of pride based on extravagant claims to spirituality evident in the church at Corinth, resulting in dissension and quarrelsomeness among the members. The Apostle was certain God would correct this. Lightfoot graphically states Paul's meaning: "If you are sound at the core, God will remove the superficial blemishes."

This may be a gentle rebuke to those in Philippi who would contend over a minor point or would rate themselves too highly. They are not arrogantly to take it on themselves to set everyone else straight, for if any is at fault on any subject, *God shall reveal* it to them (cf. John 7:17). Those who are truly "mature" *(perfect)* will refuse to judge others, recognizing the difference between a "babe in Christ" and mature manhood (1 Cor. 3:1-2; Eph. 4:11-16). It is true that "normally we judge others in relation to our own level of attainment; somewhat less often we judge with reference to Christ; very rarely indeed do we form our judgments with reference to the progress an individual has made since he became a Christian."[73] Possessing the spirit of Christ is that which is of supreme importance.

While God will be patient with the sincere, and will give them further light, there is an important condition which must be fulfilled. One must be obedient to the light already received. Stated differently, "fidelity to truth already attained is a condition of receiving further and fuller truth" (Maxie D. Dunnam). Consequently, one should not be surprised if the Holy Spirit asks for obedience to what one already knows (cf. Gal. 6:16, 25). This is the meaning of Paul's counsel. *Nevertheless,* or notwithstanding the minor points of disagreement, *whereto we have already attained, let us walk by the same rule, let us mind the same thing* (16). *Stoichein (walk)* is a technical expression, indicating Christian conduct, and means to march together in file and in the same direction. *Attained* is not the same as those words used in either 11 or 12. Originally it was employed of arrival beforehand, or rapid arrival. The meaning, however, is clear.

Paul is simply saying that having come thus far, the thing to do is to proceed in "the same path."[74] The plea is for a continuous and consistent Christian conduct.

An Appeal for Purity and Unity
Philippians 3:17—4:9

Paul has addressed remarks to the legalists (3:1-16) who, though placing emphasis on law and codes of conduct, have failed to enter into the fellowship of Christ's sufferings. Certain libertines, however, seem to have gone to the opposite extreme and rejected all law, using their pseudo-relationship to Christ as a justification for all kind of acts. Because freedom from the bondage of the Law does not mean license to sin with impunity, Paul is compelled to attack these antinomians. Further, in the opening verses of chapter 4 he addresses the threatening disruption in the fellowship at Philippi. Thus he makes a strong plea for purity and unity.

Some Personal Examples
Philippians 3:17-21

> 17 Brethren, be followers together of me, and mark them which walk so as ye have us for an ensample.
> 18 (For many walk, of whom I have told you often, and now tell you even weeping, that they are the enemies of the cross of Christ:
> 19 Whose end is destruction, whose God is their belly, and whose glory is in their shame, who mind earthly things.)
> 20 For our conversation is in heaven; from whence also we look for the Saviour, the Lord Jesus Christ:
> 21 Who shall change our vile body, that it may be fashioned like unto his glorious body, according to the working whereby he is able even to subdue all things unto himself.

The goal and aim of Paul and his associates is the practical conduct of the believers in the churches. Thus lest any at Philippi should feel that the quality of life he has been describing is not clear, or not concrete, enough, he sets before his readers some patterns of behavior, both positive and negative. He knows that it is in a life, preeminently the life of the Lord Jesus, and not in a written code, that the pattern of Christian ethical teaching is embodied. With Christ as the Supreme Model in mind, the Apostle gives some examples to be followed and others to be avoided.

1. *Brethren, be followers together of me, and mark them which walk so as ye have us for an ensample* (17). If this sounds egotistical, it should be recalled that to the Corinthians Paul gave a qualifying element: "Be ye followers of me, even as I also am of Christ" (1 Cor. 11:1). His addressing the Philippians as *brethren* is probably designed to mitigate the Apostle's strong words. *Peripatein,* literally, "walking about," indicates the ordinary circumstances of daily life. *Summimētai (followers),* or "co-imitators," is not used elsewhere in the New Testament. The prefix *sum* may simply mean "all of you." Thus Lightfoot has suggested: "Vie with each other in imitating me." It seems more likely, however, since Paul changed from *me* to *us*—evidently referring to Timothy and Epaphroditus and others—that he is saying, "Look at others who follow me, for in so doing you will become an imitator of me."[75] This interpretation is consistent with his admonition to *mark them,* an apparent allusion to the line in the stadium which guided the runner (cf. 3:14). The meaning is simply: Let other Christians whom you can observe be your line or mark. Paul is not suggesting that others follow him in his achievements, his failures, or his limitations, but rather in the fact that he has been *apprehended*— "laid hold of" (Weymouth, NASB)—by *Christ Jesus.*

2. Admittedly, examples must be chosen wisely (18-19). The conduct of some in the church at Philippi was an open scan-

dal. They lived gluttonous and immoral lives and used their Christian faith to justify themselves. Who those people were is not altogether clear. It is possible they were Judaizers, but more likely they were Gnostics, or those influenced by their teaching. They believed that matter, including the body, is evil. Therefore one could treat it with contempt—asceticism—or appease in undisciplined fashion its appetites. Or these persons may have been those who misuse Christian liberty and turn it into unchristian license. Such persons claim that Christian faith excludes all law and covers even continuing and willful sinning—thus opening the door for the exploitation of lusts and passions of all sorts. It has even been suggested that the problem was not so much at Philippi, but rather where Paul was in Rome; and he took this opportunity to warn the Philippians.

Whoever they were, Paul describes them: *whose end is destruction, whose God is their belly, and whose glory is in their shame, who mind earthly things* (19). Their final destiny will be eternal condemnation. Moffatt declares that *apōleia (destruction)* "is their fate," to indicate the inevitable consequences of allowing liberty to degenerate into license (Gal. 5:13; Rom. 6:1, 12-13, 15, 23; 16:18; Jude 4). The end of their conduct will be complete moral ruin—they are "doomed" in advance. *Destruction* does not mean annihilation, but the loss of all that makes life good and beautiful, both in the present and in the life to come. *Whose God is their belly* may refer to those who insist on the distinction between clean and unclean foods, now obsolete (Rom. 14:14-17; 1 Cor. 8:8).[76]

The chief concern here, however, is with the antinomians. If *belly* refers to the womb, as some have thought, then Paul is referring to gross immoralities which mask under the name of Christian. The meaning would include materialism of every sort which would make an idol out of the gratification of the senses. The real objects of their worship are the lower appetites of the body. The source of their depravity is that they *mind earthly things*. Their goals, thoughts, desires, and interests are fixed solely upon the temporal, the things of time and sense. As a consequence, these persons have inverted the true scale of values so that they can actually *glory . . . in their shame.* "Man fallen is but man inverted; his love is where his hatred should be, and his hatred where his love should be; his glory where his shame should be, and his shame where his glory."[77]

Paul's disturbance arises out of the fact that these so-called believers in the church are more than merely advocates of false doctrine. By their lives of sinful self-indulgence they have brought into disrepute the Cross and all it represents. Thus the Apostle speaks of those *of whom I have told you often* (cf. 3:1), *and now tell you even weeping, that they are the enemies of the cross of Christ* (18). They are akin to those who say: "We have fellowship with him" while they "walk in darkness" (1 John 1:6); or, "Let us do evil, that good may come" (Rom. 3:8). Although they claim to be friends of Christ, they are not crucified with Him, and thus are the enemies of His cross, which is the symbol of death to self and sin. Obviously this example is to be avoided and, hopefully, corrected. Nonetheless, according to Paul's example, it is in the spirit of *weeping* and not harsh censoriousness that one must view inconsistencies in others (cf. Luke 19:41).

3. In contrast to those who mind earthly things, the true Christian is exalted above them (20-21). He is enabled to "set [his] affection on things above" (Col. 3:2); *For our conversation is in heaven* (20). *Politeuma (conversation)* means "commonwealth" or "citizenship" (ASV). As the Philippians are citizens of Rome with all its rights and responsibilities, though in a foreign territory, so the Christian is now a citizen of the great community of heaven (cf. Eph. 2:19). Moffatt translates the verse: "We are a colony of heaven." The Philippians might never have seen the imperial city of Rome, but they were under its protection and lived according to its laws and enjoyed its privileges. So Christians forming "a colony of heaven" are under its care. "To it they owe their allegiance. In its register their names are enrolled.

Their conduct is regulated by its laws. Their hopes are centered on its glories" (Charles Erdman).

Huparchei (is), "subsists," is the same word *(being)* which is applied to Christ Jesus in 2:6 (cf. Gal. 4:26; Heb. 11:13, 16; 1 Pet. 1:1; 2:11). It points to the fact that the Christian's heavenly citizenship is not a result of his own doing in any present moment, though it exists in the present moment, but is always dependent on the prior grace of God.

The Christian finally will be exalted even more since from heaven he looks for, or "expects and awaits earnestly" the coming of *the Lord Jesus Christ* (cf. 1 Cor. 1:7; Heb. 9:28). *Whence* can refer to *conversation* (citizenship) or to *heaven.* It seems stronger to interpret this as meaning that from our capital city, which is situated in the heavens, we anticipate the coming of the Savior who will bring about man's final salvation and *shall change our vile body. Vile* in the 17th century simply meant "cheap" or "without value." The word describes the mortality and temporality of the body. The body, through God, is subject to decay and death. Thus it is better to read that "the body of our humiliation" (ASV) will be changed *that it may be fashioned like unto his glorious body,* that is, "the body of his glory" (ASV; cf. 1 Cor. 15:44).

The two Greek terms for "form" (cf. 2:6, 8) are both used in this verse. *Metaschēmatisei (shall change* or "transform") indicates that Christ will change the "appearance" of the body. It will be a completely new kind of body, like the body of the exalted Christ, which cannot now be fathomed (cf. 1 John 3:2). And yet its new outward appearance, according to the usage of *summorphon* (fashioned or "conformed" [ASV]) will be appropriate to its inner spiritual character.[78] "The spirit will then have an organ of expression suited to the holiness of its nature and the happiness of its estate" (Rees)—a complete likeness to Christ (Rom. 8:29). The end product of God's redeeming activity, which is continuous throughout our Christian experience (2 Cor. 3:18), will then have been achieved: Christ will have taken shape *(morphē)* in us (cf. Gal. 4:19). This exaltation of the heavenly citizens will in turn bring about the exaltation of Christ, for it is wrought *according to the working whereby he is able* (literally, "the energy of his being able") *even to subdue* ("subject" [ASV]) *all things unto himself* (21). Paul is making the point that the power of Christ (cf. Col. 1:29) to change the bodies of believers is more than adequate since it is able to subject not only the recalcitrant elements in the believer's person, but *all things,* even the entire universe, *unto himself* (cf. 1 Cor. 15:27-28; Heb. 2:5, 9).

This ultimate end of the true believer stands in sharp contrast to those who are doomed to destruction by their self-indulgence and sin. Knowing which examples to follow and which to shun should be clear.

PHILIPPIANS 4

Several Significant Exhortations

Philippians 4:1-9

1 Therefore, my brethren dearly beloved and longed for, my joy and crown, so stand fast in the Lord, my dearly beloved.
2 I beseech Euodias, and beseech Syntyche, that they be of the same mind in the Lord.
3 And I entreat thee also, true yokefellow, help those women which laboured with me in the gospel, with Clement also, and with other my fellowlabourers, whose names are in the book of life.
4 Rejoice in the Lord alway: and again I say, Rejoice.
5 Let your moderation be known unto all men. The Lord is at hand.
6 Be careful for nothing; but in every thing by prayer and supplication with thanksgiving, let your requests be made known unto God.
7 And the peace of God, which passeth all understanding, shall keep your hearts and minds through Christ Jesus.
8 Finally, brethren, whatsoever things are true, whatsoever things are honest, whatsoever things are just, whatsoever things are pure, whatsoever things are lovely, whatsoever things are of good report; if there be any virtue, and if there be any praise, think on these things.
9 Those things, which ye have both learned, and received, and heard, and seen in me, do: and the God of peace shall be with you.

Though the Epistle is friendly and informal, a certain general order of thought is discernible. Paul has spoken of his personal situation in Rome, given pertinent admonitions to his readers, discussed his plan regarding Timothy and Epaphroditus, and warned the Philippians against the legalists and the antinomians. He now addresses certain individuals in the church, appealing to them to live in Christian harmony. His remarks are connected with the great truths advanced in the preceding paragraph, as the word *therefore* indicates. The first verse probably belongs in the previous chapter. In either case it serves as a bridge to what the Apostle now wants to say. The exhortations here are both direct and indirect.

1. In the light of the examples just given and the marvelous prospect of the true believer, Paul exhorts the members at Philippi to *stand fast in the Lord* (1). In the preceding chapter the Apostle uses the metaphor of running. Now he employs a military expression: *stand (stēkete)*, as a soldier in the midst of battle (cf. Eph. 6:10-19). Regarding their love and labors the Philippians must ever be advancing. As to faith and fidelity, they must stand immovable, true to their Christian ideals and profession.

The appeal is an affectionate one. Paul glories in the Philippians. He accepts them as brothers in Christ regardless of their individual spiritual attainments and differences of gifts or graces. Accompanying this brotherly relation there also is brotherly love, twice expressed in the tender words *dearly beloved.* He ardently desires to see them. *Epipothētoi (longed for)* does not occur elsewhere in the New Testament and indicates the special fellowship which exists between Paul and the Philippians. His converts at Philippi will be his crown, his wreath of victory at the end of the Christian race (cf. 1 Cor. 9:25; 1 Thess. 2:19), or his crown at the final feast on the ultimate day of reward (cf. 2:16). They will be witness to his triumphant ministry, the seal of his apostleship (1 Cor. 9:2), and the proof that his labor had not been in vain in the Lord (1 Cor. 15:58).

2. He implores Euodia and Syntyche to *be of the same mind in the Lord* (2). *Euodias* is a man's name, but the proper reading is "Euodia" (all versions), a woman's name, as is *Syntyche*. It appears then that these are two women, as also suggested by the reference to *those women which laboured with me in the gospel* (3). They may be two of the "women which resorted" to the "river side, where prayer was wont to be made" (Acts 16:13), when the church at Philippi was begun. Since Paul normally did not allow ladies to preach (1 Tim. 2:12), they probably are deaconesses.

Numerous explanations have been given as to who these persons are. The improbable suggestion has been made that they are simply names representing opposing groups, but the names do not stand in opposition. Euodias means "prosperous" or "sweet fragrance." Syntyche means "affable" or "fortunate." The cause of their dissension is unknown. It may have been a doctrinal difference related to Christian perfection just discussed. More likely is the view that their zeal and activity occasioned some accidental friction, and they allowed the irritation to develop into dislike, distrust, and estrangement. It is possible that the two are in a lawsuit. Whatever the difficulty, they are admonished to be of the same mind in the Lord. *Phroneō (mind)* is used in 1:7; 2:2 (twice), 5; 3:15 (twice), 16; 4:2, 10 (twice). As indicated previously, it means more than to think; it is a disposition. Paul is calling for a moral unity regardless of any intellectual differences which may obtain. The mind they are to share is one which subordinates personal interest to the good of the body of believers, and is exemplified in the lowliness of the incarnate Lord (2:3, 5). The phrase *in the Lord* implies that outside Him there can be no unity. One cannot love man without loving God.

3. Paul implores a third party to "help these women" resolve their differences (3). *I entreat thee also, true yokefellow, help. Synzygos (yokefellow)* has been interpreted as a proper name, and thus a play on words similar to *Onesimus* ("serviceable") in Philemon 11.[79] The meaning would then be,

"Act according to your name." All kinds of suggestions have been made as to who this *yokefellow* is: Paul's wife, the husband of Euodia or Syntyche, Lydia, Silas, Timothy, Epaphroditus, the minister of the Philippian congregation, or Luke, whose home is thought to have been in Philippi. Whoever it is, that one is to be a peacemaker (cf. Matt. 5:9). The ministry of reconciliation is an exalted form of service.

It is not known who Clement is, although Clement of Rome has been mentioned (an unlikely possibility). But the women had labored with him and with Paul, so he is well known to the congregation. Other nameless helpers are alluded to as *my fellowlabourers.* Though unknown to us, their names *are in the book of life. Book of life* was a Jewish phrase used sometimes to describe the roll of an army. Because these persons are members of the Lord's army and have done battle with Paul against a common enemy, their names are recorded in God's book of records. Christian service may be unnoticed by men, but God takes note and will praise at the last (1 Cor. 4:5).

4. Having concluded the personal exhortations, Paul addresses the whole church with a stirring call to *rejoice in the Lord* and to be fair-minded in their relations with *all men* (4-5). Nothing so destroys joy as contention and misunderstanding; so this exhortation may relate to the unpleasant situation in Philippi. More likely, however, Paul is summarizing the character, spirit, and conduct of the Christian life. Twice in the letter he urges these Christians to *rejoice in the Lord* (3:1 and here). This second time he repeats the call—*again I say, Rejoice* (cf. Ps. 37:4; 1 Thess. 5:16). The repetition suggests that conditions in Philippi were not conducive to rejoicing. But in spite of circumstances—disagreements and persecution—rejoice. The Apostle adds, *alway.* The joy of the Lord is not a fleeting quality but a permanent accompaniment of the indwelling Spirit of Christ.

The Greek word *epieikes (moderation)* has been variously translated: "patience," "softness," "gentleness," "the patient mind," "modesty," "forbearance," "magnanimity." It describes restraint of passions, soberness, or that which is suitable. It may mean a good disposition toward other men (cf. Romans 14). In 1 Tim. 3:3 and Titus 3:2 the word is used with an adjective meaning "disinclined to fight." The idea then is that of "forbearance," not insisting on one's rights, but acting with consideration for one another.[80] In things which are nonessential the Philippians are not to run into extremes but to avoid bigotry and animosity, judging one another with charity (Matthew Henry). "Fair-mindedness" seems to capture the primary meaning—a charitable attitude toward the faults of others. One must be merciful in his judgments of others' failures since all facts surrounding them cannot be known. There must be a willingness to yield under duress in nonessentials, and a refusal to retaliate when attacked. This spirit is to be shown to *all men* both inside and outside the church.

The Lord is at hand may be a warning used in the Early Church. If so, Paul is saying, "What is the purpose of the rivalries? Bear with one another that God will bear with you when the Lord comes" (Lightfoot). The clause, however, has been viewed as a promise of the Lord's nearness, and interpreted in connection with the following verse.

5. If the Lord is nearby, and He is, then why worry? (6-7). Thus the Apostle exhorts: *Be careful for nothing; but in every thing by prayer and supplication with thanksgiving let your requests be made known unto God* (6). The implication is that the cure for anxiety is to be found in believing prayer. Though one may plan for the future (1 Tim. 5:8), he is not to be anxious about anything (Matt. 6:25)—"Be anxious for nothing" (NASB). The secret to this quality of life is prayer and supplication. "Care and prayer ... are more opposed than fire and water" (Bengel). *Prayer* is general and is based on divine promise, involving devotion or worship. *Supplication* is a special entreaty in time of personal need and appeals to the mercy of God. It is the acknowledgment of conscious need. True *prayer and supplication* breathe with

thanksgiving for every event, whether of prosperity or affliction. One prays for forgiveness—it is promised; he suppli-
cates for the recovery of his child—that is mercy which
exceeds the bounds of grace.[81] These requests, definite and
precise petitions, are to be made known unto God *(pros ton
theon);* better, "in the presence of God" (Weymouth). Here
perhaps is a subtle reminder of God's continuous presence.
In view of the conflict at Philippi, Paul more than likely is
saying, "When others don't treat you kindly, pray. Rather
than grow anxious about it, let it be known to God."

To fretful and distraught believers the primary result of
true prayer is the enjoyment of God's peace which He has
promised to all who trust Him (Isa. 26:3). God's peace is
known first in the grace of reconciliation. Then the peace of
God follows directly from peace with God through our Lord
Jesus Christ (Rom. 5:1) who made that peace by the blood of
His cross (Col. 1:20). Thus Paul assures the Philippians:
*The peace of God, which passeth all understanding, shall keep
your hearts and minds through Christ Jesus* (7); literally, "in
Christ Jesus" (ASV).

Thanksgiving and peace go together (cf. Col. 3:15).
Though one doesn't obtain all he requests, the peace of God
keeps the heart, the seat of the will. The heart does not keep
the peace of God. *Shall keep* is a military metaphor. God's
peace will stand guard over the Philippians, even as Philippi
is guarded by a Roman garrison. The verb *passeth (hu-
perechousa)* is related to the noun translated *excellency* in
3:8. In both cases, absolute uniqueness is meant, not mere
relative superiority. This protective peace "surpasses every
understanding," including all anxious forethought (cf. Isa.
26:3; John 14:27) (Lightfoot). The phrase "in Christ Jesus"
suggests that one cannot be so guarded outside Him. We
enjoy God's gift of peace and protection only by obedience to
Him and submission to His authority.

6. Knowing, even before the arrival of modern psychology,
that we are what we think, Paul gives one final exhortation
about thinking and doing (8-9). To help bring about the

unity and harmony he has in mind, he says, *Think on these things.* However, the verb *think (logizesthe)* means more than "keep in mind" (Moffatt). It means to "take into account" in such a way that the objects of reflection shape one's conduct. Paul is not primarily interested in mental activity for its own sake; he is constantly promoting ethical and behavioral reformation (cf. Rom. 12:2).

The terms used by Paul are not only features of Stoic religion by and large; they are also found in the Septuagint, except for the word translated *good report.* Thus while the Old Testament patterns are guiding his thought, Paul urges the Philippians not to ignore their value, no matter where they are taught. Certainly, the Christian must never be "less good" than the unbeliever, without at the same time making claims to spiritual superiority because of one's own good works.

Finally (to loipon) may mean nothing more than "and so." Thus the ethical terms employed continue the thought of the peace of God in verses 8-9. If inner peace is to be enjoyed, certain steps must be taken. Thus, he exhorts, *whatsoever things are true* (in thought, disposition, and deed), *honest* (serious, elevated, or worthy of honor), *just* (right in any given situation, duty performed), *pure* (chaste as in 1 Tim. 5:2, but also domestic purity in general), *lovely* (beautiful, winsome, inspiring, or worthy of being loved), *of good report* (fair-speaking or reported with the best construction—not "well spoken of" but "speaking well of"; the things which are fit for God to hear); *if there be any virtue, and if there be any praise* (anything which elicits the approval of God—as in Rom. 2:29), *think on these things* (8). Virtue was of central importance in the Greek vocabulary of ethics. Thus Lightfoot interprets Paul as saying, "Whatever value may reside in your old [pre-Christian] conception of virtue," maintain it.

But, as we have seen, the Apostle intends to give the Philippians more than subjects for meditation. He calls for obedient action and again cites himself as a pattern: *Those things, which ye have both learned, and received, and heard, and seen in me, do.* Paul's faithfulness to Christ under all kinds of circumstances has earned him the right to speak. Further, it should be noted that the term *received (parelabete)* is a technical term for the receiving of a tradition (cf. 1 Cor. 11:23; 15:3). Before the formation of the New Testament and its acceptance as authoritative, the Christian tradition as a standard of belief and behavior was embodied in the teachings and example of those in whom the ethical practice of the Lord was to be found. These things were *learned, received, heard,* and *seen* in the Apostles, including Paul. *And the God of peace shall be with you* (9). A life modeled on these patterns of apostolic example and teaching will be blessed with the gift of God's peace. In verse 7 Paul portrays the peace of God; here he promises the God of peace himself, or the "God who gives peace" (Weymouth; cf. Heb. 13:20; 1 Thess. 5:23). There is no higher incentive to *think on these things.*

Closing Word of Gratitude and Grace
Philippians 4:10-23

The final section of this letter is a strong witness to the sufficiency of Christ and displays the support of His people for each other.

Expression of Appreciation for the Philippians' Gift
Philippians 4:10-20

10 But I rejoiced in the Lord greatly, that now at the last your care of me hath flourished again; wherein ye were also careful, but ye lacked opportunity.
11 Not that I speak in respect of want: for I have learned, in whatsoever state I am, therewith to be content.
12 I know both how to be abased, and I know how to abound: every where and in all things I am instructed both to be full and to be hungry, both to abound and to suffer need.

13 I can do all things through Christ which strengtheneth me.

14 Notwithstanding ye have well done, that ye did communicate with my affliction.

15 Now ye Philippians know also, that in the beginning of the gospel, when I departed from Macedonia, no church communicated with me as concerning giving and receiving, but ye only.

16 For even in Thessalonica ye sent once and again unto my necessity.

17 Not because I desire a gift: but I desire fruit that may abound to your account.

18 But I have all, and abound: I am full, having received of Epaphroditus the things which were sent from you, an odour of a sweet smell, a sacrifice acceptable, wellpleasing to God.

19 But my God shall supply all your need according to his riches in glory by Christ Jesus.

20 Now unto God and our Father be glory for ever and ever. Amen.

The didactic portion of the letter is complete, and Paul turns to the initial purpose in writing, namely the expression of gratitude for the gift which the church at Philippi has sent to him by Epaphroditus. Because some time has elapsed since Paul received the gift, and also because he has only indirectly alluded to it earlier in the letter (1:5; 2:25-30), some have thought that these verses are part of a previous correspondence from the Apostle to the Philippians. But the conclusion is not necessary. It is quite normal to express one's thankfulness at the close of a highly personal letter which moves informally from one topic to another. To the Apostle other things were first in importance, namely, the unity of the church at Philippi. The entire letter may be viewed as an expression of his appreciation of their love. If all that has preceded has prepared the minds of the readers for this message of gratitude, then the last place in the letter is the place of prominence, and this personal word may be thought of as being climactic.

As for Paul's delay in responding, it may well be that this is his first opportunity to do so. Further, the period of time that has passed since the arrival of Epaphroditus is unknown. It could be, however, that Paul, with an apparent uneasiness with regard to monetary matters, has difficulty in expressing adequate gratitude for the financial support he has received through the years from his friends. After all, the church in Philippi was poor and had given beyond their resources. Nonetheless, the message of thanks is a rare combination of affection, dignity, and delicacy—an embodiment of ideal Christian courtesy.

1. Paul's gratitude is rooted in his joy (10-12). This keynote of the Epistle he strikes for the last time—*I rejoiced in the Lord greatly.* He knows that Christian love is the motive that prompted the gift and that Christ has inspired the Philippians' spirit of generosity. Their care of him periodically over a number of years has *flourished again,* a horticultural figure describing a plant which revives and blossoms in the spring. Once again, as before, the Philippians demonstrated their love for Paul. No clue is given as to why they had not done so sooner, but evidently the reason was outside their control. Perhaps they had no one by whom to send the gift, or were in "deep poverty" (2 Cor. 8:1-2) and financially unable to do so. Whatever the reason, Paul, in contrast to the apparent spirit of some at Philippi, refuses to be easily offended. He excuses what one of smaller spirit might have interpreted either as willful or neglectful delay. *Wherein ye were also careful, but ye lacked opportunity* (10*b*). *Ephroneite (ye were . . . careful)* means "thoughtful" in the sense of definite concern (cf. 1:7). Paul uses the imperfect tense which suggests his willingness to believe that the Philippians all along had desired to minister to his needs, but were hindered.

Assuring the Philippians of his own well-being, though until recently they have been unable to contribute to it, and seeking to dispel any thought of personal disappointment at their lack of aid, Paul states: *Not that I speak in respect of want: for I have learned, in whatsoever state I am, therewith to be content* (11). In the original the verse reads, "In the circumstances in which I am," indicating his present prison situation. *Autarkēs (content)* has no equivalent in English, but should be taken in the sense of "competence."[82] While this may be a Stoic term, it is Christ who is the secret of his serenity and victory (1:21). The tense makes clear that what he had learned came to him in a moment of time, at his conversion, and not through discipline and mental concentration as the Stoics advocated. His sufficiency results from his intimate relationship with the living Lord.

The Apostle is adequate for every situation, having learned that circumstances as such neither add to nor detract from his higher happiness. He seeks to discover the will of God in every situation. *I know both how to be abased, and I know how to abound: every where and in all things I am instructed both to be full and to be hungry, both to abound and to suffer need* (12). Literally, "in everything and in all things" (ASV), that is, in each particular event of life and in the sum total of all of life. *Tapeinousthai (abased)* carries the thought of a voluntary acceptance of a lonely situation, and was used in classical Greek of a river running low (cf. 2 Cor. 11:7).[83] Paul knows what it is to have plenty, as an animal with ample fodder (Matt. 5:6), or to be hungry—a possible allusion to his working with his hands.[84] *Memuēmai (I am instructed)* is taken from the language of the pagan cults which initiated candidates into their "mysteries." Paul has been "initiated" by every type of experience, both pleasant and unpleasant (2 Cor. 11:23-28), and he does not value the one above the other.

2. The source of Paul's strength is Christ—"I am strong for all things in the Christ who empowers me" (13, author's translation). "Christ" is omitted in some manuscripts but is clearly implied. Because Paul apparently refers to abundance in verses 12 and 18, it has been suggested that he has come into the inheritance of property, making it possible for him to afford the high cost of his trial. Thus, so runs the suggestion, he can say, "I am equal to everything."[85] But there is no basis for such speculation. The meaning is far more profound. Paul can do "all things" which he is called upon to perform in the line of duty or suffering. His union with Christ provides strength to sustain his apostolic work and to advance the progress of the gospel. The verse should be interpreted as a brief summary of Gal. 2:20 (cf. also John 15:5; 1 Tim. 1:12). Until now Paul has been using the language of Stoicism (11-12), which maintained that man can

of himself overcome all outward pressures. This the Apostle roundly denies. His sufficiency is of Christ, who continuously infuses power *(dunamis)* into him. He can be grateful for any and all circumstances, because they are the occasion for the revelation of Christ's power.

3. Lest the Philippians should assume that his "Christ-sufficiency" has made their gift superfluous, the Apostle delicately assures them of his genuine appreciation (14-16). *Notwithstanding ye have well done, that ye did communicate with my affliction* (14); better, "have fellowship with my tribulation." *Thlipsis (affliction)* is a technical term for the tribulation to come on the earth at the end of the age (Mark 13:19; 2 Thess. 1:6). The Philippians, then, have not only offered succour to their Apostle friend, they have also shared in the apostolic trials which precede and prepare for the end. Their participation with his trouble is one of the many ways that God has used to make him strong. *When I departed from Macedonia* (cf. Acts 17:14, probably 12 years before), which was the beginning of the gospel for the Philippians, *no church communicated with me as concerning giving and receiving, but ye only* (15). The Apostle may mean that at that time no other church had fellowship with him by their gifts. We know he refused to accept gifts from the Corinthian church (1 Cor. 9:15-27; 2 Cor. 11:9). Here again is the language of commerce—credits and debits. Of all the churches under Paul's care, only Philippi considered keeping an account with him. They had given, and he had returned the favors with spiritual gifts (cf. 1 Cor. 9:11; Philem. 19). Paul is not likely suggesting that no other church had remembered him, but probably that the congregation at Philippi is the only one who has this double transaction, the two-way exchange of blessings—material gifts passing from the church to him, and spiritual blessings flowing the other way. *For even* (better, "also") *in Thessalonica ye sent once and again,* that is, "more than once" (Moffatt), *unto my necessity* (16). Thessalonica was a luxurious community which Paul had visited after leaving Philippi, approximately 100

miles distant. There Paul had supported himself (1 Thess. 2:9; 2 Thess. 3:7-9), and was aided by the neighboring Philippians, whereas the Thessalonians themselves had contributed little. Such expressions of generosity could not be soon forgotten.

4. The gifts, however, are only of secondary importance (17-18). *Not because I desire a gift: but I desire fruit that may abound to your account* (17); literally, "not because I seek after the gift, but I seek after the fruit that abounds to your account." *Karpon (fruit)* commonly bore the sense of interest on an investment. For their gifts to Paul (2 Cor. 12:14), God added the interest to their credit. This is the Apostle's way of saying with Jesus, "It is more blessed to give than to receive" (Acts 20:35; cf. Luke 6:39). He who gives always receives more than he who receives. The Philippians by their generosity have stored up for themselves treasures in heaven. Paul is saying that giving with the right motivation will bring appropriate dividends. Expressing this spiritual truth is a remarkable way to say, "Thank you."

Referring specifically again to the recent gift, Paul says, *But I have all, and abound: I am full, having received of Epaphroditus the things* [perhaps clothes or other necessary items] *which were sent from you* (18a). *Apechō (I have)* is a technical expression used in drawing up a receipt (cf. Matt. 6:2, 5, 16; Mark 14:41; Luke 6:24). The sense, then, is this: "Your debt to me is more than paid, for which I give you a receipt." The Philippians' thoughtfulness which was directed to Paul he regards as *an odour of a sweet smell, a sacrifice acceptable, well pleasing to God* (18b), an obvious allusion to the pleasant fragrance in the Temple produced by the burning of incense to God (2 Cor. 2:15; Heb. 13:16). Here is a gentle reminder that all sincere Christian service and stewardship which entails sacrifice and self-denial is an act of worship in which God takes pleasure. The motivation for such giving is seen at the highest possible level, namely, to please God. If God were pleased with this offering of sacrifice, surely the Philippians must understand the Apostle's genuine gratitude and appreciation.

5. God will, in turn, reward their sacrifice (19-20). *My God shall supply all your need according to his riches in glory by Christ Jesus* (19); literally, "will fill up all your need . . . in Christ Jesus." The Philippians may have assisted Paul to their own impoverishment, suggested by the connection with the preceding verse by the word *but (de)*. Paul is assuring them of the faithfulness of God, who will supply their needs as He has the Apostle's. Whatever their deficiences, God will supply. The gifts of the Philippians are a loan, which has been drawing compound interest. Paul cannot repay it but his God, whom he serves, and who receives the sacrifice, will supply all their needs, both material and spiritual (2 Cor. 9:8), on his behalf (Lightfoot). This He will do *according to his riches* (cf. Eph. 3:16), that is, not just "out of" His wealth, but on a scale that is worthy of His wealth.[86]

In glory has been connected by some expositors with *riches;* by others with *shall supply*. Vincent thinks the latter is better, *glory* then indicating the "element and instrument of the supply." However, according to certain meanings of *glory* (Heb., *kabhodh*) in the Old Testament, the two words *riches* and *glory* are virtually synonymous, so that *glory* is equivalent to wealth (cf. Gen. 31:1; Isa. 10:3). From this view, the phrase could mean "glorious riches." Maclaren's comment is illuminating: "When Paul says 'riches in glory,' he puts them up high above our reach, but when he adds 'in Christ Jesus,' he brings them down amongst us."

Contemplating the unlimited resources of God, Paul breaks forth in rapturous praise: *Now unto God and our Father be glory for ever and ever. Amen* (20); better, "Now unto our God and Father be the glory for the countless ages of eternity. Amen." Paul no longer speaks of *my* (as in 19) but of *our,* indicating the common bond between himself and the Philippians. The joy of the Apostle reflected in the entire Epistle could not help but produce this doxology, and is

Paul's fitting response to all the things that give him joy in his prison experience.

Final Greetings and Benediction

Philippians 4:21-23

> 21 Salute every saint in Christ Jesus. The brethren which are with me greet you.
> 22 All the saints salute you, chiefly they that are of Caesar's household.
> 23 The grace of our Lord Jesus Christ be with you all. Amen.

It has been conjectured that these last verses were written by the Apostle's own hand, rather than dictated to a scribe, as was possibly the case with the rest of the letter. One would expect in a personal letter such as this one, to find in the closing salutations a number of names. But Paul mentions none, as he sometimes did (cf. Romans; Colossians; 2 Timothy). In view of the developing parties at Philippi he possibly omits them so as to avoid giving distinction to some and not to all. Paul is careful to include the whole Christian community—*Salute every saint in Christ Jesus* (21*a*). Some expositors grammatically connect *salute* with *in Christ Jesus* as in other Epistles (e.g., Rom. 16:22; 1 Cor. 16:19). But in view of 1:1 it seems better to understand the verse as the Authorized Version implies. *The brethren which are with me greet you* (21*b*); literally, "salute you" (ASV). Not only do Paul's associates (including Timothy and others) send greetings but *all the saints,* evidently meaning those of the Roman church itself—*chiefly they that are of Caesar's household* (22). It is known that "Caesar's household" was a general term for those employed in various types of government service. They resided all over the empire, and many were slaves. The reference may be to the men who have guarded Paul—some of whom perhaps he has introduced to Christ. It is conceivable that a few of these are natives of Philippi and have an interest in their home city. This might explain the use of *chiefly,* or "especially" (ASV).

The closing benediction suggests that Paul intends the letter to be read to the assembled congregation. Thus he pronounces a parting blessing, *The grace of our Lord Jesus Christ be with you all. Amen* (23). Instead of *pantōn (all)*, some manuscripts read *pneumatos* (singular), "your spirit" (ASV), perhaps a final but subtle entreaty to unity. The Epistle began with *grace* (1:2) and now closes with *grace.* This grace alone could create the fellowship which is shared so tenderly by Paul and his beloved Philippians.

The Epistle to the
COLOSSIANS

Introduction

Authorship

In the Early Church the authenticity of Colossians was never questioned. Eusebius, fourth-century church historian, states that the book was universally acknowledged to be of apostolic origin. It was widely quoted by the church fathers. The Epistle was cited by Justin Martyr, and was known to Irenaeus, Clement of Alexandria, and Tertullian at the end of the second century. The latter quoted from it about 30 times, and in a way which demonstrates his own belief in its Pauline origin.[1] The clear connection of the book with Philemon, the Pauline authorship of which is undoubted, strengthens the claim that it was written by the same Apostle.

Not until the 19th century was the genuineness of the Epistle questioned. It was argued by F. C. Baur (1762-1860) and the Tubingen school he founded that the Gnostic system attacked in the Epistle was not in place until the second century, and therefore the letter could not have been written by Paul. While it is true that the false doctrines of Cerinthus were not developed till after the Apostle's time, the incipient seeds of the heresy were present earlier. It is these "floating ideas" Paul addresses, though clearly they were not in developed form.

Others have doubted the Pauline authorship of Colossians because of its connection with Ephesians. That there is a relationship is obvious, but some maintain there are certain anti-Pauline ideas in Colossians, which is a poor imitation of Ephesians. Still others (such as German critic W. H. L. DeWette) view Ephesians as a "verbose expansion" of Colossians by a disciple of Paul.

However, there are important differences which indicate that the author is not merely trying to keep Ephesians in line with an acknowledged apostolic document, or vice versa. John Eadie has responded to this kind of reasoning convincingly:

> There is ... far less similarity than is commonly supposed—all that is special about each of them is wholly different, and even in the paragraphs where there is similarity, there is seldom or never sameness, some new turn being mingled with the thought, or some new edge being given to the admonition. ... The one letter is general; the other is special; the one is didactic, the other controversial. The one presents truth in itself, the other develops the truth in conflict with parallel error. And there is no servile imitation, no want of life and freshness.[2]

Further, it has been claimed that the references to angelology have little or no direct parallel in Paul's other Epistles, and thus Colossians was not written by him. This connection, however, is inaccurate because Paul refers to angels at least 12 times in his Epistles (in addition to Acts 17:23), and speaks of angels only once in Colossians, and then in the context of the heresy he repudiates. His concern is to show that no angel can share in Christ's redemptive work and that Christ cannot be relegated to the level of angels.

A final objection to Pauline authorship is that the style is too un-Pauline. H. Dermot McDonald has responded to this objection thus:

> It is certainly true that Colossians contains forty-six words not used elsewhere by the apostle. But since most of these are connected with the heresy and its refutation, their peculiarity can be accounted for by their appearance in this context. On the other hand, there are eleven Pauline words found in Colossians which are not used by any other New Testament writer—a fact which can be used as an argument for the opposite conclusion. That the Apostle, as we believe, wrote from Rome and

that Timothy had a share in the composition of a letter provide a reason for the enlarged vocabulary.[3]

The style of Colossians, which appears to be ragged and does not always take account of strict grammar, has been contrasted with the supposed clearer language sequence of Paul's earlier letters. However, Paul's letters are not always tidy and even (see, e.g., 2 Cor. 9:12-14). G. H. P. Thompson has observed:

> The ragged style of Colossians could be due to the haste with which Paul dictated the letter, or the tension under which he labored, as he tried to deal with the critical situation at Colossae from his distant imprisonment at Rome. The composition may also owe something to the work of Timothy. . . . But it is not possible from the style alone to draw any conclusion that Colossians was written after the death of Paul.[4]

There have been other attacks on the genuineness of the Epistle, such as the supposed differences of theological thought and expression (e.g., regarding the person of Jesus, or the broader meaning of "reconciliation," etc.). However, these are recent objections and are not formidable. There is no sufficient reason to deny the Church's claim and the Epistle's claim (1:1) of Pauline authorship. If Paul did not dictate it word for word, certainly it was commissioned by him.

Place and Date of Writing

Colossians tells us that Paul was in prison (4:18), but does not tell us where. Tradition has it that the Epistle was written from Rome during the imprisonment alluded to in Acts 28:16, which lasted at least two years. This tradition has been challenged more recently using the following line of reasoning.

It has been advanced that because Colossians and Philemon are clearly related to each other, they likely were written in the same period. Philemon is referred to indirectly in Col. 4:9 ("with Onesimus"), and the names of persons with Paul who send greetings at the close of the letter to Philemon also occur in the greetings at the end of Colossians (4:10-14). Further, Archippus is spoken of in Philem. 2, and for him Paul has a "special word" in Col. 4:17.

Though these letters were probably written about the same time, it is sometimes thought that Onesimus likely escaped to a place closer to Colossae such as Caesarea or Ephesus. The journey to join Paul would have been too long had the Apostle been in Rome. Thus, so the view goes, Colossians was written from either Ephesus or Caesarea.

There is little evidence to suggest Paul was imprisoned at Ephesus. Paul endured a number of imprisonments (2 Cor. 11:23) and went through a difficult time at Ephesus (1 Cor. 15:32). But nowhere in speaking of this period of his ministry (e.g., 2 Cor. 1:8-10) does he mention an actual imprisonment at Ephesus.

Evidence exists for Paul's imprisonment at Caesarea (Acts 23:33-35), but it is not necessary to assume Onesimus could not have gone to Rome. There were adequate facilities for travel in the ancient world. Philem. 18 suggests that Onesimus had robbed his master of money, and he may have thought he could remain hidden better in Rome than in Asia Minor. The hope expressed in Philem. 22 of paying an early visit to Colossae would have seemed as plausible to Paul from Rome as from Caesarea.

Appeal has been made to the difference in mood between Colossians and Philippians to support the claim that Paul wrote the Colossians from a different place than Rome. According to this argument, Philippians may have been written from Rome, but Colossians should be assigned to an earlier imprisonment at, say, Caesarea. However, whatever differences of atmosphere or mood there may be can be accounted for by the different situations being addressed.

None of these arguments is sufficient to counter the firm tradition that Colossians was written from Rome. This still seems to be the most likely option, and for our purposes we accept that both Colossians and Philemon were written from Rome during the imprisonment described in Acts 28. Probably Tychicus delivered our present letter to Colossae.

If the letter were written from Rome, its date will depend on the time of Paul's imprisonment there, probably about A.D. 59 and following. Tacitus, the Roman historian, writing in the time of the Emperor Trajan (A.D. 98-117), speaks of an earthquake which devastated Laodicea in A.D. 60. Eusebius speaks of a similar disaster at Colossae and Hierapolis after the burning of Rome in A.D. 64. Whether there was more than one such disaster is uncertain. If Colossians were written after this event, there would likely be some reference to it. The writing of Colossians probably occurred about A.D. 60-62.

The Tri-Cities of Colossae, Laodicea, and Hierapolis

The three towns of Colossae, Laodicea, and Hierapolis referred to by Paul in 4:13 lay along the banks of the Lycus River in western Phrygia, the Roman province of Asia, which today is the western part of Turkey. Colossae and Hierapolis were about six miles apart on the north side of the river. Laodicea was south of the river about 10 miles from Colossae and 13 miles from Hierapolis. Thus they formed a sort of triangle.

In Paul's time Colossae was the least influential commercially of the three, although in its earlier days it had been prosperous as a wool and weaving center. It had been described as a "great city" by Herodotus in the fifth century B.C., and as a "populous city, both wealthy and large" by Xenophon in the fourth century B.C. By the time of the Christian era its influence had declined.

Laodicea, the capital of Phrygia, was a city of some size, splendor, and trade, and had a rich and active population. It was surrounded by fertile country, being watered by the Lycus River and two other smaller streams. The scourge of the area, however, was the frequency and severity of the earthquakes which were notorious in the Lycus Valley. Great herds of sheep on the pasturelands supported perhaps the greatest center of the woolen industry in the world. Laodicea was well known for production of garments of the finest quality, supported by the allied dyeing trade. The city became the political center of the district and the financial headquarters of the whole area. Thus it was prosperous.

Hierapolis at one time became a trade center and was famous for its mineral springs which made a notable spa. People came by the thousands to drink of the water and bathe in its medicinal qualities. Hierapolis was the native city of the Stoic teacher Epictetus, who was a slave coming into young manhood when Epaphras first came to this area. Because Epictetus' writings show some remarkable similarities in language with the Epistles of the New Testament, it is possible to speculate that he may have met Epaphras or heard his preaching of the gospel.[5]

Originally the tri-cities were of equal importance, but time changed this. When Paul wrote his Epistle, Colossae was a small town. In spite of this, J. B. Lightfoot in his commentary on Colossians, *St. Paul's Epistles to the Colossians and to Philemon,* has said it was the most important town to which Paul ever wrote a letter. Had the heresies there remained unchecked, it could have meant the ruination of the Christian faith.

The ancient region of Phrygia was a spawning ground of enthusiastic cults and wild prophets of new forms of religion. The people were inclined to wild superstitions and were attracted to any mania that claimed a knowledge of, or fellowship with, the spirit world. Deficiencies of intellectual culture left the populace creatures of whim and impulse. No doubt these tendencies troubled the Apostle and prompted his strong and careful exposure which is seen in chapter 2.

We know that similar deliriums prevailed in the province later. The teachings of Montanus originated there about the middle of the second century and spread rapidly. The leading feature of Montanism, declared heretical by the Church, was a claim to ecstatic inspiration—the gift of prophecy, the adoption of a transcendental mode of morality, and the exercise of an austere discipline.

The Church in Colossae

The question as to who originated the Christian community addressed in this Epistle has not been answered conclusively. Acts 16:6 states that Paul and his companions "had gone throughout Phrygia," and 18:23 that he "went over all the country of Galatia and Phrygia in order, strengthening all the disciples." From these references it is concluded by some that Paul must have reached Colossae. However, it is nowhere stated that he was either in Colossae or even near it.

On his third journey we know Paul was three years in Ephesus. But there is nothing in the biblical record to warrant supposition that Paul preached in Colossae. His apostolic journeys never approached it. Among the reasons Paul never visited Colossae would be difficulties of travel, important work that needed to be done in other places, or simply the guidance of the Spirit. While Paul does state that he had suffered for the Colossians, he does not say he ever preached to them. However, special circumstances gave him a tender interest in them.

During the time Paul was in Ephesus, the entire province of Asia was evangelized (Acts 19:10). Colossae was about 100 miles from Ephesus, and probably the church was founded at this time. No doubt Paul had a hand in directing the organization. The church may have been founded by Timothy, but the greater probability is that it was by Epaphras, whom the Apostle says "is for you a faithful minister of Christ" (1:7; also 4:12-13). If Epaphras were not the founder, he was certainly the minister in charge.

The church at Colossae seems to have been predominantly a Gentile church. Paul's phrases such as "alienated and enemies in your mind" (1:21), or his reference to making known the mystery of Christ among the Gentiles (1:27) when the reference is clearly to the Colossians suggests that the church was mainly a Gentile church. Further, in 3:5-7 he gives a list of their sins before they became Christians, and these are characteristically Gentile sins.

It must be said, however, that in these tri-cities many Jews lived among the population. So many came here from Palestine that those at home complained that they had left

the rigors of discipline for "the wines and baths of Phrygia."
At one time the Jewish population in Phrygia may have been
as large as 50,000.

The Occasion and Purposes of the Epistle

Paul's knowledge of the church at Colossae was provided by Epaphras, who reported to the Apostle in prison of
the success of the mission and brought greetings from those
who had never seen his face (2:1). The Epistle was written in
the light of this report, and to expose the errors which the
believers were being asked to adopt.

The errors addressed by Paul grew up in the church and
were produced by a combination of circumstances and influences. Had they come from outside they would have been
resisted and rejected by the church. The fact that they were
nursed in the bosom of the church itself made them all the
more dangerous.

Given the Phrygian tendencies and the Jewish characteristics of the times, including the desire to enter the spirit
world through speculation and attain to sanctity by ascetic
penance, it is not necessary to claim that these false teachers were Jews without a Christian profession—as some have
held. Nowhere are they spoken of as unbelievers.

The main tenets of the Colossian heresy are not sys-
tematically described, so we are left to reconstruct them
from the allusions in the Epistle. These would be clearer to
the readers, of course, than to us. The teaching was described by its proponents as a "philosophy," described by
Paul as "vain deceit" (2:8). They appealed to a secret "tradition" handed down from some remote antiquity, giving it an
aura of ancient wisdom.

The system evidently rested on a doctrine of angelic
beings called "the elemental spirits of the universe" (2:8,
RSV), who were to be worshiped (2:18). These spirits composed a celestial hierarchy, their ranks denoted by "thrones
... dominions ... principalities ... authorities" (1:16, RSV).
All together they constituted the *plērōma* ("fulness," 1:19;

2:9) of divine activities and attributes. They offered men redemption.

Practically, this transcendental doctrine encompassed an asceticism coupled with the bondage of a Pharisaic legalism. With traces of Jewish influence, this new religion judged men "in questions of food and drink or with regard to a festival or a new moon or a sabbath" (2:16, RSV). Some of its legal requirements were codified into a set of taboos— "Do not handle, Do not taste, Do not touch" (2:21, RSV). The language of 2:11 implies that it required its adherents to be circumcised.

Apparently this doctrine had some elements of a mystery cult, in the light of Paul's statement that the leader of the group goes about "taking his stand on visions" (2:18, RSV). This phrase has been shown to have some connection with the mysteries by some Anatolian inscriptions. Further, the frequency with which the Apostle speaks of Christian truth as a "mystery" (1:26; etc.) indicates that the "philosophy" was connected with a mystery cult.

The false teachings at Colossae were of a refined nature. They did not insist apparently on circumcision as a positive Mosaic rite, but as the means of securing spiritual benefit. It seemed to be one of those ascetic austerities by which purity of heart was sought. Distinctions in meat and drink, the observance of holidays, and so on were not imposed as a Pharisaic yoke but were regarded and cherished as elements of a discipline which hoped to attain religious insight by a more certain and speedier way than that which the gospel presented.

The object of the false teachers was to secure spiritual protection by communing with the world of spirits. It aimed to have what the gospel promised, but without the assistance of the Christ which that gospel revealed. It took Christ out of His central Headship and dethroned Him from His mediatorial eminence. Eadie has said that the error of these false leaders "was not in denying, but in dethroning Christ— not in refusing, but in undervaluing his death, and in seeking peace and purity by means of ceremonial distinctions and rigid mortifications."

The errors promulgated in Colossae were wrapped up in important truth and were therefore dangerously attractive. They were not a refutation of the gospel but a sublimation of it. They wanted to introduce into the church certain mystic views and certain forms of a supereminent pietism, which had grown up with a spiritualized and theosophic system. "They were not traitors, they were fanatics" (Eadie).

It has been claimed that these teachings grew out of Epicureanism, Pythagoreanism, or Stoic and Platonic philosophies. However, we are reminded of the numbers of Jews who colonized in these portions of Asia Minor, of whom many passed over into the church still zealous for the law. Also, we see the terminology employed by the Apostle in describing these errors—"circumcision," "handwriting of ordinances," "festivals, new moons, and sabbaths," "a shadow of things to come." Therefore it seems safe to conclude that the false teaching had a Jewish source which had been carried into the church.

The false teachings outlined by the Apostle may be allied with the Christianized Essenes who were likely to become mystics in doctrine and ascetics in practice. The Essenes were philosophic Jews, who in trying to get at the spirit of their system, and to reach its hidden nature, wandered from their real purpose.

We may conclude that while the errors seem to have sprung up with Jewish converts who maintained much of Mosaic ceremonialism, they were yet in harmony with practices widely spread over the East, particularly in Phrygia. Perhaps it was Essenic Judaism modified by introduction to the church, expanding itself into an Oriental system through sympathy with views around it. In addition it identified its angels with emanations, and placed Christ among them, while at least coming close to admitting the sinfulness of all things material.

These ideas later were shaped into an organized system but at this time existed only in seed or germ. In chapter 2

Paul refers in the singular to the party holding the errors condemned by him. Thus he either marks out one noted leader or merely individualizes for the sake of emphasis and communication.

In contrast to these erroneous views, Paul attempts to show that Christ alone embraces in himself all the functions that are falsely ascribed to the angelic beings of this system. He freely gives all the blessings of redemption which men vainly seek to win through cultic rites and by ascetic observances. He argues that the gospel, like the "knowledge" *(gnōsis)* proclaimed by these teachers, is also a "mystery." But it does not depend for its authority upon an ancient tradition—it has "been hid from ages and from generations." But God himself has now revealed it, making known "to his saints" (1:26) His hitherto secret purpose to break down the barriers of race and religious privilege by extending to Gentiles as well as to Jews the glorious blessing of the Christ who was promised to Israel.

The Apostle declares that taboos and prohibitions may create an impression of wisdom and superior piety, but in reality they are powerless to check the gratification of the self. They belong to that lower level of the moral life which was under the dominion of lesser beings—"the elemental spirits." To such a life those who have participated in the death of Christ have become dead. Artificial rules in themselves no more apply to them than to Him. Risen with Him to a new life, they have their minds and hearts fixed on heaven, where He is. Their moral life is governed by the sense of its hidden, heavenly nature, and by the hope of the coming revelation of Christ in glory—a glory which will be manifested also in them (2:16—3:4).

Three purposes are discernible in Colossians. (1) Paul wants to express personal interest in the Colossian Christians. Though he has never visited them (2:5), he feels they are converts of his missionary party and that he is spiritually responsible for their doctrinal safety. (2) Primarily, Paul seeks to warn the Colossians against these Gnostic teachings and their undermining influence on the doctrine of the person and work of Christ. So he enlarges on his views of Christology—the most thorough presentation of Christology in the New Testament. He emphasizes the deity and preexistence of Christ; His work in creation and the upholding of the universe; His headship over the Church; and so on. (3) Paul attempts to show how a well-rounded Christian life is based on one's true relationship to Christ.

In accomplishing these purposes the Apostle declares some basic but profound truths which are at the heart of the gospel and must continue to constitute the fabric of Christian preaching and teaching. These may be summarized as follows:

1. God is the Father.

2. Jesus Christ, coequal with the Father (1:2-3), is the Son of God (1:13), the fullness of Deity permanently dwelling in Him (2:3, 9).

3. Jesus is involved with the Father as Creator and Reconciler of "all things" (1:16, 20). He is the mediate Creator of the cosmos, having existed before anything was made. As God's "Other Self" He is in direct contact with the material world.

4. By means of His death, in relation to the Church, He is the Savior, the Redeemer (1:21; 2:13-14). He is the Head of the Church, which is His Body and instrument for redeeming and ruling the world (1:18; 2:19).

5. As the Father's "beloved Son" Christ secures our redemption and guarantees forgiveness of sins (1:13-14). He nailed to the Cross the bonds of legal demands which threatened us, canceled their condemnation (2:14), and by His death defeated and shattered the evil powers ranged against us (2:15). Peace He made by "the blood of his cross," so to reconcile all things to God (1:20). This gospel or "good news" is the mystery of God's love now made known to men by Christ.

This is the Christ whom Paul declares "we preach" (1:28). And this is the Christ "received" (2:6) by "faith" (1:4; cf. 2:5, 7, 12), and who dwells in the believer as "the hope of glory" (1:27).

6. Morality roots itself in union with God by faith in the Son, not by ascetic practices as the Gnostics taught. Reconciled in and by Christ, the believer is to live and act as a redeemed person. Having received Christ, we are to live in Him (2:6). The believer has died to the old life of sin and self, and is risen again in Christ to a new life of moral worth and ethical action. Christ is "our life" (3:4) with whom our life is hid in God (3:2).

7. This hidden life is to be revealed openly in all our relationships of home and family (3:18-21), between employer and employee (3:22—4:1), and in every human relationship (4:5-6).

Unquestionably, the Epistle to the Colossians has unique doctrinal significance and value. Occasioned by a pretentious but transitory error, it remains to us an imperishable treasure. It has fresh force of application for our times as ancient forms of error recur, evidenced by preoccupation with cults, astrology, the spirit world, and "additional attachments" to the redemptive work of Christ.

This Epistle has abiding value for every generation of Christians because it forces us to deal with the absolute preeminence of Christ. It insists that the clue to the meaning of the universe is *Jesus Christ.* The key verse may well be 1:18: *that in all things he* [Christ] *might have the preeminence.* The message of Colossians may be summed up in the declaration of 3:11: *Christ is all, and in all,* or as Phillips gives it: "Christ is all that matters for Christ lives in all."

Topical Outline of Colossians

Greeting (1:1-2)
  Power and Authority of Apostleship (1:1)
  Responsibility of Apostleship (1:2)

Thanksgiving and Prayer (1:3-14)
  A Subject for Praise (1:3-8)
  Prayer for Spiritual Insight (1:9-14)

The Supremacy of Christ's Person (1:15-23)
   Christ Is the Image of God (1:15a)
   Christ Is the Lord of Creation (1:15b-17)
   Christ Is the Head of the Church (1:18)
   Christ Is the Reconciler of All Things (1:19-20)
   Christ Makes His People Holy (1:21-23)

Excursis: The Christian Minister's Exciting Task
(1:24—2:7)
   Joy in Suffering for Christ's Church (1:24-27)
   The Ultimate Goal of Ministry (1:28-29)
   Concern for the Saints (2:1)
   Intercessory Prayer for the Saints (2:2-5)
   A Fervent Admonition and Warning (2:6-7)

The Supremacy of Christ's Teachings and Redemption
(2:8-23)
   Guard Against False Doctrines (2:8)
   Acknowledge God's Full Revelation in Christ (2:9-10)
   Accept Christ's Atoning Benefits (2:11-15)
   Exercise Your Freedom in Christ (2:16-19)
   Summary: A Penetrating Question (2:20-23)

The Superior Quality of the Christian's Life (3:1-17)
   Life with the Risen Christ (3:1-4)
   Eliminate the Negative (3:5-9)
   Accentuate the Positive (3:10-17)

The Superior Quality of the Christian's Relationships
(3:18—4:18)
   In the Family (3:18-21)
   In the Working World (3:22—4:1)
   In Difficult Circumstances (4:2-4)
   In an Unbelieving World (4:5-6)
   In the Circle of Believers (4:7-14)
   Final Instructions (4:15-17)
   Grace: The Last Word (4:18)

Greeting

Colossians 1:1-2

COLOSSIANS 1

Power and Authority of Apostleship

Colossians 1:1

> 1 Paul, an apostle of Jesus Christ by the will of God, and Timotheus our brother,

We must keep in mind that Paul is writing to a church he had not founded and had never visited. Therefore in dealing with the "Colossian heresy," one of the most formidable challenges to Christ and His Church encountered in all his ministry, it was imperative to establish his authority. To do this he appealed to the Highest Authority, God himself, and by Him claimed the right to speak.

The salutation is typically Pauline. We may observe that of his 13 letters in the New Testament, Paul uses the title "Paul, an apostle of Jesus Christ" exclusively seven times. In Romans and Titus, he presents himself as "servant and apostle"; in Philippians, as "servant"; and in Philemon, as "prisoner." In the two Thessalonian letters he uses no title at all. Particularly in this letter it was crucial that Paul clearly identify his credentials.

1. *The Divine Commission* (1). Though in a Roman prison, Paul still knew who he was—"an apostle of Christ Jesus"

(ASV). One who is sent on a mission for another, a messenger, a minister or ambassador with powers, an extraordinary emissary—that was an apostle. The Apostles formed the highest rank of ministers in the Early Church (1 Cor. 12:28), and the title indicated a position of authority and leadership. The term originally applied to the Twelve (Luke 6:13; John 6:67). Paul could not claim apostleship because he had not been one of the original apostles. Nor had he been so selected or commissioned.

a. Rather, his apostleship was *by the will of God.* He owed his apostleship to an experience on the Damascus Road when he had met the risen Christ face-to-face (Acts 9:1-9; Gal. 1:15). His office and task had been given to him direct from God.

Paul's language in his other writings describing apostleship is informative: "called . . . apostle" (Rom. 1:1; 1 Cor. 1:1); apostle "through the will of God" (2 Cor. 1:1, ASV); God has "set" or "placed" apostles in the Church (1 Cor. 12:28, Williams); God "gave some, apostles"—He "gives" the office (Eph. 4:11). The implication seems clear—ordination for the Christian ministry is indelible.

I did not choose this calling, Paul says. The calling chose me. "I am made a minister," and as such, my assignment is to "fulfil the word of God" (1:25). An important function of the Apostles was that of preaching the gospel (1 Cor. 1:17). They also had the task of founding and supervising communities of Christians (1 Cor. 9:2). Paul felt he had no other business—none at least that could ever serve as a substitute for these divinely given tasks.

No man can make another a minister. Only God can do that. The primary test is not whether one has completed a prescribed course of study or earned a divinity degree; but, rather, has he or she seen Christ face-to-face in a living encounter? An old Jewish priest said of the office which he held: "It was not my father or my mother who installed me in this place, but the arm of the Mighty King gave it to me." Every true minister acknowledges and knows this divine installation.

Not only in the Christian community but also to the Jew, the word "apostle" was well defined. It meant a special messenger, with a special status, enjoying an authority and commission that came from a body higher than oneself. Paul knew full well that a Jewish *apostolos* would normally be sent from a group (perhaps the Sanhedrin) and would have received his commission from the high priest or some similar high official.

When the Apostle went on his journey to Damascus to bind the Christians (Acts 9:2), his apostolate was of this nature. But no longer was it so. His authority now was from above, and his assignment was to open men's eyes and "turn them from darkness to light, and from the power of Satan to God, so that they may receive forgiveness of sins and a place among those who are sanctified by faith" in Christ (Acts 26:18, NIV).

b. Paul never forgot the *Source* of his call to be an apostle. Consequently he was faithful in the drought season. The real reason for his ability to toil and suffer (at Lystra and elsewhere) was that he was certain his task had been given him by God. Paul had an experience of being commissioned. Thus he became known not just as *"an* apostle," but as *"the* apostle." "Three cubits in stature, he touched the sky" (Chrysostom).

> *A desert way,*
> *A burning sun,*
> *And—Saul.*
> *A sudden light,*
> *A heavenly voice,*
> *And—Paul.*

The minister's task may be one of which all men will know; it may be one of which no one will ever hear. But it matters not, if it is from God. It is this sense of divine commission which makes one give priority to ministry and keeps primary attention from being given to other labors and sidelines.

Though sure of his call to be an apostle, Paul always felt his own *unworthiness* for the position (1 Cor. 15:8-9). The more intense the sense of divine vocation, the greater should be the spirit of humility. Though not all are called to be members of the clergy, all believers are commissioned to be "ambassadors for Christ" (2 Cor. 5:20) in reconciling the world to God.

2. *Man with a Message* (1). If Paul never forgot *who he was*—an apostle; if he never forgot the *Source of his call*—God himself; he also never forgot the *heart of his message*—"Christ Jesus." His message was not a principle but a Person. He lifted up the exalted title of "Christ" (1:27), and then added, "whom we preach" (v. 28). Paul Rees observes: "Not 'what,' mind you, but 'whom.'"[6] Preaching is more than talking *about* Christ. It is Christ himself being ministered to people.

To the Corinthians Paul earlier had written: "I determined not to know any thing among you, save Jesus Christ, and him crucified" (1 Cor. 2:2). "For Christ did not send me to baptize, but to preach the gospel—not with words of human wisdom, lest the cross of Christ be emptied of its power" (1 Cor. 1:17, NIV).

a. Paul knew Christ *is* the gospel. Thus he deliberately put Christ side-by-side with God—"an apostle of Christ Jesus by the will of God." The King James Version uses the order "Jesus Christ." While both are found in different sources, according to the best texts "Christ Jesus" is the correct order. The heretics in Colossae, forerunners of the later Gnostics, refused or failed to give Jesus His rightful place. Christ's sovereignty was being compromised, so Paul seeks to bring the church back to full acknowledgment of Christ's Lordship.

b. The Apostle had no struggle with the deity of Jesus. He had seen God "in Christ, reconciling the world unto himself" (2 Cor. 5:19). Christ was the center of his message and is for every true preacher and believer. He was not timid or hesitant in exalting Jesus as the Christ. Certainly Lightfoot is correct in asserting, "Feebleness is the last charge which can be brought against this apostle."

3. *Fellow Laborers with the Lord* (1). Paul did not forget his brother: *and Timotheus our brother.* How gracious for the Apostle to refer thus to Timothy. He was Paul's "true child in the faith" (1 Tim. 1:2, RSV). Apparently on Paul's first missionary journey Timothy had been won to Christ at Lystra (Acts 14:6-7), and on his second journey he had chosen this "disciple" as one of his traveling companions (Acts 16:1-3).

Paul did not refer to Timothy because he needed the sanction of his partner. Rather, it was his large spirit and desire to promote fellowship which caused him to mention the young associate. *Brother* here, literally, "the brother," does not mean "fellow apostle" but "fellow Christian," and indicates something of the warmth of Paul's personal regard for his companion. This reference to his junior partner says a great deal about the great Apostle and about the fellowship of Christian believers. "Though Paul is a special messenger of the Lord Jesus Christ, an apostle of the highest rank, he is yet merely one among many members of the Christian brotherhood."[7]

Responsibility of Apostleship
Colossians 1:2

> 2 To the saints and faithful brethren in Christ which are at Colosse: Grace be unto you, and peace, from God our Father and the Lord Jesus Christ.

Apostleship not only brings a more than human peace and authority; it also carries with it heavy responsibility.

1. *Preaching to Real Needs* (2). Paul always kept before him the *persons whom he was addressing:* "To the holy and faithful brothers in Christ at Colosse" (NIV). The Apostle plainly says he had never seen the Colossians (2:1). He learned of their needs and the dangers confronting them through Epaphras who had preached first in the Lycus Val-

ley after his conversion in Ephesus. Pastor Epaphras carried on his heart the burden of the churches at Colossae, Hierapolis, and Laodicea (4:13). It may be that Paul had sent Epaphras, following his conversion, from Ephesus to Colossae as his personal representative. If so, the Colossians were indebted at least indirectly to Paul for their knowledge of the gospel.

Whatever the situation was at Colossae, Epaphras felt it necessary to discuss the matter with his spiritual mentor. As a result, Paul clearly was having agony of heart over the Colossians, Laodiceans, and others who had not seen his face. What news did Epaphras bring which stirred the Apostle to write this bold and forceful Epistle?

Disturbers had come to the Lycus Valley, and 2:8 implies that there was a leader who tried to make spoil of these believers. They used persuasive talk which was leading astray some not versed in doctrine and in the art of dabbling in philosophic language. Evidently even some of the elders of Ephesus were seeking to "draw away" the disciples after themselves. It is astounding that sheep will follow a wolf to their own destruction. These "savage wolves" (NASB, NIV) were "not sparing the flock" (Acts 20:29).

The heresy at Colossae was not fully developed Gnosticism as we know it several centuries later, but a kind of incipient Gnosticism. These early Gnostics sought salvation by *gnōsis* (knowledge) as well as by the ritual of the mysteries. They claimed to have a richer and fuller revelation than ordinary Christians. This was accompanied by a pride of knowledge which led to contempt of others. This contemptuous and condescending attitude was contrary to the spirit of Christ and stirred Paul to indignation. Further, it was a dangerous claim which he felt responsible to confront.

Paul was not afraid of truth, whatever its source. He does not plead for less knowledge but more. All through Colossians he urges his readers to obtain additional knowledge, particularly of God and His will (9-10; 2:2).

a. The fundamental doctrinal error of these disturbers at Colossae was in teaching that *matter is evil.* Since the good God could not create evil (including matter), they postulated a series of emanations, aeons, spirits, and angels that came between God and matter. They reasoned that one aeon came from God, another aeon from this aeon, and so on till there was one far enough away from God for God not to be contaminated by the creation of evil matter and yet close enough to have power to do the work. (Paul may have had these aeons in mind when he condemned "endless genealogies." See 1 Tim. 1:4; Titus 3:9.)

When these Gnostic-like thinkers became interested in Christianity, they faced the problem of what to do with Christ. Some put Him in the center of these aeons, others at the bottom of the list.

Converted Gnostics interpreted Jesus in two different ways. (1) The "docetic" Gnostics (from *dokeō*, "to seem" or "appear") denied the actual humanity of Jesus. They thought Jesus only *appeared* to have a body and was simply an aeon or angel. His body was illusion. He was not really born, nor did He really die. (2) The other branch of Gnosticism is called *Cerinthianism* (after Cerinthus, its chief advocate in later years of the first century). This view denied the identity, the unity, of Jesus and Christ (the Logos). These thinkers thought Jesus had a natural human life, but the aeon Christ came upon Him temporarily at His baptism in the form of a dove and later left Him on the Cross.

b. Ethically, this Gnostic error that matter is essentially evil took a double turn. (1) One wing argued for *asceticism* as the method of escape from sin and sensuous things. Paul writes to expose the folly of treating the body as essentially sinful. (2) The other group took the opposite extreme of *antinomian license.* The way to overcome sensuality, they insisted, is to indulge it to excess, even to exhaustion. The Apostle shows the danger of this view and the need and possibility of a clean life for the new man in Christ.

c. To combat these errors Paul asserts that in Christ "are hid all the treasures of wisdom and knowledge" (2:3).

Hence the worship of angels is wrong and sinful, as well as superfluous. The Apostle gives a full-length portrait of Christ as Creator and Head of the universe in nature and in grace (15-16). He writes the church at Colossae that in Christ all the fullness *(plērōma)* of the Deity lives in bodily form (2:9). Jesus had a real human body and shed His blood on the Cross (22).

Paul's position is emphatic and clear. The eternal, creating Christ (Logos) became the historic Jesus. His was no phantom existence. He was real flesh and blood and lived among men. Charles Wesley's lines, sung by millions every Christmas, catch Paul's meaning:

> *Late in time behold Him come,*
> *Offspring of a virgin's womb.*
> *Veiled in flesh the Godhead see;*
> *Hail th'incarnate Deity!*

The Epistle to the Colossians was designed to be read in church (4:16). It is not a literary production, but a church Epistle for reading and public use. In this it comes close to preaching. Paul wrote and preached for real needs of real people in real-life situations.

He who would preach must ever keep his hearers before him. Preaching to a congregation without addressing its needs is like fighting in a sham war that has no opposition or issue. Likewise, personal witnessing which does not speak to the hearer's personal needs may be an exercise in futility.

2. *Christ's Holy Ones* (2). Observe that Paul is writing to the "holy . . . brothers" (NIV). *Hagiois (saints)* is literally "holy ones." It refers to those who have been set apart to the service of Christ and are different from the world. They belong to, and are like, God. They are His purchased possession and His peculiar property. The term is the equivalent of believers or regenerated ones, and indicates those who have been "washed" from sin and set on the road to moral and spiritual maturity (1 Cor. 6:9-11; 1 Pet. 1:2). "Holy . . . brothers" at Colossae means the church of true Christians at Colossae.

a. "Saint" (holy one) expresses the state of the Christian in Christ. One is a "saint" in biblical usage only because he is *in Christ.* This is one of Paul's favorite phrases and fairly summarizes his theology. Its meaning stands in contrast to "demon possession" (see Mark 1:23; literally, "in an unclean spirit," or, according to Phillips, "in the grip of an evil spirit").

To be *in Christ* is to be possessed by Him, to be under His control and influence. It is to be held in the heart of Christ. The phrase should be understood as being in the "power of another." (Note that to be *in Christ* is the opposite of being "in Adam" [1 Cor. 15:22].)

As the spirit of a person can transform the total being of another without violating his freedom or individuality, so the Spirit of Christ can transform into new creatures those who are in Him (2 Cor. 5:17) without denying to them full freedom or the fulfillment of their personality.

b. In all Paul's letters, "in Christ" is found 34 times; "in Christ Jesus" 48 times; and "in the Lord" 50 times. Whatever the emphasis, these always affirm that the saint's true life is the life of the risen Christ within him ("Christ in you, the hope of glory," 27). The "fruit" of this life is Christlikeness.

In this sense, every believer is sanctified, or made holy (1 Cor. 1:2; 6:11). "It is the Spirit who sanctifies; but He does so inasmuch as He roots us in Christ and builds us up in Christ. Therefore saints are sanctified by, or of, the Spirit; but they are sanctified (or holy) in Christ Jesus."[8]

3. *The Good News* (2b). Paul knew *(a)* who he was. He knew *(b)* the Source of his call. He knew *(c)* the content (the Person) of his message. He knew *(d)* the value of his associate Timothy and of his colaborers. He knew *(e)* the needs of his hearers at Colossae. But he also knew *(f)* the gospel, the Good News, and what he wanted to say. (Here are six necessary qualifications for effective preaching.) He condensed his concept of the gospel in his greeting: *Grace be unto you, and peace, from God our Father.*

a. Grace *(charis)* is God's love toward sinners, not because of their merit, but because He is God. This is Paul's master word and key in all his writings. Grace is the sum total of all that Christ has done for man. Grace is the inward compulsion that drove Christ to the Cross. And it is the essence of a truly Christian life. Not only does God provide salvation initially; He continues to give. The result of grace is gracious—"and grace for grace" (John 1:16).

"Grace" has many meanings: graciousness, gracefulness, generosity, gratitude. According to William Barclay, there are two main ideas in the word "grace." (1) The first is that of *sheer beauty.* It always suggests beauty and charm. Because the Christian life results from grace, it is both lovely and attractive. Too often goodness exists without charm, and charm without goodness. Grace combines both.

(2) The second idea in grace is that of *undeserved generosity.* "The law was given by Moses, but grace and truth came by Jesus Christ" (John 1:17). It is a gift. Man doesn't deserve it, nor can he earn it. God's goodness and love alone prompt His blessings. Thus when Paul prayed for "grace" to fall on his friends, he was saying, "May the beauty of the undeserved love of God be on you, so that it will make your life lovely too."[9] Everything grace touches becomes "something beautiful, something good."

b. Paul also prays for peace. The Hebrew word for peace *(shalom)* and the equivalent Greek word *(eirēnē)* mean far more than the absence of trouble, and more than freedom from tribulation (John 16:33). Contrast the Roman (Latin) word *pax.* In the Roman Empire peace was maintained by soldiers stationed everywhere with swords drawn. They kept the peace *(pax),* but it was an "uneasy peace," merely the forced cessation of open hostility. Christ's "peace" is blessedness in the midst of the storm on the outside.

The "peace" Paul has in mind connotes a sense of total well-being that comes from a right relationship with God, from accepting God's gift. It means everything which is to a man's highest good, which will make his mind pure, his will resolute, and his heart glad. It is that assurance of the love and care of God which, even if his body were tortured, would keep a man's heart in peace and joy.

"Peace" is the promised gift of Christ to His troubled disciples. On the Cross Jesus willed His mother to John the Beloved; His spirit back to His Father. But to His disciples Jesus said, "Peace I leave with you" (John 14:27). "Peace" was Jesus' first greeting to His assembled followers when He rose from the dead (John 20:19).

c. *Grace and peace* is the divine formula for adequacy. And the order is not accidental. Grace always precedes. God's peace is never enjoyed where God's grace has not been received and retained. Never once did Paul write a salutation in which peace precedes grace. Paul had been torn at the seams till he met Christ and experienced His boundless grace. Inadequacy causes men to break up; fullness or adequacy resulting from grace holds life together.

One of secular man's favorite words is "efficient." Paul's word is "sufficient." Someone has suggested that efficiency is playing the keyboard; sufficiency is keeping a song in one's heart. Efficiency is building the boat; sufficiency is the ability of the river and sea to float it.

Here is where Paul got his light, his power, and the courage to handle opposition, strain, and the attacks upon him. Grace was the secret of his mental and spiritual health.

Man seeks peace where it is not—a new thrill, drugs, the passionate worship of success, a new partner in marriage, and so forth. But peace is harmony. Harmony with oneself is *integrity;* harmony with life itself is *gratitude;* harmony with people is *brotherhood;* harmony with God is *faith.* All this adds up to peace of soul—the gift of Christ.

We talk a great deal about peace of mind. But the basic issue is a religious one. "What are we afraid of?" is answered by "What and whom do we believe in?" And this is the business of religion. So Paul says this "grace and peace" is *from God our Father and the Lord Jesus Christ.* Observe that there is no reference to the Holy Spirit here. He *is* that peace that "passeth all understanding" (Phil. 4:7). Peace is the in-dwelling of the Holy Spirit.

Thanksgiving and Prayer

Colossians 1:3-14

A Subject for Praise

Colossians 1:3-8

> 3 We give thanks to God and the Father of our Lord Jesus Christ, praying always for you,
> 4 Since we heard of your faith in Christ Jesus, and of the love which ye have to all the saints,
> 5 For the hope which is laid up for you in heaven, whereof ye heard before in the word of the truth of the gospel;
> 6 Which is come unto you, as it is in all the world; and bringeth forth fruit, as it doth also in you, since the day ye heard of it, and knew the grace of God in truth:
> 7 As ye also learned of Epaphras our dear fellowservant, who is for you a faithful minister of Christ;
> 8 Who also declared unto us your love in the Spirit.

Gratitude follows greeting in all of Paul's Epistles except Galatians. It was a common practice for Paul to express gratitude for blessings. The Apostle was overjoyed with the good news which Epaphras brought from the Colossians. He had never been to Colossae and had never met these Christian people. But reports rejoiced his heart.

"We always thank God ... when we pray for you" (3, NIV). Before he warns and rebukes, Paul first gives the Colossians credit for all the good he can find in them. Not a bad habit to form. Paul may have had prayer lists, for he regularly carried these and other saints in prayer to the throne of grace.

1. Paul was grateful because the Colossians were in possession of the three cardinal Christian graces—faith, love, hope. He had been told of their *faith in Christ Jesus* (4), their Christ-centered faith; of their *love* which they had "for all the saints" (4, NIV)—their unity with God and each other was to be admired; and of their *hope* which the gospel had brought to them (5).

The first, faith, is in Christ; the second, love, is within the Christian community; and the third, hope, is "stored up for you in heaven" (5, NIV). Faith and love are based on hope, a fact which gives stability to the Christian not only today but tomorrow as well. Of this triad Lightfoot says, "Faith rests on the past; love works in the present; hope looks to the future."

The phrase *for the hope* (5) in the Greek has the force of "on account of the hope." The text itself is not clear as to whether this refers to the *love . . . to all the saints* or to *we give thanks.* Some feel that the first would make the Christian's motivation selfish since it would be based on hope of reward. However, reward cannot be totally removed from the Christian life. While the hope of reward and blessings laid up in heaven is not the highest motivation for faith and love, it nurtures them nonetheless. Alexander Maclaren has put it well: "Both are made more vivid when it [hope] is strong. It is not the light at which their lamps are lit, but is the odorous oil which feeds their flame."[10]

Perhaps a better way to think of this "hope" is to say that in spite of the difficulties encountered because of one's faith, the Christian walk is ultimately superior; in spite of the world's evils and injustices, God's way of love and righteousness will have the last word. William Barclay captures the thought beautifully: "The Christian hope is that God's way is the best way, that the only happiness, the only peace, the only joy, the only true and lasting reward are to be found in the way of God. . . . The Christian hope is the certainty that it is better to stake one's life on God than to believe the world."[11]

2. Paul was grateful because the Colossians were another example of the power of the gospel "all over the world" (6, NIV). The true gospel is universal, meeting man's needs everywhere. False gospels are limited, growing out of local circumstances, and displaying narrow characteristics. The gospel of Jesus has two marks: *(a)* it produces "fruit" by transforming men's lives, and *(b)* it "grows" or spreads. Where these evidences are absent we would do well to ask ourselves if we are in fact preaching the *gospel.*

Prayer for Spiritual Insight

Colossians 1:9-14

> 9 For this cause we also, since the day we heard it, do not cease to pray for you, and to desire that ye might be filled with the knowledge of his will in all wisdom and spiritual understanding;
> 10 That ye might walk worthy of the Lord unto all pleasing, being fruitful in every good work, and increasing in the knowledge of God;
> 11 Strengthened with all might, according to his glorious power, unto all patience and longsuffering with joyfulness;
> 12 Giving thanks unto the Father, which hath made us meet to be partakers of the inheritance of the saints in light:
> 13 Who hath delivered us from the power of darkness, and hath translated us into the kingdom of his dear Son:
> 14 In whom we have redemption through his blood, even the forgiveness of sins:

After the thanksgiving Paul revealed his deepest desire for the Colossians. His prayer for them was definite, precise, and persistent. The Colossians had a problem so he brought it to the Lord. His request was fourfold.

1. *For Knowledge of God's Will* (9). He says, "We have not stopped praying for you and asking God to fill you with the knowledge of his will through all spiritual wisdom and understanding" (9, NIV). The antidote for the false claim to knowledge by the Gnostics was additional knowledge, richer knowledge, which comes from the God who makes His will known.

The knowledge referred to is far more than intellectual knowledge, even of God's will. It is spiritual understanding and involves knowing God's will in practical, everyday issues. Paul often insisted that by yielding ourselves to God we can know His will (Rom. 12:2; Eph. 5:10, 17). And Jesus, too, put obedience to God's will as a prerequisite to further discernment (John 7:17).

Knowing God's will, then, has a moral aspect. Paul understood this well. That's why he wanted increasing knowledge of Christ (Phil. 3:8-10). The master passion of his life was to know Christ better. An intimate knowledge of Jesus not only brings wisdom in the broad sense, but "understanding," the ability to apply it to life's daily decisions, the capacity to make sound moral judgments.

2. *For a Life Worthy of the Lord* (10). Definite benefits derive from receiving "spiritual wisdom and understanding." Paul desired this for the Colossians that they "may live a life worthy of the Lord and may please him in every way: bearing fruit in every good work, growing in the knowledge of God" (10, NIV). Spiritual enlightenment is shown by a worthy walk. "Doctrine and ethics are for Paul inseparable."[12]

Jesus also taught that a tree is judged by its fruit. Knowledge of God is not an end in itself, but the means to growth in the likeness of God. Obedience to God's will is an organ of knowledge, but spiritual intelligence should lead into fuller likeness to God.

3. *For Power for Their Task* (11). Spiritual wisdom and understanding provide power commensurate to one's responsibilities: "being strengthened with all power according to his glorious might so that you may have great endurance and patience" (11, NIV).

The word translated "power" *(dynamei, might)* is kin to our word *dynamite*. Here it is used as a play on the root idea of power: "empowered with all power." It comes from God alone. He gives it out of His might and resources. This power is proportional not simply to the recipient's need, but to the divine supply. There is an undiminished supply of God's power for the continuous needs of the saints.

Literally, the verse reads, "being empowered with all

power according to the might of His glory." God's "glory" *(shekinah)* among the Old Testament saints was the bright light over the mercy seat. No man could look on it and live. That same "shekinah" can rest on the Christian, making him invincible against all attacks of the enemy.

This "empowering with power" (present tense, denoting continuous strengthening) brings "great endurance and patience." God's glory, which is mighty, is like the sun. It is always shining, always working—though clouds and darkness may temporarily obscure it. The word "patience" here means "remaining under," staying at one's post of duty, but uncomplainingly and without succumbing to the temptation to desert. In other words, this power will save from cowardice or despondency. It enables one to hold on, not to become a quitter. It reinforces one to be long-suffering, enduring for a long time and putting up with more than could be expected.

4. *For a Spirit of Gratitude* (12-14). These graces are to be exhibited with joy: "joyfully giving thanks to the Father" (11-12, NIV). Peake has put it this way: "The remedy [for impatience] is that the Christian should be so filled with joy that he is able to meet all his trials with a buoyant sense of mastery."[13]

And what are the grounds for the Christian's joyful gratitude? They are the work of the Father, "who has qualified you [some manuscripts read 'us'] to share in the inheritance of the saints in the kingdom of light. For he has rescued us from the dominion of darkness and brought us into the kingdom of the Son he loves, in whom we have redemption, the forgiveness of sins" (12-14, NIV).

The analogy of the inheritance of Canaan, the allotment of the Promised Land, must not be far from Paul's mind (Heb. 3:7—4:11). Just as the Israelites were delivered (redeemed) out of the darkness of Egyptian bondage, so Christians have been "rescued" from the darkness of sin— and brought into light. It is the kingdom of light where the saints have their inheritance. We were slaves in the land of darkness, says the Apostle, but God rescued us from this thralldom.

The verb "brought" (*translated* or "transferred" [NASB, RSV]) was used by classical writers for the removal of whole bodies of men, like colonists or military personnel who had been conquered. God did more than rescue us from the power of darkness. He "transported" us, brought us out, changed our habitation. So He carried us over *into the kingdom of his dear Son.* He brought us out that He might bring us in.

The Gnostics claimed special illumination and revelation, but it is all darkness in comparison with Christ's way of light. The mission of the Son is to reveal the Father. He is the Son of God's love (1 John 4:9), and in Him we already *have redemption . . . the forgiveness of sins.* The word translated *forgiveness* means removal of the barrier of sin. Sinful man can't remove it, but Christ can—and did! He has reconciled us with the Father.

Is it any wonder that Paul was thankful? Shouldn't every Christian be grateful, too? By His forgiveness Christ has removed the barrier—the Red Sea of sin's penalty and power—which separated us from His kingdom of light. And He has carried us over into His domain of liberty and life.

My heart was distressed 'neath Jehovah's dread frown,
And low in the pit where my sins dragged me down.
I cried to the Lord from the deep, miry clay,
Who tenderly brought me out to golden day.

He gave me a song; 'twas a new song of praise.
By day and by night its sweet notes I will raise.
My heart's overflowing; I'm happy and free.
I'll praise my Redeemer, who has rescued me.

He brought me out of the miry clay;
He set my feet on the Rock to stay;
He puts a song in my soul today,
A song of praise, hallelujah!

—H. J. ZELLEY AND
HENRY L. GILMOUR

The Supremacy of Christ's Person

Colossians 1:15-23

Having given his greeting, thanksgiving, and prayer, Paul now comes to the heart of his letter. This majestic passage of Scripture is the Apostle's answer to the Gnostics who were disturbing the church at Colossae. To understand these verses we must keep in mind their erroneous thinking.

As noted earlier, these Gnostics believed that matter—this world—is evil. They reasoned that God, being good, could not have created it. They thought God sent forth a series of powers, or aeons, or emanations. The further away from God they became, the more ignorant of Him, and hostile to Him, they were. One of these emanations created the world. Paul disagrees. He does not close his eyes to evil *in* the universe, but he denies that this *is* an *evil* universe. He insists that God *did* create the world, and His agent in creation was no ignorant and hostile emanation, but Jesus Christ, His Son (16). He would have been able to sing: "This is my Father's world," meaning the "Father of our Lord Jesus Christ."

The Gnostics held that Jesus Christ was by no means unique. He was simply *one* among many of these emanations between God and the world. Paul maintains, in contrast, that in Jesus Christ all fullness dwells (19); that in Him there is the fullness of the Godhead "in bodily form" (2:9, NIV). Jesus is not a partial revelation of God. Rather, He is unique and in Him is the fullness of God.

Further, the Gnostics held that Jesus had only a phantom existence. He could not have had a real body of flesh and blood, since matter is evil. Jesus was simply a spirit who took a bodily form. But Paul leaves no doubt as to his contrary view. He speaks of Jesus reconciling man to God by His "physical body through death" (22, NIV).

For the Gnostics man discovers his own way to God. But the way is obstructed by these emanations which the soul must overcome. To bypass these barriers special knowledge and secret passwords were needed which the Gnostics claimed they alone could supply. This meant that for them salvation is intellectual knowledge for the intellectually elite. Consequently, it cannot be for every person since simple people cannot understand it. Thus the Gnostics divided mankind into "spiritual" and "earthly," and only the spiritual (those with special knowledge) can be saved.

To counter these teachings, Paul writes that salvation is not knowledge and is not secured by knowledge in any ordinary sense. Rather, salvation is trust or faith in God's actions on behalf of man. It is redemption and the forgiveness of sins. Since this is what salvation is, it is not beyond the reach of any man. Paul's aim was to proclaim Christ, to warn every man, to teach every man, and to "present every man perfect in Christ Jesus" (28), however wise or untutored he may be.

Against this background of errors affecting the Colossian church, Paul makes some bold claims concerning the preeminence of Christ. Already he has said Christ is the Redeemer, or Deliverer. To this he adds several other great truths.

Christ Is the Image of God

Colossians 1:15a

15 Who is the image of the invisible God,

The word *image (eikōn)* means the exact, inner, essential likeness of God.[14] It is a derived likeness as the parental likeness in a child. However, it "does not imply a weakening or a feeble copy of something. It implies the illumination of its inner core and essence."[15]

Three ideas combine in this word "image": *derivation, representation,* and *manifestation.* That is, so Paul Rees points out in *The Epistles to Philippians, Colossians, and Philemon,* Christ comes from God, represents God, unveils God. An image can be a representation. But a representation, if it is perfect, can become a manifestation. H. Dermot McDonald, in his *Commentary on Colossians and Philemon,* observes that as the *manifestation* of God, Christ makes the Invisible visible—God is perfectly revealed in Him; as the *representation* of God, Christ makes the visible intelligible (see John 1:18, NEB). "In Christ, then, the Invisible has become visible and the Unutterable knowable."

Moses learned that God is invisible to man when he asked to see the glory of God pass by. God dwells in light unapproachable, whom no one has seen or can see (1 Tim. 6:16). Yet we see God in Christ. Thus Phillips phrases verse 15*a* this way: "Now Christ is the visible expression of the invisible God." Jesus himself said: "He that hath seen me hath seen the Father" (John 14:9). "In the exalted Christ the unknowable God becomes known" (Peake).

Paul is affirming that Jesus is the perfect revelation or manifestation of God. He reveals the nature of God. He shows what God is. One cannot claim to know God while denying the Son. With this affirmation Paul pulverizes the Gnostic heresy.

1. Jesus is the fulfillment of Jewish thought and dreams. Old Testament and intertestamental writers often spoke of "Wisdom." It was said that wisdom is the "image" of the goodness of God. William Barclay captures the Apostle's thought dramatically: It is as though Paul turns to the Jews and says, "Now you've been writing and dreaming about this divine wisdom which is as old as God, which made the world, and which gives wisdom to men. In Jesus Christ this Wisdom has come to men in bodily form for all to see."

2. Jesus is the fulfillment of Greek thought and longing. The Greeks talked and wrote about the *Logos,* the Reason of

God. Philo, one of their writers, repeatedly called the invisible and divine Logos the "image" *(eikōn)* of God. Again Barclay suggests it is as if Paul addresses the Greeks and says: "For the past 600 years you have dreamed and written about the mind, the Word, the Logos of God. You called it God's *eikon.* Well, in Jesus Christ that Logos has come plain for all to see."

3. Jesus is what God intended man to be. If these thoughts were too lofty for the Colossians, they would certainly know the creation story which says, "God created man in his own *image"* (Gen. 1:26-27). Man was designed to be the *eikōn,* the image of God. Jesus shows what God is, but, says the Apostle, He also shows manhood as God planned and created it prior to sin. Jesus is the perfect manifestation of man, the goal of his ultimate destiny.

4. Jesus fully reveals what God is. Even if Paul's readers did not know the creation story, they surely knew that one form of the word *eikōn* was the word used in Greek for a portrait. In meaning it was close to our word "photograph." Further, the Colossians and their troublers would know that when a legal document or a promissory note was drawn up, "it always included a description of the chief characteristics and distinguishing marks of the contracting parties, so that there could be no evasion and no mistake" (Barclay).

Paul is saying to the most unsophisticated, "You know that with any legal agreement, there is always included a description, an *eikōn,* by which the participants may be recognized. Now Jesus is the portrait of God. In Him you see the personal qualities and the unparalleled traits of God. If you want to know what God is like, look at Jesus."

But lest his hearers take the analogy too far, and think of the portrait as only a sketch, Paul says Jesus is the *plērōma* (the completeness, the fullness) of God (19). Jesus is not simply a brief outline of God; not a summary of God; not a miniature version of God. He is more than a mere portrait. In Him is present all that makes God to be God. He is the complete and ultimate Revelation, and no other special knowledge as advanced by the Gnostics is required to know God.

Christ Is the Lord of Creation

Colossians 1:15b-17

> the firstborn of every creature:
> 16 For by him were all things created, that are in heaven, and that are in earth, visible and invisible, whether they be thrones, or dominions, or principalities, or powers: all things were created by him, and for him:
> 17 And he is before all things, and by him all things consist.

In these verses Paul takes great care to assert that Jesus not only has priority *in* the creation, but priority *to* the creation. He is not himself a creature, for as the Agent of creation He had a share in creating everything.

1. Two ideas are present in Paul's use of *firstborn (prōtotokos)* in the phrase "firstborn over all creation" (15, NIV): priority to all creation and dominion or sovereignty over all creation.[16] Christ was not only present at the formation of all things; He is still present to sustain all things (Heb. 1:2-3). H. Dermot McDonald unites these two ideas beautifully in his statement: "Not only does He [the firstborn] not belong to the order of created realities, but rather the order of created realities belongs to Him."

When it was said that Israel was the "firstborn" son of God (Exod. 4:22), it meant that Israel was the chosen, the most honored and favored child of God. The word was also used as a title of the Messiah: "I will make him my firstborn, higher than the kings of the earth" (Ps. 89:27). With this in mind Paul is saying that Jesus is the firstborn of all creation, and the highest honor which creation holds belongs to the Son. To the Colossians, he is denying that Jesus is one of the angels or aeons. So far from being *one* of them, He *created* them. He is "not only superior to every creature, but He is himself the agent in the work of creation."[17] He is as far above them as the Creator is above the creature.

2. But Paul has a further word to add. The universe stands created *for him* (16). Christ is not only Creator, He is also the Goal and End of creation. "The conditions of existence are so ordered that without Christ it cannot attain its perfection."[18] He is the Alpha and the Omega of the Father's creative purpose. The world was created in order that it might ultimately belong to Jesus Christ.

3. Now Paul climaxes and summarizes this part of his argument: Jesus "is before all things, and in him all things hold together" (17, NIV). Christ is the Beginning and the End of creation, but in between He holds the world together (see Rom. 11:36). He makes the universe to be a cosmos—a world of order—and not a chaos. He is the Sphere in which all things have their existence. What we view as scientific laws, such as the law of gravity, are really divine laws. They are the laws which make this a predictable and reliable world. Without Christ we could never have put a man on the moon. Every law of science and nature is an expression of the thought of God. Without Jesus the universe would disintegrate into chaos and nothingness.

It is a majestic canvas on which Paul paints, and the representation of the Lord given here as the exalted Creator and Sustainer brings great comfort in times of transition such as ours. This truth is of immeasurable practical significance for the Christian believer in an age of space enterprises and the releasing of unknown forces of nature. For the Christian, the universe is not terrifying because its Creator is his Lord. "For a man redeemed by Christ, the universe has no ultimate terrors; he knows that his Redeemer is also Creator, ruler and goal of all."[19]

Christ Is the Head of the Church
Colossians 1:18

18 And he is the head of the body, the church: who is the beginning, the firstborn from the dead; that in all things he might have the preeminence.

This is one of the key verses of the Epistle to the Colossians. Paul is anxious to demonstrate to the Gnostics the superiority of Jesus in every realm, whether it be material or spiritual. He has just declared that Jesus is supreme over created matter. Now He asserts that He is supreme in the realm of spirit. There is an obvious parallel between Christ's relation to the world as His material creation and His relation to the Church as His spiritual creation. To both He is the *firstborn,* the sovereign. As with His relation to the cosmos, He also is the Source, the power, and the goal of the life of the Church.

In this Epistle there are four references to the Church (18, 24; 4:15, 16). By the term "church" Paul denotes those who have experienced the redemption or deliverance accomplished in Christ and who have acknowledged Him as Lord. The Church is made up of those who are "in Christ," and to be in Christ is to be a part of the Church.

1. Christ is the Head of the Church, which is His Body. This figure of speech is found in 1 Corinthians where the mutual relations of church members are emphasized. It is also prominent in Ephesians where the emphasis is laid on the Church itself. Here in Colossians the primary thought is centered upon Christ as the Head of the Church.

Here is a vivid suggestion of the unity which exists between Christ and the community of God's people. The Church is the organism through which Christ acts. Physically the body is dependent on the head. It is the servant of the mind and the brain. It moves at the head's bidding. Without the head the body is powerless and dead. So Jesus as the Head of His Body is the directing and dominating Spirit of the Church. Every action of the Church must be governed and directed by Him.

But there is a more sobering thought. The head is dependent on the body to carry out its plans. If a man abuses or misuses his body he can make it incapable of serving the mind. Herein is a warning. The Church can become so listless and undisciplined that it becomes unfit to be the instrument of Christ, who is her Head.

2. Christ is the *beginning* of the Church, "the firstborn from among the dead" (NIV). He is not the beginning in the sense of being the first believer in the community of faith. He is not merely the first Christian. More profoundly, it is in Him and through Him and unto Him that anyone is a Christian. *Beginning* does not denote merely the first in a series, but the source to which the series can be traced and by which it is sustained. Christ, then, is the originating power of the Church. He created the world, but also the Church.

> *She is His new creation*
> *By water and the word.*
> —SAMUEL J. STONE

Here the figure of speech is changed from the Church as a Body, of which believers are the members, to that of a family, of which Christ is *the firstborn from the dead.* Christ was the first to rise from the dead never to die again. The term *firstborn* implies that others will follow. The family is composed of those who share with Christ His resurrection life, which is both spiritual and physical, present and future.

Christ is the firstfruits of those who slept (1 Cor. 15:20, 23) and the Prince of Life. He is the Conqueror of death (Heb. 2:10, 14), and because of that victory He will finally abolish death (1 Cor. 15:24, 26). He is the King over life and death, the life-giving Spirit (1 Cor. 15:45). Paul's thoughts here can be illustrated clearly from 1 Corinthians 15 and Romans 8.

3. Supremacy belongs to Christ because of His resurrection. Christ is first in creation, first in the Church. Now Paul states that He was resurrected "in order that" (Weymouth) He might be supreme in *everything.* Whether in nature or grace, His preeminence is absolute. The purpose of God for His Son in this eternal program is clear—that He alone should stand forth as Lord (cf. Phil. 2:9-11). He is to be supreme in all respects and at every point. H. M. Carson has written: "Lord of creation and Lord of His Church, He must

be Lord in the lives of His own, with a sovereignty which brooks no rival."[20]

The writer to the Hebrews acknowledged that we do not yet see all things subjected to Him, but we do "see Jesus . . . crowned with glory and honour" (Heb. 2:9-10). "The believer knows that while the *rule* of Christ has not yet been established in every human heart, the *over-rule* is an actual fact even now (cf. Rom. 8:28)."[21]

Christ Is the Reconciler of All Things

Colossians 1:19-20

19 For it pleased the Father that in him should all fulness dwell;
20 And, having made peace through the blood of his cross, by him to reconcile all things unto himself; by him, I say, whether they be things in earth; or things in heaven.

The Apostle has shown the preeminence of Christ as the image of God, as the Creator and Sustainer of the universe, and as the Head of the Church. Now he shows Him to be preeminent in His redeeming work. One cannot miss Paul's cosmic sweep of thought as he contemplates God's work of redemption in Christ.

1. None but a divine Savior could reconcile a world unto God. This seems to be the meaning of the Apostle in speaking of the *fulness* (19) which dwelt in Jesus. Numerous interpretations of this fullness have been suggested, but the most natural way of understanding it is to say it denotes the sum total of the powers and attributes of God. All these are said to reside in Christ. In Him dwelt all the fullness of God as Deity. The word *dwell* indicates a permanent residence in contrast to an unreal or transient incarnation.

It may be that the term *fulness* was a technical term used by the Gnostics to refer to the totality of aeons and emanations which they supposed emanated from the transcendent God and served as intermediaries between God and man, heaven and earth. Against this view Paul proclaims that all the fullness of God himself resides permanently in Christ. This fullness is not diffused among many. Rather, Christ is the one Mediator between God and man and as such provides reconciliation for all who believe.

The subject of "was pleased" (NIV), God, is omitted from the text and must be supplied by the translators. There can be little question that God *the Father* is in the mind of the Apostle (for similar thought and expression see Phil. 2:13; 2 Thess. 1:11; Eph. 1:5, 9; Matt. 3:17; Luke 12:32; 1 Cor. 1:21). The Old Testament tells us that God chose to dwell in the Temple: "Why gaze in envy, O rugged mountains, at the mountain where God chooses to reign, where the Lord himself will dwell forever?" (Ps. 68:16, NIV). But now, says Paul, He chooses to meet with men in the Human Being, Jesus of Nazareth. "Here and nowhere else is the complete being of God, His true nature and character, to be found."[22] Only one who is thus divine could effect reconciliation for man.

2. Christ is engaged in the work of reconciling the world to God. Reconciliation was the purpose of His coming. This saving work has its origin in the love and grace of God. It is the Father who planned the reconciliation (2 Cor. 5:18-21). He has taken the initiative—"while we were yet sinners, Christ died for us" (Rom. 5:8). He came seeking man and undertook the work of reconciliation—"God so loved the world, that he gave his only begotten Son" (John 3:16). He has provided the atonement for man's sin.

Reconciliation includes the removal of all estrangements or barriers between God and men. Both the sinful impenitence of men and the divine displeasure with sin have been overcome by the death of Christ, who *made peace through the blood of his cross* (20). The word translated "having made peace" *(eirēnopoiēsas)* is found only here in the New Testament, but the idea of Christ and His work as the Maker and Giver of peace is throughout (see Luke 1:79; John 14:27; 16:33; 20:19, 21, 26; Acts 10:36; Rom. 1:7; 15:33; 16:20; Eph. 2:14). Peacemaking and reconciliation are parallel words in this verse. The Cross, which is the medium of reconciliation, is the supreme revelation of God's love and evokes from man a responding love.

> *Love so amazing, so divine,*
> *Demands my soul, my life, my all.*
> —ISAAC WATTS

3. This reconciliation has cosmic significance. *To reconcile* has the force of restoration, as to a primal or original state of harmony and unity. Six times in the passage beginning at verse 15 (vv. 15-20) the cosmic Christ is highlighted by the phrase *all things.* "Through him" was the creation of all things; "through him" is the reconciliation of all things. All things, both material and spiritual, have their restitution through Him.

The precise meaning of Paul's declaration that reconciliation extends even to *things in heaven* is unclear. Some have thought the angels in heaven were under sin and needed to be reconciled to God. Origen, the third-century universalist, taught that at last even the devil and his angels would be reconciled to God. Others think Paul's language does not refer to anything definite but is simply a lavish expression of Christ's redeeming work. None of these views is satisfactory.

One of the most provocative suggestions (which comes from Theodoret through Erasmus) is not that the heavenly angels were reconciled to God, but that they were reconciled to men. They were angry with men for what they had done to God, resented man's rebellion, and wanted to destroy men. But Christ did away with the wrath of the angels when they saw in the death of Jesus how much God still loved men. At least men, if not angels, sometimes act this way—slow to forgive and quick to berate, destroy, and attach blame.

However we may view this subject, Charles Erdman's observation is sound: "The main idea is clear and majestic. It is the purpose of God, in the gift of his Son, to abolish all the disorder of the universe and to bring into perfect and abiding harmony all powers and beings in heaven and on earth."[23] The reconciling work of Christ, then, is intended for the whole universe, including nature and the effects of sin itself. We may observe that when Paul speaks of the creative work of God, his order is "in heaven and on earth" (16, many versions). When speaking of reconciliation, the order is "on earth or in heaven" (NEB, RSV, Williams) as if "to indicate that those things which stand closest to the redeeming cross are the first to experience the effects of its healing power."[24]

Whatever the meaning of this profound passage, Paul Rees is correct in saying: "There is something cosmic about the Cross. It has not been the same universe since Christ died and rose again."[25]

Christ Makes His People Holy

Colossians 1:21-23

> 21 And you, that were sometime alienated and enemies in your mind by wicked works, yet now hath he reconciled
> 22 In the body of his flesh through death, to present you holy and unblameable and unreproveable in his sight:
> 23 If ye continue in the faith grounded and settled, and be not moved away from the hope of the gospel, which ye have heard, and which was preached to every creature which is under heaven; whereof I Paul am made a minister;

According to the Nestle Greek text the long sentence that began with Paul's prayer for the Colossians in verse 9 ends at verse 20. We know, of course, that the original Greek had no punctuation, but Nestle's placing a full stop after 1:20 underscores the practical turn which Paul now takes in his thinking. He wants to make clear the application of his great truths of Christology to the Colossians, so he addresses them, *And you* (21), as if to say— "you also, you Gentiles." As we have seen, Paul never spoke or wrote in a vacuum, but spoke and wrote to specific issues significant to his hearers or readers.

1. Alienation from God is one of the terrible effects of sin in the human heart. Ephesians 2 and 4 describe the nature of this alienation as being a state of "fallenness" including ev-

ery man. Because of sin, man begins life with his back to God. "Alienation" suggests this is not man's original condition; it is something man becomes. Sin is not an essential part of man's nature. It is an unnatural intruder into the cosmic order, although man has welcomed it and consequently has developed an attitude of hostility to God. He has become God's "enemy."

Before turning to Christ, Paul reminds the Colossians, "You ... were ... hostile [to God] in your minds" (Weymouth). The word indicates personal hostility. "The attitude of hostility toward God grows out of the sense of resentment of God's goodness in contrast to one's sins and out of the fact that men are 'darkened in their intellect' (Eph. 4:18)."[26]

2. Opposition to God is shown in wicked deeds. In time, the consequence of a state of hostility will be the performance of wicked deeds. The seat of man's enmity to God is the mind, where we think, imagine, reflect, and will. Paul says that "the mind of the flesh is enmity toward God" (Rom. 8:7, lit.). A corrupt mind has its sphere of development in evil deeds. The Apostle does not paint the picture of man's sinfulness with exaggeration. On the contrary, a review of history indicates he has used restraint. God's holiness creates prejudice and opposition to His plan of salvation which reveals man as a sinner in need of a pardon he cannot win by his own deeds. It is a pardon which urges in him a holiness which requires a total revolution of his life-style and desires. Paul's purpose was to highlight the Colossians' present state of grace in contrast to the old life of sin. "Once you were alienated" (NIV), but *now* you are *reconciled.*

3. Christ's death has made possible a new relationship with God. By *now* Paul means "in the present order of things," not "at the present moment." While Christ's death on the Cross becomes effective for a given person only at the point of faith and acceptance of the reconciling work in Christ, God has laid the foundation through Christ for a complete reconciliation. Whether Paul refers to God or Christ in the

phrase *hath he reconciled* is immaterial, for it is the Triune God who acts in the deed of the Cross "for us men and for our salvation" (cf. 2 Cor. 5:19; Heb. 9:14). As McDonald puts it, God has entered into "man's hopeless situation" and stepped "into the terrible quagmire of man's sin."

The medium of God's reconciling work is the death of Christ on the Cross—*in the body of his flesh through death* (22). One word might have sufficed to make Paul's point, but he uses both *body* and *flesh*. Probably Paul is prompted to this strong assertion by the Gnostics' denial of the actual humanity of Christ, or their view that Christ was merely an angelic aeon. In the Incarnation, the Son of God assumed genuine human nature; on the Cross this same human body died. Thus, the Incarnation finds completion in Christ's death on the Cross.

4. God's program in reconciliation is *to present you holy and unblameable and unreproveable in his sight.* There is no unanimity in the interpretation of this verse. Lightfoot and others see the "presentation" as denoting a sacrificial idea— "without blemish and without spot." Ellicott and Abbott[27] think the word conveys no such idea and that the meaning is not favored by the context. Some writers feel the "presentation" spoken of has judicial significance and refers to one accused in a court of law and acquitted (as in 1 Cor. 8:8; 2 Cor. 4:14; Rom. 14:4; 2 Tim. 2:15). It is true that the word *unreproveable* (*anegklētous,* or "irreproachable") has the idea of "not being called to account" (cf. 1 Cor. 1:8; 1 Tim. 3:10; Titus 1:6). Thus, according to this view, as one accused before a court of law is pronounced "not guilty," so one who has been reconciled to God is without blame (Rom. 8:33).

Whether Paul meant to be this precise with his figure of speech, the overall meaning is clear. The purpose of reconciliation is to make us acceptable to God and to declare us without blame. This is the meaning of Paul's great word "justification"—"in Christ" we are accounted as righteous and made acceptable to God. Christ is our justification or "righteousness" (1 Cor. 1:30).

This "presentation" or justification is a present reality as in Eph. 1:4. And yet it also has a future reference as suggested in Eph. 5:27. Thus F. F. Bruce has written, "The sentence of justification passed upon the believer here and now anticipates the pronouncement of the judgment day."[28] It is not inappropriate to view the "presentation" as being eschatological, referring to the great consummation when Jesus returns on clouds of glory. In 2 Cor. 4:14 the Apostle speaks of the day when the Lord Jesus shall "raise . . . us" up and "present us" (see also Eph. 5:27). The reconciled will be presented with Him—literally, "set alongside Him"—without shame or blame (1 Cor. 1:7-8; Eph. 1:7; 1 Thess. 3:13; 5:23; 1 John 2:28).

Abbott has stated that the adjectives used by Paul— *holy*, "blameless" (Williams), *unreproveable*—"are best understood of moral and spiritual character." "Holy" means separated to God's service, wholly yielded to Him; "blameless" means spotless or unblemished; "unreproveable" means no one will be able to call one to account or pick flaws in him. A. T. Robertson states: "These three adjectives give a marvelous picture of complete purity (positive and negative, internal and external). This is Paul's ideal when he presents the Colossians 'before him' . . . , right down in the eye of Christ the Judge of all."[29]

Maclaren frames a beautiful summary of the meaning here: "All the lines of thought in the preceding section lead up to and converge in this peak. The meaning of God in creation and redemption cannot be fully fathomed without taking into view the future perfecting of men."[30] "Perfection is there to be received as God's gift and to be verified in the life of Christians" (Eduard Lohse).

5. This great hope is conditioned on continuous loyalty to Christ and the gospel—*if ye continue* (23). Paul affirms the Colossians by acknowledging that they are presently in the faith. He stresses the positive aspect of their relationship to Christ and thereby expresses confidence in them. Yet he is aware that the heretical teachers are exercising pressure to

coerce them to loosen their hold on Christ, to acknowledge some substitute for Him; and he reminds them that their reconciliation and ultimate presentation to God is conditioned on their fidelity to the gospel they have received.

The promises of the gospel carry a conditional element and point to the necessary conditions which must be fulfilled in order to inherit them (see John 7:17; Col. 3:1). The conditional clause here means that if salvation is all of grace, it is also all of faith; and, as Eadie puts it, "The loss of faith is the knell of hope." G. Preston MacLeod has observed: "The promises of the Gospel always place this two-fold responsibility on those to whom they are proclaimed: a) to fulfil the conditions of attainment; and b) to exhibit the consequences of attainment."[31]

Hendriksen holds together the divine and human aspects in salvation in this succinct statement: "Divine preservation always presupposes human perseverance. Perseverance proves faith's genuine character, and is therefore indispensable to salvation. To be sure, no one can continue in the faith in his own strength (John 15:5). The enabling grace of God is needed from start to finish (Phil. 2:12 13)."

6. Paul suggests to the Colossians that in order to withstand the attractions of the Gnostics they must remain *grounded and settled* in the faith. He seems to be using the figure of a building and warns that only by being established on Jesus, the firm Foundation, will they not be *moved away,* or "not constantly shifting" (Lightfoot). The tense of the verb suggests that the process can go on almost imperceptibly as when a ship is loosened from its moorings and drifts into dangerous waters (see Eph. 4:14; Heb. 6:19). The Colossians have heard the gospel from Epaphras. Now they must remain true to it.

The gospel, Paul says, has been preached *to every creature.* The phrase emphasizes the universality of the genuine gospel, in contrast to the narrow exclusivism of the Gnostics whose message was only for the initiated few. The Colossians were not to be sidetracked by the heretics who desired to get them on a side issue.

The very mention of this universal gospel and of the glorious prospect of being presented blameless before God at the last day conjured up for Paul an appreciation of the great privilege he had in being a minister of such a gospel. Almost abruptly Paul introduces his own relationship to it— *whereof I Paul am made a minister.* In what follows, as a sort of excursion, he will specify in greater detail what is involved in being a minister of Christ. When not under the necessity of defending his apostolic authority, Paul was content to be identified with all who labor in the gospel as servants of Christ.

Excursis (Apostle's Aside): The Christian Minister's Exciting Task

Colossians 1:24—2:7

This section is a kind of aside from the main argument in Colossians. Paul's appeal to the Colossians to *continue in the faith* turns his mind to his personal relationship with the gospel, and the thought of this sets his soul aflame. He views himself as a steward appointed to make known to the Gentiles the gospel of grace which has transformed his own life. Fulfilling this ministry makes heavy demands, but no work or affliction is too great in order to accomplish what is required of him. Here the heart and soul of Paul is revealed as a worthy model for every minister of the gospel.

Joy in Suffering for Christ's Church

Colossians 1:24-27

24 Who now rejoice in my sufferings for you, and fill up that which is behind of the afflictions of Christ in my flesh for his body's sake, which is the church:

25 Whereof I am made a minister, according to the dispensation of God which is given to me for you, to fulfil the word of God;
26 Even the mystery which hath been hid from ages and from generations, but now is made manifest to his saints:
27 To whom God would make known what is the riches of the glory of this mystery among the Gentiles; which is Christ in you, the hope of glory:

1. *Paul's Joy in Suffering* (24). The word *now* is temporal and emphatic—even *now* the chains were around Paul's wrists. Whatever inconvenience and suffering should come to him, as they do to many ministers at some time or another, he had only joy because he had a part in Christ's magnificent work. He did not nurture the attitude of a martyr, but found joy in service because he was in the line of duty. He thought of the sufferings through which he was passing as completing the sufferings of Jesus Christ himself.

Jesus died to create and cleanse His Church; but the Church must be strengthened and enlarged. To suffer for the Church, in Paul's view, is a privilege and an honor, for it is sharing the work of Christ. We must not infer that Paul felt Christ's sufferings and reconciling work are incomplete. Paul's own statement in 2:14-15 would contradict such an inference. Christ's work for our salvation is throughout the New Testament seen as a completed, once-for-all work. The word Paul uses for *afflictions (thlipseōn)* is never used in the New Testament to describe the actual sufferings of Christ on the Cross. Further, by Paul's expression *fill up that which is behind* [lacking] *of the afflictions of Christ* he does not mean his afflictions were imposed by, or endured for, or even after the style of, Christ. He means something more profound.

Paul sees a divine purpose in what he had to endure for the sake of the Colossians. By his sufferings something was added to the afflictions of Christ. The word translated *fill up* or "complete" *(antanaplēroō)* is found only here in the New Testament, although its simple compound *(anaplēroō)* occurs several times and conveys the idea of a deficiency (1 Cor. 14:16; 16:17; Gal. 6:2). Paul obviously is not speaking of Christ's work as Reconciler, but probably as the supreme Example of service. Even Christ, however, could not bear in this sense all possible afflictions which must be undertaken for the sake of His Body, the Church. Thus Paul expresses his own suffering as a minister who contributes his share. "Jesus did not exhaust all the sufferings to be endured, nor did He suffer so that his followers do not have to suffer."[32] Thus McDonald states: "As the Servant of the Lord, Christ's ministry is, indeed, complete in its atoning efficiency, but in its ministerial utility it has to be carried on by his servants." This the Apostle was willing to do *for his* [Christ's] *body's sake* (24).

2. *Paul's Commission to Ministry* (25). Rather than dwell on his sufferings, the Apostle repeats his statement that he has been *made a minister.* However, in verse 23 he refers to himself as a minister "of the gospel." Here he speaks of himself as a minister of the Church: *Whereof I am made a minister, according to the dispensation of God.* The word translated *dispensation (oikonomia)* means "stewardship" (NASB). Thus Paul's ministry accords with the stewardship or "economy" of God (see 1 Cor. 4:1-5; 9:17; Titus 1:7; 1 Pet. 4:10; Eph. 3:2). This is what enabled him to endure hardship—it was for the sake of the gospel and the Church. He suffered because he was a minister of the gospel. He served because he was a minister of the Church. Ralph Earle has said: "In a very real sense it is still true today that only a suffering ministry can be a saving ministry."[33]

This ministry was *given* to him by God *for you,* that is, for the Gentiles. He was not pursuing a self-chosen career but had responded to a divine call. The Apostle had been given the special assignment of declaring the gospel to the Gentiles, and he gloried in this ministry. His "trusteeship" (Williams) was from God to whom he was accountable (1 Cor. 4:1-5). By being faithful to him he will *fulfill the word of God* or fill full the gospel by carrying on its universal mission and message.

3. *Paul's Disclosure of the Mystery* (26-27). Paul calls *the word of God* (25) *the mystery which . . . now is made manifest to his saints* (26). He was the steward of this mystery for the

sake of God's people. This was not a new idea for Paul, who expressed it in Eph. 3:9 and Rom. 16:25. And, of course, the word *mystery* was used by the mystery religions, including the Gnostics, who understood it in terms of secrecy and initiation. The Apostle was comfortable in taking some of the terms of the mystery religions and investing them with his own meanings. Whereas these religions were confined to a limited circle of persons, the Christian "mystery" was fully and freely communicated to all by both revelation (Eph. 3:5) and by preaching (4:4; Titus 1:3).

Why the gospel was hidden from those in earlier ages may not have a simple answer. It is a fact, however, that men did not and could not know the God and Father of Jesus until Christ revealed Him. Certainly we know that God, who is unchanging, initiated the revelation of himself in Jesus (John 3:16). G. Preston MacLeod has suggested perhaps the most plausible reason men did not come to the truth earlier:

God did not reveal himself in Jesus in earlier ages and generations because mankind had not been brought to the level of moral and spiritual maturity necessary to understand and respond to the gospel in Christ (see Acts 17:30; Heb. 1:1). As it was, the generation to which Jesus came rejected him. He won to himself only a small remnant through whom he founded the Church and sent it forth to "make the word of God fully known."
What holds back the kingdom is not the "delaying tactics" of God, but the unresponsive wills of men.[34]

God has chosen His people, the *saints*, that is, Christians in general, to make known this *mystery* (Moffatt translates it "open secret"). What a joy! What a responsibility! The source of this revelation is solely in God's will—and Paul exults, *what is the riches of the glory of this mystery among the Gentiles* (27). This is a favorite figure of Paul's—"that he might make known the riches of his glory" (Rom. 9:23); "the riches of his glory" (Eph. 3:16); "according to his riches in glory" (Phil. 4:19). He uses the same Greek term each time as here. "The expression does not mean the glorious riches, but rather how rich is the glory" (Peake).

And how rich, indeed, is this glory now manifest—
Christ in you, the hope of glory (see Eph. 3:17). Here is the
content of the mystery which has been made known: *Christ
in you.* This indwelling of Christ by His Spirit as *the hope of
glory* is the central fact of Christianity. Paul is talking about
a transforming experience with Christ, a spiritual union and
vital communion with Him. Jesus is the "Shekinah" *(glory)*
of God, and He shines in our hearts so that we see the glory
of God in the face of Christ (2 Cor. 4:6). The indwelling
presence of Christ "constitutes in himself a pledge or promise of future glory" (Peake). He is the assurance of all that
we will become, and affords a firm hope that we will "share
in that fulness of glory that is yet to be displayed on the day
of 'the revealing of the sons of God'" (Bruce).

The Ultimate Goal of Ministry

Colossians 1:28-29

> 28 Whom we preach, warning every man, and teaching every man in all
> wisdom; that we may present every man perfect in Christ Jesus:
> 29 Whereunto I also labour, striving according to his working, which worketh
> in me mightily.

1. Paul's goal in preaching was to lift up Jesus (28). Christ
was his message. With an unerring instinct for centralities,
he moves from the *mystery* and the *hope* to Christ who is the
Source of both these spiritual realities. "We proclaim him"
(NIV), he says. The verb means to "tell out" with certainty
and conviction. In contrast to the troublers who mumbled
their mysteries in secret places, Paul says, "We are no mut-
tering mystery-mongers. From full lungs and in a voice to
make people hear, we shout aloud our message. We do not
take a man into a corner, and whisper secrets into his ear; we
cry in the streets, and our message is for 'every man.'"[35]
　　But Paul knew he must not only proclaim the gospel, he
must shepherd the sheep. The care of the saints involves
warning (nouthetein, admonishing) *every man.* He feared
that the Colossians might be rent by the wolves at Colossae.
Thus, more positively, he wanted to *teach—every man in all*

wisdom. Three times in this verse he uses the phrase *every man.* Every man has some need for correction, for instruction in practical, everyday Christian living. There is also some possibility of growth through such instruction.

Both correction and instruction are needed to *present every man perfect in Christ Jesus.* The word *perfect (teleion)* is used in the New Testament to indicate "complete and without flaw" (Matt. 5:48), and also to denote the mature Christian in contrast to the babe in Christ (1 Cor. 2:6). Because the verb *present* here looks to the future, the Apostle seems to be referring to the day when the effects of sin will be finally removed. In the meantime, "What Paul desires is to reduce the gap between spiritual immaturity and the ultimate perfection which will dawn upon every child of God."[36] He wants to move every believer to that relative perfection which is characteristic of adults no longer babes (Heb. 5:14), and which Paul claims for himself and others (Phil. 3:15).

2. To accomplish this goal, Paul was giving himself completely (29). This is indicated by his use of two terms: *labour* and *striving.* The first is the terminology of the faithful worker, the second is the terminology of the disciplined athlete motivated by the final prize (see also 2 Tim. 2:5-6). He will continue to work and train himself in order to sharpen and exert all his powers in this task. It is noteworthy that Paul uses the present tense. Though he is imprisoned, he refuses to succumb to melancholy or to view his work as terminated or even suspended. He continues to exalt his Savior (Acts 28:20-31; Philem. 10), to write letters, and to pray and praise (3). He will invest all his energies into building up the faith as he once had dissipated them against, in John Newton's immortal words, "the faith he had long laboured to destroy."

However, this phenomenal display of energy is not the result of his own determination. Rather, Christ is working in him *mightily.* The minister "strives"; Christ "strengthens." This divine potential is available to all believers (Phil. 2:13), though it is appropriated only by a few.

Concern for the Saints

Colossians 2:1

> 1 For I would that ye knew what great conflict I have for you, and for them at Laodicea, and for as many as have not seen my face in the flesh;

The opening word *for* in this verse suggests this is not the place for a chapter division. That the idea of 1:29 is continued is seen in the fact that the meaning of *striving* is carried forward in the word *conflict,* which may be rendered "struggling" or "striving." Thus the NIV gives the verse: "I want you to know how much I am struggling for you and for those at Laodicea, and for all who have not met me personally."

Before dealing directly with the doctrinal intrusion of the teachers of the Colossian heresy, Paul reminds his readers of his deep concern for them in the hope that they will not think he is speaking in merely some official capacity. His words of counsel grow out of a deep desire to help them.

1. Paul's struggle for the saints has its center in his own spirit as he reached out in prayer to those who were far away. His striving for the Philippians took the form of providing an example of fortitude and patience in enduring persecution. Here the struggle is more internal. Paul is particularly thinking of believers in the three towns of Colossae, Laodicea, and Hierapolis—some manuscripts add "those in Hierapolis," though the latter at this point may not have been affected by the false teachers. He shares the soul travail of Epaphras, who has been wrestling in prayer for these believers (4:13).

The word Paul uses—*conflict (agōn)*—is the word from which we get *agonize* and *agony.* It means "deep and earnest solicitude, accompanied with toil and peril" (Eadie). The marginal reading of the Authorized Version gives us the word "care." Paul's soul was in perpetual distress for the Colossians. He knew what was at stake, and he could not be there to defend against the Gnostic onslaughts. The Apostle was in great conflict and passion of spirit for the Colossians.

2. Paul was not embarrassed by his concern. On the contrary, he wanted them to know the depth of his love for them—*I would that ye knew.* He avoided the two extremes which are undesirable for any minister of the gospel: *(a)* an icy indifference or refusal to allow one's true concern to show; and *(b)* a shallow loveliness which grows out of mere human enthusiasm and only appears to be concerned. The first is ineffective; the second is short-lived and lacks authenticity.

Paul Rees has captured the true biblical concept of ministry to others in these words:

> The more we are ruled by the love of Christ the more care we feel for people. And let it be added, for people as *persons.* Not as *things* to be used, nor as *agents* to be employed, nor as *prospects* to be sold, but as *persons* to be served for their own sake and for Christ's. . . .
>
> But what if they do not want our service, or our care, or our love? What if, indeed, they strike back at us with resentment, or bitterness, or hatred? . . .
>
> Do we withhold love? No. Or, worse still, do we replace it with a bitterness that we hurl back at those who are bitter towards us? Never.
>
> This is part of love's pain. It is prepared to take risks. It is willing to get hurt. It imposes no conditions and asks no reward.[37]

Though he had never seen these Colossians, Paul was anxious for them. The false teachers in Colossae would divide their loyalties between Christ and ceremonialism, between Christ and astrology, and between Christ and asceticism. Phillips gives Paul's concern thus: "I wish you could understand how deep is my anxiety for you."

Intercessory Prayer for the Saints

Colossians 2:2-5

> 2 That their hearts might be comforted, being knit together in love, and unto all riches of the full assurance of understanding, to the acknowledgement of the mystery of God, and of the Father, and of Christ;
> 3 In whom are hid all the treasures of wisdom and knowledge.
> 4 And this I say, lest any man should beguile you with enticing words.
> 5 For though I be absent in the flesh, yet am I with you in the spirit, joying and beholding your order, and the stedfastness of your faith in Christ.

These verses pose a considerable textual difficulty for the interpreter. There is a multiplicity of variant readings and texts, particularly verses 2-4. However, although the interpretation remains dubious in certain details, the general sense is clear.

Paul was struggling. The great Apostle's struggle was a struggle in prayer. In 1:9 he writes: *We ... do not cease to pray for you.* Though he was in prison and limited because of his forced confinement, he could pray for the Colossians. What he could not do himself, he turned over to God. Unable to deal personally with the false teachers at Colossae, he wrestled in prayer with God on behalf of the saints there. This caring side of Paul's ministry which expressed itself in intercessory prayer is instructive for every believer, particularly for those who have answered God's call to ministry.

Paul Rees has observed that "many of us know something of the *nestling* side of prayer—sweet, comforting, nourishing communion with God. But few of us are acquainted with the *wrestling* side of prayer—lining up with God in holy combat against the dark, destructive forces that are loose in the world." Then very pointedly and personally, he asks: "Quite honestly, how long has it been since the passion and heat of your caring drove *you* to your knees, there to join with God in His concern for someone far from light, or deep in sorrow, or shackled by evil? When was the last time—if ever—there were any tears to give a holy saturation to your prayers?"[38]

It is in this spirit of intercession that Paul expresses a

desire, issues a warning, and rejoices in confidence in the Colossians.

1. Paul expresses a deep desire that the Colossians might be strengthened in their hearts because of Christ (2-3). *Comforted* (2) translates *paraklēthōsin* (lit., "called to one's side"), which here means "to encourage, strengthen" (Thayer). "Comfort" in the current sense is too weak to translate adequately the Greek term here used. Originally "comfort" (from the Latin *confortare*) meant "to encourage to action, not to console in misfortune."[39]

The word *hearts (kardiai)* includes the intellect, will, and emotions. The prayer, then, is that the Colossians will be strengthened in their inner man, "cheered" at the level of their deepest being to be able to understand the fallacies of the Gnostics, willfully reject their intrigues, and be fortified in their emotions against these false teachings and teachers at Colossae. That they press on to maturity is the end for which Paul strives.

a. From this individual fortification Paul prays that the Colossians will find strength to develop a conscious unity among themselves, cemented by love. Error, or the threat of error, brings suspicion and division. Persons are tempted to wonder if others have been infected, and if so to what extent. Soon understanding is lost and fellowship is broken. Paul was anxious that the churches in the Lycus Valley experience no such disruption but remain in affectionate oneness, bound together in love.

The phrase *being knit together (symbibasthentes) in love* is translated by Moffatt: "May they learn the meaning of love!" This is because the word in the Septuagint has the sense of "instruct" (as in 1 Cor. 2:16; Acts 19:33). If this is the meaning, Paul is instructing them in love, not as a spiritual dictator, but as a concerned friend. He hopes they will receive his instruction in the same spirit in which it is given, not with resentment at his intervention.

b. It is only as the Colossians are grounded in love that they will "acquire the power to apprehend 'with all the saints' the fulness of God's revelation" (Bruce)— *all riches of the full assurance of understanding.* In the human realm of person-to-person relationships, knowledge and understanding precede love. But in the divine realm love is the foundation of knowledge and understanding. Pascal said: "In order to love human things, it is necessary to know them; in order to know those that are divine, it is necessary to love them."

Paul's prayer is that the Colossians will be persuaded or convinced—that they comprehend the truth. Anything less than this certainly makes the mind susceptible to false influences and impressions. This *assurance* alone gives solace of mind and heart. Thus the Apostle describes its value by the term *riches,* for it is a form of intellectual and heart wealth. The word *acknowledgement* is better rendered "knowledge" (RSV) or "true knowledge" (NASB). True knowledge is to know Christ, the mystery, and His purposes for the world, in contrast to the limited and unfounded ideas of the false teachers. The key to Christian maturity is to know Christ in the full knowledge of faith.

c. Verse 3 gathers the four cant words of the heretics into one sentence—*wisdom, knowledge, all, hid*—and claims for Paul's gospel what the Gnostics erroneously promised. Christ is the Source of wisdom and knowledge. In Him are hidden all the treasures of divine knowledge and of the divine attributes. Literally, the verse reads, "in whom are all the treasures, hidden" (cf. ASV). They are hidden only in the sense that they are *gathered* in Him, not in the sense that they are not available to men, or are for only a select few. God's mystery, Christ, is openly unveiled for all to see who will allow their minds to be quickened by the truth.

2. Paul issues a solemn warning (4). Sometimes intercession becomes so intense, it bubbles beyond conversation with God. In Paul's case it climaxed in a warning against those who would lead his fellow believers astray with *enticing words.* The Greek term used here *(pithanologia)* is not found anywhere else in the New Testament. However, we gain the meaning from an early papyrus document which

describes an attempt of thieves to retain their stolen goods with what we would call "glib talk." The verb means to produce reasons to prove anything likely or probable. The implication is that Gnostic teaching is supported more by the subtlety and subterfuge of its advocates than by the truth of its doctrines. The gospel, in contrast, needs no disguise or special presentation—the proclaimer relies only on its truth (1 Cor. 1:17; 2:1-5).

It is noteworthy that heretical teachers and teachings commonly profess "to simplify what is obscure, unravel what is intricate, reconcile what is involved in discrepancy, or adapt to reason what seems to be above it. Or it deals in mystery, and seeks to charm by a pretence of occult wisdom, and the discovery of recondite senses and harmonies" (Eadie).

It was against this kind of delusive rhetoric that the Apostle reminds the Colossians to be on guard and wishes them to come to a *full assurance of understanding* (2).

3. Paul rejoices in his confidence in the Colossians (5). Though he cannot be present with the Colossians in their time of testing, Paul is able to communicate his deep concern and states that he is with them "in spirit" (NIV). He is one in the fellowship of the Spirit with the Colossians in their common faith in Christ. His pastoral instincts cause the Apostle to speak a word of praise and to express his confidence in the Colossians. Far from accusing them of apostasy, he believes that they are standing firm in the faith. Verses 4 and 5 seem to imply that doctrinal error has not made significant inroads into the congregation.

The terms used by Paul, *your order, and the stedfastness,* are thought by some to be military terms. If this is correct, then Paul is comparing "the Colossian church to an army under attack, keeping its lines unbroken, showing the firmness which derives from confidence in the commander."[40] Others feel that the military is not in Paul's mind, but rather he is thinking of a "well-ordered condition" which characterizes the church (see 1 Cor. 14:40) whose faith is supported by "firmness" (NBV, RSV, Williams).

Whichever view is adopted, the meaning is essentially the same. Paul's spiritual presence with them enabled him to see their "orderly array" (NEB) and consistency. To the Thessalonians he wrote of the contrasting disorder produced by those who had succumbed to idleness (2 Thess. 3:6-7, 11), and to the Corinthians whose fellowship was disrupted over spiritual gifts (1 Corinthians 12; 14). He may be referring to both these types of disorder—private or personal, and doctrinal. The Colossians' orderliness at this point had excluded error and preserved unity. Paul rejoiced that their faith in Christ was "solid" (Moffatt, Phillips, Weymouth), and he had confidence that it would remain so.

A Fervent Admonition and Warning

Colossians 2:6-7

> 6 As ye have therefore received Christ Jesus the Lord, so walk ye in him:
> 7 Rooted and built up in him, and stablished in the faith, as ye have been taught, abounding therein with thanksgiving.

Verse 6 is connected in thought with 1:21-23. Once the Colossians were estranged from God, but now in Christ they have been reconciled with the prospect of being presented holy before God, provided they continue in the faith. Now Paul admonishes them to this steadfastness with a fresh statement of the preeminence of Christ and of their vital relationship with Him. He has commended them for their order and steadfast faith, and now he adds a word of counsel.

1. The Colossians had not merely received knowledge or information about Christ, they had *received Christ Jesus the Lord* himself (6). They had received Christ in their acceptance of the preaching about Him by Epaphras. They had received in faith what they were *taught* (7), which was no mere *tradition of men* (8). The emphasis here is on the fact that they received the actual person of the Lord proclaimed to them in the gospel. So they have more than a store of

knowledge about Him, for He has been received into their hearts.

Paul uses the words *Christ Jesus the Lord* rather than "gospel," according to Lightfoot, "because the central point of the Colossian heresy was the subversion of the true idea of Christ." Thus he goes beyond the mere facts about Christ to the believer's experience of Him as the living Lord. The Colossians had received the gospel, and in doing so they had received Christ himself. Whatever men receive in the gospel, it is Christ. He is more than the object of faith. He is the sphere in which the Christian life is lived out to the glory of God.

Having received Christ they are admonished to *walk in Him* (6). "Walk" is used figuratively in the New Testament to describe the manner of one's life, or one's visible conduct. Paul employs this metaphorical meaning in his Epistles 32 times. It occurs 4 times in the Epistle to the Colossians (Earle). Consequently recent translations prefer "live"; for example, Goodspeed translates: "So just as you once accepted the Christ, Jesus, as your Lord, you must live in vital union with Him." Here the present tense is used, meaning "*continue* to live in Him." If the Colossians will do this they will be fortified against the pernicious teachings of the Gnostics. Having begun the Christian life by a commitment to Christ, they are to daily live under His Lordship.

2. Paul gives the secret of the Christian life in his phrase *in him* [in Christ] (7). Only in Christ does one come to know God. The believer is to "walk" in Him, to be *rooted and built up in him.* To underscore the growth aspect of the Christian life the Apostle puts together in rapid succession three graphic metaphors: a *man,* a *tree,* a *building.* Believers are to walk as men, to be rooted like trees, and to be built up like houses.

The meaning of the Christian walk is made explicit by Paul with the other two figures of speech. "Rooted in Christ" refers back to the Colossians' conversion. The perfect tense characterizes it as a past action whose consequences have continuing effects. God placed the Colossians in the soil of Christ which is ideal for growth. This agricultural figure is now combined with one of construction—*built up in him* (see 1 Cor. 3:9). The tense here is continuous, emphasizing that the resulting process of growth is going on in the present. If the rooting is a precise moment of faith, the building must continue to rise. Progress and fruitfulness are the standards for Christian living.

The main ideas connected with walking in Christ, then, are stability and growth. While Paul mixes his metaphors, his message is obvious: "Christ is both the ground in which the root is held (Eph. 3:17), and the solid foundation on which (1 Cor. 3:11) the building is raised" (Ellicott).

The initial action in becoming a Christian is to receive Christ. This much was past for the Colossians, but the present always calls for a continuous relationship with Christ—*so walk . . . in him.* To live in union with Him is to become established in the faith, to hold to the unchanging truth that Jesus is Lord, and to abound *with thanksgiving.* A grateful spirit indicates that one is satisfied with his relationship with Christ, and is good insurance against the temptation to depart from the faith. This kind of life in Christ will close the door against all false teachers, malcontents, and spiritual "con men."

Clearly, for Paul, helping move believers toward spiritual maturity is the exciting task of the Christian ministry.

The Supremacy of Christ's Teachings and Redemption

Colossians 2:8-23

Here begins Paul's formal refutation of the heresies at Colossae to which he has alluded previously. This section repeats the warning sounded in verse 4 but in more structured form and with stronger language. The method used to declare the caution is not that of bitter denunciation, nor that of detailed reference to the false doctrines. Rather, the Apostle seeks to meet the heretical teachings by positive affirmation of the preeminence of Christ. Thus he eloquently declares the deity of Christ and the supremacy of His teachings and redemption. Four significant imperatives are clearly enunciated.

Guard Against False Doctrines

Colossians 2:8

> 8 Beware lest any man spoil you through philosophy and vain deceit, after the tradition of men, after the rudiments of the world, and not after Christ.

Paul had learned, probably through Epaphras, the names of one or more self-named leaders who were drawing believers at Colossae away from the purity of the gospel and from total dependence upon Christ. Thus he issues a specific warning. To highlight the gravity of the danger he employs a word not found elsewhere in the New Testament, which later came to carry the idea "to kidnap." The word translated *spoil (sulagōgōn)* was used by ancient writers to describe the kidnapping of a man's daughter, the plundering of a house, or the seduction of a maid. The Colossians were in danger of becoming "captive through hollow and deceptive philosophy" (NIV) which was being spread among them. To become enslaved to this erroneous teaching is far different from the blessed captivity to Christ which they had experienced (1:13) and which McDonald calls "the fetters of freedom." "Take heed" (ASV) "lest any man *rob* you" of your doctrinal soundness is a good rendering of Paul's admonition.

This danger is ever present in the Church and evidently has been from the beginning. Writing to young Timothy, Paul spoke of unprincipled persons "of corrupt minds, reprobate concerning the faith" who "lead captive silly women" and gullible men, and who are "ever learning, and never able to come to the knowledge of the truth" (2 Tim. 3:8, 6-7). The form of expression in verse 8 seems to indicate that Paul is referring to a specific individual. More often than not in such a defection there is one person, a certain "someone," who is able to command a following of unstable believers and wields an insidious influence among them.

We can't know exactly and with certainty the specifics of the problem at Colossae. But scholars are in general agreement as to the broad, erroneous principles. This much is certain: The heresy which threatened the Colossians was Jewish. The false teachers sought to bind upon Christian believers certain Hebrew ceremonials, or what William Barclay has called "additions to Christ."

1. *A Godless Philosophy.* The heretical teachers insisted on a knowledge of *philosophy* which went beyond and superceded Jesus and His gospel. Only here is the term "philosophy" used in the New Testament. Paul was aware that speculative thought, like everything else, must be subservient to Christ, or it will pander to intellectual pride. But he is not here referring to philosophy per se, to the legitimate discipline of philosophy which seeks to "see life complete and to see it whole." Rather, he warns against the pseudophilosophy, the "so called" (Williams) philosophy of the false teachers. He labeled this imitation "falsely called knowledge" (1 Tim. 6:20, many versions). The definite article appears before *philosophy,* suggesting some individual's philosophy or ideas; further the term *and (kai)* should be rendered "even" (Kenneth S. Wuest). Thus the phrase *and*

vain deceit describes the type of philosophy Paul condemns —a mere "intellectualism or high-sounding nonsense" (Phillips).

The "philosophy" the Apostle opposes is identified also by the fact that it was handed down by *the tradition of men,* human tradition. There is nothing necessarily bad about tradition. Nonetheless this was a slap at the Gnostics who thought they had special or esoteric teaching which had been passed to them from some secret source. They claimed that there were some things Jesus communicated only to a chosen few. Paul insists that all such claims to the truth must be judged by Scripture. Nothing can be called Christian teaching which is not supported by the Word of God.

2. *A Demoralizing Determinism.* The false teachers tried to impose, in addition to Christ, a system of astrology. This is referred to by the phrase *rudiments of the world.* The word translated *rudiments (stoicheia),* "basic principles" (NIV), or "elements" (ASV margin) has two meanings.

a. It refers to things set out in a row, and sometimes was used to describe letters of the alphabet. Consequently, it commonly meant elementary instruction, the ABCs of a subject. If this is what Paul has in mind, he is suggesting that the system of rites and ceremonies insisted on by the Gnostic teachers are childish, though their proponents claim to be propagating profound and advanced knowledge. The so-called gnosis (knowledge) of these misguided instructors is regressive, a backward step rather than a progressive one.

b. The word can also mean "elemental spirits" (Moffatt, NEB, RSV) of the world, those elements which make up the material structure of the universe—as earth, air, fire, and water (see 2 Pet. 3:10-12)—with special reference to the spirits of the stars and planets. This level of thinking dominated ancient thought. Persons perceived themselves to be controlled and enslaved by an inflexible and demoralizing determinism set in motion and sustained by an impersonal influence of the stars and spirits of the world.

Almost universally persons believed there was no escape unless they could come to know the right password or secret code. The Gnostics claimed to have this secret knowledge which would bring deliverance from the fatalistic power of the stars. They admitted that Jesus could do *some* things, but He was powerless to save from the fearful grip of the heavenly bodies.

For Paul, this false teaching at Colossae "depends on human tradition and the basic principles of this world rather than on Christ" (NIV). The phrase *not after Christ* refers to the person of Christ, not merely to His teachings. The Gnostic teachers degraded Christ; true believers exalt Christ. Thus Paul's warning is prelude to his insistence on the "triumphant adequacy of Christ to overcome any power in any part of the universe. You cannot at one and the same time believe in the power of Christ and influence of the stars."[41]

Acknowledge God's Full Revelation in Christ

Colossians 2:9-10

9 For in him dwelleth all the fulness of the Godhead bodily.
10 And ye are complete in him, which is the head of all principality and power:

The Colossian heresy was guilty of *theological* error—it substituted inferior and created beings for the divine Head himself. Against this falsity Paul asserts the doctrine of the Lordship of Christ and maintains the sole sufficiency of Christ to unite God and His world. The Apostle allows no other beings a share in making possible this reconciliation. There can be no other mediators between God and man. While we cannot identify all the details of the Colossian error, it is clear that for Paul all human theories and views of life and the world which deny the supremacy and uniqueness of Christ are spurious and must be denied. Christ is the Alpha and Omega; the First and the Last; the Beginning and the End (cf. Rev. 1:8, 17; 2:8; 21:6; 22:13). He is the Ultimate One. "Other than Jesus will not do; less than Jesus will not suit; more than Jesus is not possible. . . . Everything of God is to be found in him and little of God is to be found apart from him."[42]

1. *The Fullness of the Christ* (9). The Gnostic innovators viewed the *plērōma,* the plenitude of God, as being distributed among many angelic aeons, or spiritual beings. Almost every word of Paul's response to this view is emphatic. *In him,* in Christ, and nowhere else, is the *fulness of the Godhead* to be found (cf. 1:19 for the meaning of "fulness"). God has not dispersed himself, part in this aeon, and part in that. Christ is not a mere emanation from the Supreme Being. This is the force of the word *all. Godhead* refers to the essence of Deity. This is the only place in the New Testament *theotētos (Godhead)* is used, and by it Paul affirms "the whole essence and nature of God" (Maclaren).

   a. This quality of divine being *dwelleth* in Christ, that is, "has a permanent home with or in" Christ. The Jews had difficulty in thinking of God as dwelling with men. For them the *shekinah* or glory of God was a representation or symbol of His presence, nearness, and availability. No wonder Jesus' claim of oneness with God was an offense to them (John 10:30). For Paul, God has not come upon Jesus temporarily but has taken up permanent residence in Him.

   b. Furthermore, God's fullness dwells in Him *bodily.* The term does not refer merely to the Incarnation as a single event, since the present tense is used in this verse. It certainly teaches that the Incarnation continues to be a fact. But primarily it "reinforces the idea of concentration in one place as opposed to dilution through distribution."[43] That is, "the one and only divine power that matters confronts us in the life, death, resurrection and present lordship of Jesus."[44]

   The precise meaning of *bodily* has been interpreted variously: as the glorified body, the Church as Christ's Body (Eph. 1:22-23), reality as opposed to shadow (2:17), or "in the shape of a body." Whatever view one takes, we must note that Paul does not say "in a body." It was not "into" a body that Jesus came. Rather, He became flesh and blood. His was a real incarnation—a distinguishing mark of Christianity. Paul would have nothing to do with a "docetic" Christ—a phantom body; nor with the idea that the aeon Christ came on the human Jesus at His baptism and left Him on the Cross. Rather, the Son's full union with actual human flesh is reality, without consuming the humanity or changing any of its essential properties. Jesus hungered and ate, thirsted and drank, grieved and wept, watched and prayed, bled and died (Eadie). All the qualities of God dwell in the Son of God who is also the Son of Man, the incarnate Son of God.

No stronger statement that this of the deity of Jesus and the reality of the Incarnation can be found in the New Testament. The meaning seems to be that the divine fullness "exists in Christ as a body, that is as a complete and organic whole."[45] Verse 9 has been translated: "In him there is continuously and permanently at home all the fulness of the Godhead in bodily fashion" (Wuest).

2. *The Fullness of the Believer* (10). *Complete in him* describes the true believer. The term *complete (peplērōmenoi)* is the same root word as "fulness" *(plērōma)* which has just been used of Christ. Thus by a play on words, Paul applies the idea of "fulness" to those who are the Body of Christ. Christ is both the fullness of the Godhead and the fullness of the Christian. The Apostle is not claiming deity for the saints, but that in Christ all the potential of the redeemed life is accessible to those who will receive it by faith. Thus the RSV expresses it: "You have come to fulness of life in him." The fullness of life belongs to the believer because of the fullness, the deity, of Christ. Moule's translation is beautiful: "You are filled full in Him in whom resides all fulness." Then he comments: "In his promise, presence, power, you do possess 'all things needful' for life and godliness."

a. It is only in Christ, that is, in union with Christ, and not merely "by" Christ, that we are made full. Our fullness comes from Christ's fullness. Thus John wrote: "Of his fulness we all received" (John 1:16, ASV). And in Eph. 3:19 Paul prayed "that you may be filled with all the fulness of

God" (RSV). There is a fullness to be enjoyed now, and yet an ever expanding fullness is our destiny as God's children, till we all come to the "measure of the stature of the fulness of Christ" (Eph. 4:13).

b. The words *in him* clarify the significance of the claim that Christ is the *head of all principality and power,* or "rule and authority" (NASB). Jesus' Lordship has been expressed in 1:16. The powers referred to are the superhuman forces of evil which were believed to hold a grip over human lives. In 2:15 Paul will claim these powers have been defeated. Here he anticipates and states that Christ is superior to those agencies and beings which the false teachers regarded as so powerful. Therefore believers, who alone are *in him,* need not live in fear of these unknown and unpredictable forces, nor look to the angelic intelligences for mediation or assistance of any kind. Because Christ is both Lord of creation and of the Church, Christians are foolish to look for knowledge or salvation elsewhere than to Him. He is the "head over all things to the church" (Eph. 1:22), and as Head He is the Center and Source of all life for believers (Eph. 4:15-16) and for all spiritual beings.

Accept Christ's Atoning Benefits

Colossians 2:11-15

> 11 In whom also ye are circumcised with the circumcision made without hands, in putting off the body of the sins of the flesh by the circumcision of Christ:
> 12 Buried with him in baptism, wherein also ye are risen with him through the faith of the operation of God, who hath raised him from the dead.
> 13 And you, being dead in your sins and the uncircumcision of your flesh, hath he quickened together with him, having forgiven you all trespasses;
> 14 Blotting out the handwriting of ordinances that was against us, which was contrary to us, and took it out of the way, nailing it to his cross;
> 15 And having spoiled principalities and powers, he made a shew of them openly, triumphing over them in it.

Paul has addressed in the preceding verses the *theological* error of substituting angelic beings for Christ. Now he turns to the Gnostics' *practical* error of insisting upon ritual and ascetic observances as the foundation of their moral teaching. Obviously if Christ is not supreme, then faith in Him alone is inadequate. Other things, other practices, must be added. For the troublers at Colossae this included the requirement of circumcision. They sought to impose circumcision on all believers. For them circumcision was *the* distinguishing and necessary sign of being one of God's chosen people. How short a distance it is from insisting on a given evidence that one's heart is right with God to that point of actually substituting such an evidence for one's inward relationship to Him.

1. *Spiritual Circumcision* (11-13). The intrusion of circumcision into the discussion would seem out of place since Paul's readers were largely Gentiles. Evidently the strange "philosophy" at Colossae was mixed with the insistence of some to enforce certain Jewish observances. Throughout the history of Israel there had been differing views of circumcision. Some thought the physical act of circumcision was all that was required to set a man right with God. It alone was the sign of one's membership among God's people (Gen. 17:10). But in the best Jewish teaching the great thinkers and spiritual leaders saw circumcision as only the *outward* sign of the more important circumcision of the heart, the removal of all that hinders complete loyalty to God (see Deut. 10:16). They talked of uncircumcised lips (Exod. 6:12), an uncircumcised heart (Lev. 26:41), or an uncircumcised ear (Jer. 6:10). For these inspired writers, to be circumcised meant to have a change effected in the heart and in one's whole life. Circumcision was an outward sign of an inward commitment and transformation; but the transformation was the excision from life of everything which opposed the will of God.

a. Paul knew that a priest can perform physical circumcision; but only Christ can bring about that spiritual circumcision which means *putting off the body of the flesh* (11). (The phrase *of the sins* in KJV should be omitted for lack of sufficient manuscript authority, although the meaning is not altered by its inclusion.) By the *body of the flesh*

Paul does not mean the physical body, but the "totality of the self-life, human nature apart from the renewing, purifying grace of God" (Rees). For Paul, the only true circumcision is that which is spiritual, *made without hands,* which destroys the sinful self-life, and fills one with "newness of life, and with the very holiness of God" (Barclay).

Paul had expressed this truth to the Romans. He had argued for the spiritual circumcision, the Jew in the hidden (inner) man, the circumcision of the heart as that which really counted (Rom. 2:28-29). He had shown in Rom. 4:10 that Abraham experienced this circumcision of the heart before that of the flesh. He believed God, and his faith was placed to his credit. The circumcision of the flesh was only the sign and seal of the faith which Abraham already had. Paul concluded that the new birth of the heart is Christian circumcision.[46]

b. As a part of being made full in Christ (10), the Colossians had already experienced the spiritual act of inward circumcision of the heart. The outward sign of this was their baptism, which cannot be identified with it, for it is not made with hands. Paul could move with ease from circumcision to baptism since both are initiatory rites in connection with their respective covenants, the old and the new. But more importantly, verse 12 suggests that the inner circumcision of the heart and the outward symbolic act of burial in the baptismal waters go together. The former refers to the inward and spiritual grace and the latter to the outward and visible sign. Baptism denotes one's circumcision of the heart. The entry into baptismal waters and emergence from them symbolize the fact of one's cleansing from the old life under the power of sin and the beginning of a new life lived in the power of God. In baptism the believer deliberately puts off one way of life for another. To be buried beneath the waters of baptism is to become dead to the old life of sin. To be raised from them is to be raised to new life in Christ.

c. This miracle of grace takes place only *through the faith of the operation of God,* or better "through faith in the working of God" (RSV), that is, through faith in Jesus Christ—His life, death, and resurrection. As the Savior was dead and then raised to life, so the Colossians were dead because of their sins. However, the same power which raised Christ from the dead has brought life out of death to these believers. They had been raised together with Christ, and thus were sharing the resurrection experience of their Lord.

Baptism of itself is not the means of the change from spiritual death to spiritual life. If it were, baptism would be exalted even above circumcision, and Paul would be guilty of sacramentalism like the Jews he is condemning. Baptism is the sign or dramatization of the change but does not effect the change. As A. T. Robertson puts it, "It is the Christian uniform for the soldier, the wearing of colors for Christ. The uniform is the public sign of the enlistment." The change itself is wrought by the same quickening energy which brought Christ from death.

d. The NIV renders verse 13 thus: "When you were dead in your sins and in the uncircumcision of your sinful nature, God made you alive with Christ. He forgave us [not *you* as in KJV] all our sins." Paul cannot resist including himself and other Christians, for he too had received forgiveness of sins and had been set free from the burden and curse which sins had imposed.

Observe that the "quickening" or coming "alive with Christ" follows the "forgiveness." Spiritual life apart from forgiveness is inconceivable. The KJV makes this connection clear: *And you, being dead in your sins . . . hath he quickened* [made alive] *together with him, having forgiven you* [us] *all trespasses.* Sanctification (in the broad sense, as here, as well as entire sanctification) always follows justification, and not vice versa. One does not by good deeds win God's favor or forgiveness.

Paul's argument is clear: Men were dead in their sins, powerless to break sin's bondage or to relieve its condemnation. They had no more power than dead men to overcome it, remove it, or atone for it. But what men could not do, Christ has done. By His person and redemptive work He has delivered men from the power and penalty of sin. He has raised them from death to life. This transformation is a work of grace since men had and have no goodness to deserve it and no power to effect it.

The sketch in Paul's mind is apparent. But he has yet two more graphic details to fill in the picture in verses 14-15.

2. *Sin's Debt Canceled* (14). The meaning of the forgiveness alluded to in the previous verse is here elaborated. Paul passes to the historic fact of Christ's work on the Cross which is the ground for forgiveness. The word picture used by the Apostle is that of the cancellation of a bond. Christ has "blotted out" (ASV) or "canceled the written code, with its regulations, that was against us and that stood opposed to us; he took it away, nailing it to the cross" (NIV). The giving of a certificate of indebtedness to a person from whom one borrowed was a common practice in Paul's day (cf. Philem. 19), and still is today. Such a bond *(cheirographon,* KJV, *handwriting),* bearing one's signature, stands over against the debtor until paid or canceled.

a. The *handwriting* spoken of refers to "the decrees of the law" (NEB), including the moral law (Eph. 2:15). *Ordinances,* or "regulations" (NIV), includes the entire Mosaic law. For the pagan Colossians it suggests the regulations required to keep favor with their gods or to secure their secret knowledge (21). Apart from Christ both Jews and Gentiles were viewed as being continuously in debt, never able to "catch up with their payments."

The Law stands *against us* because it makes demands which we cannot meet. Paul argued in Romans that no one has measured up to the Law's requirements or can do so. Like a harsh taskmaster the Law bids us do certain things, but does not provide the power to perform them. Then it accuses man of unfulfilled duty and reveals man's guilt. Further, the "law is against us, because it comes with threatenings and foretastes of penalty and pain. Thus, as standard, accuser, and avenger, it is against us" (Maclaren).

Our sins, then, are viewed as an obligation which we

have freely acknowledged as one who sets his signature to a bond. Jew and Gentile alike have the law of conscience "written in their hearts" (Rom. 2:15). "The bond is the moral assent of the conscience, which (as it were) signs and seals the obligation" (Lightfoot). The immediate problem Paul is addressing is that the Gnostics are trying to put new mortgages on the Colossians which they cannot keep.

b. The "good news" is that this bond of legal demands has been canceled. Two phrases in this verse illustrate Christ's deliverance from man's indebtedness and default. This bond God through Christ has blotted out and nailed to His cross.

In Paul's day a scribe, in order to save paper, would sometimes use papyrus or vellum (a substance made of the skin of animals) that had already been written upon. Because the ink had no acid in it and would lie on the surface of the paper, the scribe was able to take a sponge and wipe away the writing. It was "blotted out" as if it had never been there. Similarly, Paul declares, God (or Christ) has blotted out the bond against us, canceled it, marked it "Paid," erasing it so that it no longer exists. The record of our sins is taken away; our transgressions, sins, and iniquities He will remember no more (Isa. 43:25; 44:22; Jer. 31:34). This is not to say the moral law is removed, but its condemnation of us for not fulfilling it is taken away and its just penalty for our sins is blotted out.

Not only has the writing against us *on* the bond been removed, but also the bond or indictment itself has been taken *out of the way* (the perfect tense is used, indicating the bond remains out of the way), nailed to the Cross, executed with Christ. The Law as a condemning force was nailed to the Cross when Christ was. Hence Paul could write, "There is therefore now no condemnation to them [who] are in Christ Jesus" (Rom. 8:1). Man is no longer under the curse of the Law. Christ, having become a curse for us, has removed it (Gal. 3:10-13). By the cross of Christ, Paul could affirm that he and the world were crucified to each other (Gal. 6:14).

Nailing it to his cross is vivid language to indicate how truly and fully Christ identified with sinners, being made sin for us (2 Cor. 5:21). Through his death Christ exempts sinners from the sentence which they merit. The guilt of men was borne by Him. In canceling the bond of debt and letting it die when Christ died, God "has shown in Jesus that the relationship of human beings to himself is based on love, and not on an idea that God is the creditor and we are the debtors. God has shown that the 'cosmic powers and authorities' are not to be feared and therefore regulations to keep on the right side of them are idle."[47]

3. *Satan's Powers Conquered* (15). Almost every word is disputed by scholars in this difficult verse. However, several things may be safely asserted, and the primary meaning seems clear. The word *and (kai)* at the beginning of the verse is not in the Greek text but is supplied by the translators. Its absence implies the close connection, even the identity, of the two acts of *blotting out the handrwriting of ordinances* (14) and spoiling *principalities and powers* (15). In accomplishing the former, God simultaneously vanquished Satan (Eadie). Christ's death was not only a pardon; it was manifested power. It not only canceled a debt; it was a glorious deliverance and triumph. By His cross Christus Victor defeated Satan and all his hosts. Whatever else is being declared, this much is clear—there are no powers anywhere in the universe which are to be dreaded by man. Christ has conquered them and made a public spectacle of Satan and his powers. The believers at Colossae need not fear reprisal from the spiritual powers or angelic beings whom the false teachers worshiped. These spirits cannot harm the Colossians who do not submit to the demand to perform certain rites and ceremonies. They have been stripped of their power and authority.

a. The *principalities and powers* here are the same as those mentioned in Eph. 6:12—the demons of Satan in the atmosphere of this earth. Some have thought these are the captives taken by our Lord in His ascension as He left the tomb (Eph. 4:8). It is true that hostile powers seem to be designated. Their reign over man began with his sin and lasted until sin was atoned for on the Cross when their power was destroyed. Some have thought the reference is to angels of the Law. In either case, "If evil spirits, they are stripped of their dominion; but if angels of the Law, they are despoiled of the dominion they exercise" (Peake).

b. The meaning of the words *having spoiled (apekdusamenos)* has been debated. Literally, the Greek term means "having stripped off from himself" (see 3:9 and 2:11). Probably "disarmed" is the best translation (RSV, NIV, NASB, cf. NBV; also "discarded," NEB; and "stripped," Williams). It is the word for stripping the weapons and the armor from a conquered foe and parading them as captives, chained to the wheels of the conqueror's triumphant chariot. A Roman general, upon winning a significant battle, marched through the streets of Rome with his victorious armies, followed by those whom he had vanquished.

The *principalities and powers,* the hosts of darkness against which the Christian must carry on spiritual warfare, were not eliminated at the Cross, but their ultimate doom was sealed. In fact, Christ "made a public example of them" (RSV). "His spiritual foes, on being vanquished, were exhibited as a public spectacle." That is, Christ "has shown the fact of their complete subjugation in His triumph over them. . . . And it was no private parade, it was done *openly.*"[48]

c. The paradox of our Lord's crucifixion is thus placed in its strongest light—triumph in helplessness and glory in shame. "The convict's gibbet is the victor's car" (Lightfoot). The apparent triumph of the powers of darkness over Christ was His real and glorious triumph over them. Whatever the difficulties of exegesis, the general idea is familiar to us, telling, as in the noble old hymn *Vexilla Regis—*

> *How of the Cross He made a throne*
> *On which He reigns, a glorious king.*

Here is Paul's answer to the speculations of the divisive Gnostics who talked endlessly of aeons and angels, principalities and powers. The crucified Christ is Lord, and all hostile powers are subject to Him. In His cross the hosts of evil have met their Conqueror, for "Christ's cross is God's throne of triumph" (Maclaren). Through Christ man is free. His enemies have had their ammunition taken away from them.

The victory of the Cross still stands. Though contemporary man describes these spiritual powers differently, they are nonetheless real to him—black magic, the horoscope, drugs, cults, satanic rituals, and so on. "To any one of these it is easy to become a willing, and finally, a degraded slave. But the cross liberates from every bondage; for the cross is Christ's cosmic victory, his holy conquest, over every evil power and all human schemes. His scaffold is his throne; and his cross is his chariot. And so the person who has found release in Christ's great atonement can join the chorus: 'Thanks be to God, who continually leads us about, captives in Christ's triumphant procession'" (2 Cor. 2:14, NEB).[49]

Exercise Your Freedom in Christ

Colossians 2:16-19

> 16 Let no man therefore judge you in meat, or in drink, or in respect of an holyday, or of the new moon, or of the sabbath days:
> 17 Which are a shadow of things to come; but the body is of Christ.
> 18 Let no man beguile you of your reward in a voluntary humility and worshipping of angels, intruding into those things which he hath not seen, vainly puffed up by his fleshly mind,
> 19 And not holding the Head, from which all the body by joints and bands having nourishment ministered, and knit together, increaseth with the increase of God.

Paul moves with ease in both directions between the heights of doctrine and the everyday practicalities of Christian living. He has just spoken profoundly of the person and work of Christ, and suddenly with one strategic word—*therefore*—brings his readers face-to-face with a pressing issue relating to the believer's behavior. Paul knew full well that in time beliefs lead to certain types of behavior, and behavior presupposes some underlying assumptions and faith-judgments. Consequently, he "kept his theology tightly bound to practice and his conduct tied to doctrine."[50] Doctrinal teaching which overlooks practice is in danger of becoming sterile. Ethical teaching that has no doctrinal foundation has no convincing or staying power. At Colossae, false doctrine was producing faulty practice.

The cancellation of the bond against them (and us) and the triumph of Christ on the Cross should keep the Colossians from falling victims to the crafty teachings and views of the Gnostics. They need to realize and appropriate their Christian liberty. *Therefore,* in view of the believer's sufficiency in Christ (8-15), Paul warns the Colossians against an "enslaving ritualism" and a "false mysticism" (Erdman).

1. *Freedom from the Judgment of Men* (16-17). If the physical body is evil, as the Gnostics viewed it, two opposite conclusions may be drawn as to how to treat it. One may choose to indulge it, pamper it, ignore it, or treat it with contempt. Or one may feel it must be subservient and keep it down—starved, beaten, chained, or restrained. Or stated differently, Gnosticism could issue either in complete immorality and wild licentiousness (cf. 3:5-11) or in extreme asceticism (2:20—3:4). It is with this latter conclusion that Paul deals here.

The Gnostics wished to lay down ascetic rules and regulations about what a man could eat and drink, and about what days he must observe as festivals and fasts. Paul answers, In the light of what Christ has done for you, "Therefore do not let anyone judge you [i.e., judge against you] by what you eat or drink [better, 'in matters of eating or drinking'], or with regard to a religious festival, a New Moon celebration or a Sabbath day. These are a shadow of the things that were to come; the reality, however, is found in Christ" (16-17, NIV). A "religious festival" *(holyday)* refers to the three great annual feasts of the Passover, Pentecost, and Tabernacles. The *new moon* ushered in certain monthly celebrations. The *sabbath days* are the weekly celebration of worship and rest.

a. The false teachers evidently insisted that true believers would keep all the food laws of the Jews and would observe specific days on which certain things must be done and certain other things must not be done. They seem to have equated genuine religious faith with ritual and Sabbath observance and sought to impose their views on others. Thus Paul's admonition: *Let no man judge you* (16). Such judgments were being made, and Christians were being made to feel that if they did not comply, they were guilty of failing in their religious obligations. The pressure to conform apparently arose out of Jewish sources, from Jewish Christians who had a tendency to regard Christianity as a branch of Judaism.

In earlier letters Paul had dealt with similar matters and had warned believers not to judge one another in things that are secondary and external, but rather to allow for individual consciences and personal decision (1 Cor. 10:25-29; Rom. 14:3-4, 13, 21). He had argued for liberty in diet, and affirmed that the kingdom of heaven does not consist in eating and drinking (Rom. 14:17), while at the same time pleading for believers not to become a "stumbling block" to the less mature Christian. However, the situation at Colossae was even more complex than in Corinth and Rome, where Paul was trying to reconcile two factions of Christians. There he encouraged a voluntary limitation of one's freedom for the sake of others. Here, in addition to the fact that they were judging each other, the whole company of believers was in danger of losing freedom in Christ because of externals. The Colossians were being asked to observe certain days and times and practices as being necessary to salvation. Such prohibitions the Apostle was compelled to repudiate, otherwise the Colossians would put themselves back under the control of those powers Christ had conquered and through which such regulations were mediated.

Paul's position is emphatic: let no one "test your piety" (Eadie), or "take you to task" (Moffatt, NEB), or "pass judgment on you" (RSV, Williams) on the basis of these secondary criteria. "Allow no one to criticize your action on the ground that it is not in harmony with the precepts of the Law, or cuts you off from communion with the angels [whom some thought mediated the Law]. You have nothing to do with Law or angels" (Peake).

b. The requirements being imposed on the Colossians by the false teachers Paul labels as *a shadow of things to come; but the body is of Christ* (17). That is, the "substance" (many versions) which belongs to Christ, is future from the viewpoint of Judaism. Christ possesses the reality in contrast to the shadow. This analogy embodies two significant truths. On the one hand, the Mosaic economy which shadowed Christ was not useless and without value. It served a gracious purpose (Heb. 10:1). The Law as such was good and was our "tutor" to lead us to Christ (Gal. 3:24, ASV). On the other hand, the substance supercedes the shadow. "The shadow is the intended likeness of the substance. In other words, Christianity was not fashioned to resemble Judaism, but Judaism was fashioned to resemble Christianity."[51] Therefore, Paul asserts that in contrast to shadows, the realities so long dimly revealed belong to Christ. Why one would grasp the shadow when he has the substance is inconceivable to Paul.

c. Yet Paul does not argue that the shadow must be abandoned. He leaves the decision for observance of these things to each Christian. Already, for example, the Jewish and Gentile Christians appear to be observing different weekly sacred days, the Jews keeping the Sabbath, the Gentiles Sunday (or perhaps Saturday night after sundown). To the Romans, Paul earlier had insisted on liberty concerning this question: "Let every man be fully persuaded in his own mind" (Rom. 14:5). All of these rules and regulations are just a *shadow*. But the "reality" (many versions), *the body,* the "substance," is found in Christ. A solid body casts a shadow, but there is a difference between them. To cling to the shadow in place of Christ is to become enslaved all over again to the tyranny of the old economy and to abandon Christian freedom. Therefore Paul insists that no one should be compelled to observe a form or a ceremony. There is freedom in Christ from the judgments of men, even from believing, but misguided or unthinking, men.

2. *Freedom from False Humility and a Holier-than-Thou Attitude* (18-19). The obscurities in these verses may arise out of Paul's desire to show that he is familiar with the false teachings at Colossae, evidenced by the use of terms known to his readers but somewhat unknown to us. In any case, these teachers were demonstrating a false humility by practicing angel worship and by advocating the necessity for others to do the same. So Paul admonishes: "Do not let anyone who delights in false humility and the worship of angels disqualify you for the prize. Such a person goes into great detail about what he has seen, and his unspiritual mind puffs him up with idle notions. He has lost connection with the head, from whom the whole body, supported and held together by its ligaments and sinews, grows as God causes it to grow" (NIV). Clearly the troublemakers wanted to substitute ecstatic or esoteric experiences of some kind for Christ.

a. The verb translated *beguile* (18) ("disqualify," NIV, RSV) means "to decide against." Found only here in the New Testament, it is compounded of the verb for "acting as umpire" and "against." In speaking of *your reward* Paul may have in mind the contests of the stadium in which the victor was awarded the prize. If so, the Christian life is the arena of the contest, Christ is the Umpire who dispenses the awards, the Colossians are the participants, and the false teachers are those who impede the runners in the race in an attempt to disqualify or "rob" (ASV) them of their just reward (Lightfoot). But the idea of a prize is not always associated with the use of this word. In 3:15 the simple form of the verb *(brabeuetō)* carries the idea of "arbitrate" (ASV margin, NBV; "be arbiter," NEB)—"Let the peace of Christ rule [be the true, the official, 'umpire' (Williams)] in your hearts" (ASV). However interpreted, the fundamental meaning is clear enough. *Let no man*, Paul warns (and we may infer that he has someone particular in mind), through a self-assumed authority, call you "out" because you have not done certain things to his satisfaction or failed to measure up to his unofficially imposed standards.

b. The Gnostics were given to special visions unknown to the majority of people. This led them to spiritual pride, to a certain "class consciousness" spiritually, resulting in the adoption of a condescending attitude toward others. They appeared to be acting in "self-abasement" (18, 23, RSV, NASB), but in fact it was a "false humility" (NIV, Phillips) which claimed that no one could approach the Most High directly—not even through Christ—but must come to Him by the meditation and worship of angels. Affecting a superior reverence for God, they portrayed themselves as humble—indeed, too humble to trust in Christ alone. This was a form of humility which boasted of its particular form of asceticism. Consequently, it was a mere *shew of ... humility* (23) which had become offensive by its self-consciousness. Their humility had become a means of gaining God's favor and, perhaps worse, of manipulating others.

Paul is seeking, not to articulate the character of the false teachers, but to warn the Colossians to be on guard against them, for they seek to entrap by means of their spurious "humility." He is condemning a holier-than-thou attitude, pride because of one's so-called spirituality or holiness. This type person often sees not what God shows him, but what he wants to see. He is taken up with, or obsessed by, his own visions and revelations.

The KJV speaks of these false teachers *intruding into those things which he hath not seen.* On good manuscript authority the negative should be omitted. The meaning is "making a parade of the things which he has seen." There is general agreement that this refers to special visions claimed by the false teachers. The term *intruding (embateuōn)* has been translated by many "taking his stand on" and probably suggests the experience of a cultic initiation in which the initiate supposedly receives a vision giving him knowledge of the secrets of the divine and of the universe. From that point on he "takes his stand on visions" from which he had the key to the mysteries of life. This kind of subjective pretension to supernatural knowledge *puffed up* these deluded individuals (see 1 Cor. 8:1; 2 Cor. 12:7). Their boasts to special insight were vain, "without reason" (RSV) or foundation. Indeed, they were *fleshly* or "carnal."

c. For Paul, the basic fault of the heretics was in *not holding the Head,* which is Christ (19). The Gnostics had lost connection with Him and had substituted angelic aeons and angels in His place. Eadie describes their fatal error: "If they worshipped angels, they could not adore his [Christ's] person. If they insisted on circumcision and ascetic practices, they depreciated the merit of His work."

Peake states that "the false teachers were Christians. They did not profess to have no hold upon Christ, but their hold was not firm. All the supplies of life and energy flow from the Head, so that loose connexion with it involves serious loss and not progress in the spiritual life." Failure to hold to Christ results in the loss of unity and sustenance. Whereas the Gnostic heretic was claiming spiritual advance and strength, in reality he was growing spiritually weak, for he was in the process of severing himself from the Body of Christ, which is the Church (1:18). In the Church there is both unity and diversity; there are many members, *joints and bands,* through which the divine life flows. From Christ the whole Body is "nourished" and *knit together*—both participles are in the present tense, suggesting the process is a continuing one.

Current knowledge of physiology invests the Apostle's words with meaning and force greater than that for his first readers. The computerlike messages communicated from the brain to the members of the body and the sensations telegraphed back indicate the delicate relation between all parts of the body. When this continuity is disrupted, instant paralysis can result. Paul maintains that only in Christ can these relationships of harmonious union, proper functioning of the parts, and continuous growth be possible. Only in Him is the Body held together and enabled to develop *with the increase of God.*

Summary: A Penetrating Question

Colossians 2:20-23

> 20 Wherefore if ye be dead with Christ from the rudiments of the world, why, as though living in the world, are ye subject to ordinances,
> 21 (Touch not; taste not; handle not;
> 22 Which all are to perish with the using;) after the commandments and doctrines of men?
> 23 Which things have indeed a shew of wisdom in will worship, and humility, and neglecting of the body; not in any honour to the satisfying of the flesh.

These verses are a kind of transition between Paul's exposition of the doctrinal and ritual errors of the Gnostics that has gone before and the ethical falsities and implications which will follow in the next chapter. They are viewed in this exposition as a kind of summary of what has been said, and perhaps as a prologue to the Apostle's teaching that the gospel touches every aspect of the believer's life—both outward acts and inward attitudes. Paul maintains that the Gnostics, by insisting on certain ascetic prohibitions, in effect are advocating a return to pre-Christian or unchristian slavery at the price of giving up their Christian freedom.

1. Paul reintroduces one of his leading ideas, namely, union with Christ (20). The death of Christ abrogated the ritual law; and being one with Him in that death, the Colossians had died to that law. It therefore has no more authority over them. Paul wants the Colossians to recall the specific moment when they died with Christ. They became one with Him through faith so that Christ's death became theirs (2 Tim. 2:11). By their death with Him they are no longer alive to man-made ordinances.

The key to Paul's view is the death of Christ in relation to worldly regulations imposed by those who misunderstand the nature of true holiness. He reasons that through baptism the Christians at Colossae had died in union with Christ. They died to self (2 Cor. 5:15), to sin (Rom. 6:2), to the law (7:6; Gal. 2:19), to the world (as here and in 3:2). By use of the aorist tense Paul emphasizes the crisis moment of their conversion. They died instantaneously when in penitent faith they appropriated the truth that Christ died for them. The death of the believers with Christ is a death to their old relations, to sin, law, guilt, the world. It is a death also to the angels who had ruled their old life.

Consequently, they were liberated from the rule of the *rudiments* or "elements" (ASV margin) of the old ordinances, whether the kindergarten methods of the legalists or the personal powers of evil. The message to the Colossians is clear: "You died with Christ to your old life. All mundane (worldly) relations have ceased for you" (Lightfoot). "Why then, as though you are still in that old 'world of selfishness and sin, do you subject yourself to man-made ordinances'?"

The NIV, omitting *wherefore,* which is not in the best manuscripts, renders verse 20 in pointed and lucid language: "Since you died with Christ to the basic principles of this world, why, as though you still belonged to it, do you submit to its rules[?]" These ordinances are defined by expressions quoted from the false teachers themselves (21). The first and third should be reversed, and indicate a progression which makes the prohibitions increasingly demanding: "Do not handle! Do not taste! Do not touch!" (NIV). Eadie clarifies what the teachers advocated: "You are not to take certain meats into your hand, nor are you to taste them; nay, you are not even to touch them, though in the slightest degree—you are to keep from them hand, tongue, and even finger-tip."

Those who insist on the necessity of these injunctions for salvation are subjecting themselves to the old bondage, though Christ has delivered them from this slavery by His death on the Cross (14). To go back to these things is like the Israelites longing for the leeks and onions of Egypt. The Gnostics had degraded Christ from His mediatorial work on the Cross and from His throne of glory and power. Consequently, by their practices they had undercut faith. The emphasis in the New Testament falls on self-discipline, and not on ascetic practice, as the key to dedicated usefulness in the kingdom of God (1 Cor. 9:24-27). Such practices may have value as means to an end, or as symbols of a genuine inner self-devotion, but the error of exalting them to first place Paul denounces unsparingly.

2. Several reasons are advanced to show how these prohibitions are fruitless for the believers.

a. Too much significance, sometimes eternal significance, is attached to temporal things *which all are to perish with the using* (22). Maclaren makes an oft-overlooked point: "Dives with his purple and fine linen, and the ascetic with his hair shirt, both make too much of 'what they shall put on.' The one with his feasts and the other with his fasts both think too much of what they shall eat and drink." They are things which go to destruction and normally leave no permanent effect (cf. 1 Cor. 8:8; also Matt. 15:16-17; Mark 7:7; Acts 20:35). Such teachings of men degrade Christianity by making it a system of physical or ascetic disciplines. Verse 23 refers to this error as *will worship,* or "forced piety" (NEB). The fundamental mistake is in assuming that holiness is to be found in the outward rather than the inward. This is not to exclude deeds of righteousness and mercy, but it is to note that God's mighty work of transformation is from the center to the outer life, and not from the outer life to the seat of motive and thought.

b. Paul's chief objection to ascetic practice is that these ordinances fail in their primary purpose. Human regulations do have *a shew* ["an appearance" (Weymouth, RSV, NIV; cf. NASB)] *of wisdom* (23). They seem to make some sense and are intended for good. The Apostle does not question the value of discipline in Christian living. Of himself he said: "I keep under my body, and bring it into subjection: lest that by any means, when I have preached to others, I myself should be a castaway" (1 Cor. 9:27).

The material things are fleeting, though they have a reputation for wisdom. They lack reality. They have the outward show and "make an officious parade of religious service" (Lightfoot). The false teachers at Colossae called this fantastic display *humility*. In reality it was a kind of religious vanity.

Paul's concern is always focused at the point of the centrality of Christ. To make rules and regulations primary is to move Christ out of the center. Nothing must move the spotlight from Him. The "rules mentality," no matter how productive it may seem to be, "ultimately produces a self-centered pride in one's achievements rather than a whole-souled dependence upon Jesus Christ."[52]

The fact is that these things have no value of themselves in remedying indulgence of the flesh. They cannot "satisfy the flesh" (23). By *flesh* Paul does not mean the body but the unregenerate personality. That is, regulations cannot deal with the problem of the unregenerate nature or "restrain sensual indulgence" (cf. NIV). Outward ceremonial ritualism may only cover a brood of scorpions in the heart.

Sinful tendencies and motives may be suppressed, but by mere restraint they cannot be cleansed and redirected. Eadie states this truth beautifully:

> The body might be reduced, but the evil bias might remain unchecked. A man might whip and fast himself into a walking skeleton, and yet the spirit within him might have all its lusts unconquered, for all it had lost was only the ability to gratify them. To place a fetter on a robber's hand will not cure him of covetousness, though it may disqualify him from actual theft. To seal up a swearer's mouth will not pluck profanity out of his heart, though it may for the time prevent him from taking God's name in vain. To lacerate the flesh almost to suicide, merely incapacitates it for indulgence, but does not extirpate sinful desire. Its air of superior sanctity is only pride in disguise—it has but "a show of wisdom."[53]

Modern psychology supports this view when it claims that undue repression causes violent stimulus and difficult complexes. Overregulation intensifies the evil. The golden mean is the line of safety, and that is found by each individual in a change of heart and acceptance of the Lordship of Christ over one's life. Only then will one begin to understand the reality and power of words attributed to J. O. Mc-Clurkan: "There is a *sinful* self to be *crucified* with Christ. There is a *true* self to be *realized* in Christ. There is a *human* self to be *disciplined* by Christ."

Alexander Maclaren graphically describes the attraction and powerlessness of asceticism:

> Any asceticism is a great deal more to men's taste than abandoning self. They will rather stick hooks in their backs and do the "swinging poojah," than give up their sins or yield up their wills. ... There is only one thing which will put the collar on the neck of the animal within us, and that is the power of the indwelling Christ.[54]

To this life in Christ Paul turns his attention in the next chapter.

COLOSSIANS 3

The Superior Quality of the Christian's Life

Colossians 3:1-17

Having finished his formal refutation of error, the Apostle now turns to the more pleasant task of inculcating truth. The preceding verses, in referring to the Colossians' "death with Christ," focus on the negative. Here Paul speaks of their "resurrection with Christ," the positive side of the same experience. "Death" looks to the past, to the end of the old life; "resurrection" looks to the present and future, and suggests what the new life is and can become. The Colossians are pointed to the kind of life—a life of ethical righteousness—which develops when Christ is supreme over all secondary rivals.

The contrast of life in Christ with the sterile practices advocated by the heretics at Colossae is clearly seen. W. R. Nicholson has labeled this section, particularly verses 1-4, "the true ascetism." The Christian is shown to have a far superior program for triumphant living than that of impotent legalism. Nobler aspirations, as well as the power to attain them, characterize the believer who shares the resurrection life of Christ. As is the case throughout the letter, the focus continues to be upon Christ, here described as the Royal Figure enthroned at God's right hand. The secret of seeking and enjoying life on a higher plane is keeping one's eyes on Him.

Life with the Risen Christ

Colossians 3:1-4

> 1 If ye then be risen with Christ, seek those things which are above, where Christ sitteth on the right hand of God.
> 2 Set your affection on things above, not on things on the earth.
> 3 For ye are dead, and your life is hid with Christ in God.
> 4 When Christ, who is our life, shall appear, then shall ye also appear with him in glory.

If in verse 1 does not imply uncertainty but rather denotes a fact. Thus it should read, *"Since* you were raised with Christ." Again the Apostle appeals to the idea of "union" or "identification" with Christ. Paul Rees notes several aspects of this identification: *(a)* In a *historical* or *provisional* sense, the believer died and was raised when Christ died and arose. *(b)* In *principle* and in *fact* the believer died and rose again when by faith he received Christ as "our Life and Lord, as Saviour and Sanctifier." *(c)* In *continuing practical experience* the believer must draw on the power of this Life to make the principle *operational* in all of his relationships with God, persons, and things.[55]

Paul is referring to the Colossians' personal resurrection with Christ at the time of their conversion and baptism *(b* above). But now they must work out the meaning and application to daily living of that which they then received in union with Christ (c above).

1. *A New Value System* (1-2). Two imperatives are given by the Apostle: *Seek those things which are above,* and *set your affection on things above.* Literally, *"be constantly* seeking [and] setting." Clearly one's priorities are to be arranged with spiritual values first and Christ at the pinnacle. The Christian has a new focal point. No longer earthbound, his attitudes and perspectives are directed upward. Walking with Christ in this "Beulah land of the spirit," the Christian has new ideals to inspire and new goals in life to bind him to the highest and best. His aims are centered in heaven, where reigns Christ enthroned on *the right hand of God.*

The word *phroneite (set your affection)* means "to be mindful of, think of." Thus the exhortation is "Set your mind upon things above" (cf. NIV). It involves both thought and disposition. The Christian *must* not only *"seek* heaven," he must also *"think* heaven" (Lightfoot). This is not to say that things of earth are sinful, as the Gnostics held; but that they can become so if sought and thought on in preference to the *above* things. Harmless things can become harmful if pursued to the exclusion of, and in the place of, things eternal (Matt. 6:19-21). Things *which are above* are not necessarily otherworldly. They are anything in this life that expresses God's love and compassion, or are capable of expressing them, in our everyday human relationships. These means of exalting Christ become life's highest priority.

The believer, then, has a new set of values. He marches to a different drumbeat. Life's highest goals are those which relate to Christ at God's right hand, and not to the principalities and powers of the planetary spheres. Christ has ascended far above these. The believer lives, not by the rules and regulations of the Gnostic schismatics, but by things that are *above.* He has a new standard for judging things. What the world views as important, he no longer thinks is significant. He measures things by God's standards, not men's. He values giving above getting and serving above ruling.

Nor is this to say that earthly, historical things do not matter. On the contrary, history is the arena for accomplishing God's purposes and demonstrating His love. It is to say that these things must be viewed against the backdrop of God's ultimate purpose. The believer sees himself as a pilgrim, not as a patron of this world's schemes. He does not despise the comforts enjoyed along the way, but he does not put a premium on their value. To become attached to them is not in keeping with being *risen with Christ.*

What can wealth achieve for him who has treasure laid up in heaven? Or honour for him who is already enthroned in the heavenly places? Or pleasure for him who revels in "newness of life"? Or power for him who is endowed with a moral omnipotence? Or fame for him who enjoys the approval of God?[56]

2. *An Inner Source of Power* (3). *Ye are dead,* being an aorist indicative, has usually been translated "You died" or "You have died," and refers to a past fact. It happened when the Colossians identified themselves with Christ in His death. This is the explanation Paul offers for the change in taste, for the transformation, and for the adoption of a new system of values. The Colossians' natures have been changed. They have died with Christ as pictured in baptism. When they entered the water of baptism, they were buried with Christ, and they arose with Him to live anew. The Greeks commonly spoke of one who had died and had been buried as being "hidden in the earth." The Christian has died a spiritual death in baptism, but his *life is hid with Christ in God.*

Or the Apostle may have a different metaphor in mind. The word translated "hidden" *(kekruptai)* is part of the verb *apokruptein,* from which the adjective *apokruphos* comes. The false teachers called their books of wisdom *apokruphoi* —"secret" or "hidden" books, "apocryphal" writings. Paul may be making a wordplay here. If so, he is saying: "For you the treasures of wisdom are hidden in your secret books; for us Christ is the treasury of wisdom, and we are hidden in Him" (Barclay).

However the expression is understood, *hidden with Christ* does not primarily carry the idea of concealment, since Christians are to be lights to the world (Matt. 5:14-16). Further, the Apostle has spoken against the secret mysteries of the false teachers. The phrase indicates that this power for living is both eternal and invisible—it is a matter of inner experience. It suggests the Christian has hidden resources, that is, resources unknown to the world. He draws his "inspiration from heavenly places and obey[s] a heavenly throne" (R. E. O. White). To say this life is "hidden" is no argument against present enjoyment. One may drink cool water from the stream and be unable to know its distant source. Nonetheless, just as the risen Christ is hidden now in the life of God, so those who belong to Christ are "hidden" from the comprehension of the world.

3. *A Glorious Destiny* (4). Though Christ's kingship is hidden in the sense that it has not been finally and openly demonstrated, in the future Jesus will be "manifested" (ASV; better than *appear*) and shown to be the undisputed Lord of the universe. The rightness of the Christian view of life will be demonstrated. The resurrection of Jesus is the pledge of this final victory. That which is hidden will be revealed, that which is not comprehended will be understood. The world cannot understand or appreciate the Christian, whose true greatness is hidden to the unbeliever. The world does not understand the risen life of Christ any more than it understood the life of Christ himself (John 14:17; 15:18-19). But the day will come—the only reference in the Epistle to Christ's second coming—when the verdicts of men in time will be overturned by the judgments of God in eternity.

Paul does not say merely that we share life with Christ. He speaks of *Christ, who is our life.* This is a good summary of the Apostle's testimony: "Christ liveth in me" (Gal. 2:20), as the Source of life, and "To me to live is Christ" (Phil.

1:21). Spiritual life is not only being "with Christ," or sharing His life; it is also unity with Christ in the bosom of the Father. Christ is himself the essence of the Christian's life.

But though Christ is our life here and now (1 John 5:12), *when Christ . . . shall appear, then shall ye* [we] *also appear with him in glory.* "We know that, when he shall appear, we shall be like him" (1 John 3:2). We shall be glorified with Him. Paul spoke of this great day as "the manifestation of the sons of God" (Rom. 8:19). The glory will come as the "crown of the hidden life" (Ellicott). "Then shall the righteous shine [blaze] forth as the sun in the kingdom of their Father" (Matt. 13:43). The final destiny of the believer will be realized, the first installment of which Jesus spoke in the presence of His disciples: "I have given them the glory that you gave me" (John 17:22, NIV).

The unbelieving world which now persecutes and ignores will one day be blinded with the dazzling glory of Christ's final revelation, and justice in history will prevail. In that day the believer will be like his Lord, having seen Him face-to-face.

> *Face-to-face with Christ my Savior,*
> *Face-to-face—what will it be,*
> *When with rapture I behold Him,*
> *Jesus Christ who died for me?*
> —CARRIE E. BRECK

Meanwhile the believer lives his risen life in Christ "by the faith of the Son of God" (Gal. 2:20). He goes on living the life hid with Christ in God, secure and protected so long as he remains in Him, and with the solid hope of his ultimate vindication.

Eliminate the Negative

Colossians 3:5-9

5 Mortify therefore your members which are upon the earth; fornication, uncleanness, inordinate affection, evil concupiscence, and covetousness, which is idolatry;

6 For which things' sake the wrath of God cometh on the children of disobedience:
7 In the which ye also walked some time, when ye lived in them.
8 But now ye also put off all these; anger, wrath, malice, blasphemy, filthy communication out of your mouth.
9 Lie not one to another, seeing that ye have put off the old man with his deeds:

In the opening verses of chapter 3 Paul has given several indicatives: "You have died" (3); "you have been raised" (1, many versions); *your life is hid with Christ in God* (3). These indicatives describe a set of facts which God in Christ has established.

But the Apostle also gives some imperatives which are a "series of functions in which our faith is to be continuously engaged":[57] *seek those things which are above* (1); *set your affection* (i.e., mind, disposition, the best of your thoughts) *on things above* (2). Now comes the transition which is characteristic of all Paul's writings, namely, the transition from theology to ethics—or better, the clear articulation of the applications to daily living of the theology he has been proclaiming, for theology and ethics cannot ultimately be separated.

1. *Live by the "death principle."* To clarify the ethical demands placed on the believer, Paul adds a third imperative: *Mortify therefore your members which are upon the earth* (5). *Mortify* is no longer a good rendering, since it is currently used broadly to include self-denial and a variety of disciplines. The Greek term *nekrōsate* here means "to deprive of power, destroy the strength of" (Thayer). A better translation is: "Put to death what is earthly in you" (Arndt and Gingrich).

The use of *therefore* points back to 2:20 and 3:2, where the principle of death to sin and the world is stated. The meaning is: "Make dead, therefore, every part of *your members,* whether body or mind, which is against God and hinders you from accomplishing His total will in your life." Rom. 8:13 expresses the same idea: "If ye through the Spirit do mortify the deeds of the body, ye shall live." Jesus graphically taught the same thing in saying that one should cut off his hand or foot, or destroy an eye if these were the occasion for sin (Matt. 5:29-30).

Paul's demand of the Colossians is clear. Since you have died, your old sinful self has been nailed to the Cross. Now in a once-for-all, specific commitment, determine that the principle of death will govern the use of every instinct, every appetite, of your being. The ascetic schemes offered by the false teachers at Colossae are futile; the death principle alone leads to life.

Neither Paul nor other writers of the New Testament assert that the body with its drives and urges is sinful. "The fact that the body can be cleansed and sanctified (cf. 1 Cor. 6:13, 19-20; 2 Cor. 7:1; see Rom. 6:13; 12:1) is decisive against any identification of sin with the flesh" (McDonald). The *members* of our body are not evil in themselves, as the Gnostics held. However, they give sin its opportunity and can become the occasion for sin. As A. T. Robertson has said: "It is only when we allow our bodily appetites to drag us down that they do us harm." The perversion and selfish use of these God-given drives and functions is sinful, and these misuses spring from an ego infected by sin. To tolerate a disposition that puts the rule of appetite above the rule of Christ and the death principle is to be "carnally minded" and leads to death (Rom. 8:6). Paul Rees has said: "It is this disposition that must drop its proud head at Calvary and say 'finished.'"

2. *Discipline Bodily Appetites* (5-7). Paul catalogs five specific vices or perversions which the believer must carry to the guillotine, or "make dead": "sexual immorality, impurity, lust, evil desires and greed" (NIV). (See similar lists in Eph. 5:3-4; Gal. 5:19-21; Rom. 1:26-32; 1 Thess. 4:3-6).

a. *Fornication* is a precise translation of the term *porneian* (from which is derived our word *pornography*), but Paul seems to have in mind broader connotations than sexual deviations. Thus "immorality" seems to be the meaning (see 1 Thess. 4:3; 1 Cor. 5:10; 6:9, 18; 2 Cor. 12:21; 1 Tim.

1:9-10). Paul's world, much like our own, regarded the sexual appetite as something to be gratified, not controlled. The Christian ethic brought a new virtue of chastity and purity. The believer who is mastered by Christ cannot be controlled by unleashed passions and desires.

b. "Impurity" *(uncleanness)* refers to a more subtle form of evil than a physical act of sin. It includes every manifestation in sight, word, and deed, of a contaminated spirit (cf. Gal. 5:19-21; Eph. 5:3-5).

c. "Passion" (ASV) *(inordinate affection)* is a word which may be used in either a good or bad sense. Obviously it means the latter here. The Greeks used it to refer to all ungovernable affections.

d. "Evil desires" *(evil concupiscence)* describes passions which are out of control, includes all evil longings, not merely sexual desires, for things to which one is not entitled. Gal. 5:19 refers to the desire of the flesh which leads to sinful actions. Uncontrollable passion and evil desire must be ended.

e. Covetousness (pleonexia) is basically the desire to have more of anything, whether evil or not. It is "greediness" (Eph. 4:19). Paul seems to mean the love of money—the opposite of the desire to give. It is an insatiate desire which will not be quelled until Christ rules the believer.

This spirit Paul labels *idolatry,* "the attempt to use God for man's purposes, rather than to give oneself to God's service" (Moule). The sin of idolatry is "placing anyone or anything higher than the will of God in our priorities" (Demarest).

For these things *the wrath of God* will surely fall on *the children of disobedience* (6). The terrible retribution that comes, even in this life, for sins of lust and greed, are obvious to the careful observer. Avarice deprives the soul, and sexual vice destroys both soul and body. Much is said today of God's all-embracing love. But the Scriptures also speak of His all-consuming wrath. Maclaren has put it well: "If there is no wrath, there is no love; if there were no love, there would be no wrath." God's wrath comes upon one's disobedience *because* of His love. These consequences of unconquered sin cannot be escaped. "The wrath of God and the moral order of the universe are one and the same thing" (Barclay).

Verse 7 is a joyous note in the midst of a rather somber context. Paul refers to the transformation in the life of the Colossians who once *walked,* or lived ethically, in the manner of life described above. The message of the gospel is that we who are "by nature the children of wrath" (Eph. 2:3) have been "saved" (Eph. 2:8) and "delivered" (1 Thess. 1:10) from the wrath of God. Such remembrance of past forgiveness and the knowledge of the divine wrath are incentives to the Colossians to "put *to death*" (many versions) what is "earthly" (5, cf. NIV).

3. *Do Away with the Deeds of the Old Life* (8-9)

The word rendered *put off (apothesthe)* or "put . . . away" (ASV), refers to the changing of one's garments or putting off old clothes. It gives the picture of discarding sins like an old, worn-out garment that is no longer fitting or appropriate. Lay them aside, Paul admonishes. The reference also may be to the baptismal practice of putting off one's old clothes at baptism in exchange for a new and pure white robe.

Put off is another aorist imperative and means to be rid of these things definitely and completely. Let these things be gone forever. In verse 5 Paul begins with action and moves upward to desire. In the list of particular evils here he begins with emotions and attitudes and moves downward to actions. He focuses at this point, not on external things relating primarily to one's sexuality, but rather to those pertaining to attitudes and relationships.

The Christian must put off:

a. Anger (orgēn)—a spirit of personal resentfulness and provocation. It is a slow-burning anger which one nurtures and keeps burning—perpetual resentment, holding a grudge which refuses to be pacified.

b. Wrath (thumon), or "rage"—sudden outbursts or explosions of passion and temper which, like straw, are quickly kindled and may quickly subside. Such behavior is never constructive. The Christian is to be liberated from this in Christ.

c. *Malice*—This is anger "heightened and settled" (Henry), "the vicious nature which is bent on doing harm to others" (Lightfoot). It is an all-pervading spirit of evil, malignity against another, badness of heart.

d. *Blasphemy (blasphēmia)* or "slander"—the use of speech either against God or one's fellows with intent to injure. Here the emphasis seems to be on the latter, namely, vilification of another by lies or careless gossip.

e. *Filthy communication* ("filthy language from your lips," NIV)—obscene language, "shameful speaking" (ASV), unclean talk, salacious double entendre in which some delight, smutty stories; perhaps even abusive language. Such talk is worthless; but worse, it is harmful, in contrast with that speech which edifies (see 4:6).

f. *Lying*—*Lie not one to another.* The devil is the "father of lies" (John 8:44), and the Christian is to give no "place to the devil" (Eph. 4:27). "Falsehood is not faith, and what is not faith is sin" (McDonald).

Barclay has suggested that from the prohibitions regarding speech, if we make them positive, we derive three important criteria for guiding and controlling our speaking:

"Christian speech must be *kind.*
Christian speech must be *pure.*
Christian speech must be *true.*"

And in the light of the fact that all will give account of "every idle word" they speak (Matt. 12:36), we may add, Is it *helpful?* Is it *necessary?*

Paul gathers up his thought with the metaphor of *the old man with his deeds* (9b). The expression is more inclusive than such phrases as "sin that dwelleth in me," "carnally minded," and "flesh." "It is the totality of what we are apart from Christ and his saving offices."[58] The Apostle is consumed not only with the sinfulness of the offenses he has cataloged, but also with the unreasonableness and contradictions of their presence in the life of the Colossians, or any Christian. The old and the new are incompatible. He insists that one has not really *put off* the old life unless and until he has *put off* the sinful deeds also. In Gal. 5:24 this "putting off" is spoken of as a crucifixion of "the flesh" with its passions and lusts. Life in Christ affects the center and circumference of one's being. When one becomes a Christian, there is a complete change of person. The believer puts off the old self and puts on a new self.

Accentuate the Positive

Colossians 3:10-17

> 10 And have put on the new man, which is renewed in knowledge after the image of him that created him:
> 11 Where there is neither Greek nor Jew, circumcision nor uncircumcision,. Barbarian, Scythian, bond nor free: but Christ is all, and in all.
> 12 Put on therefore, as the elect of God, holy and beloved, bowels of mercies, kindness, humbleness of mind, meekness, longsuffering;
> 13 Forbearing one another, and forgiving one another, if any man have a quarrel against any: even as Christ forgave you, so also do ye.
> 14 And above all these things put on charity, which is the bond of perfectness.
> 15 And let the peace of God rule in your hearts, to the which also ye are called in one body; and be ye thankful.
> 16 Let the word of Christ dwell in you richly in all wisdom; teaching and admonishing one another in psalms and hymns and spiritual songs, singing with grace in your hearts to the Lord.
> 17 And whatsoever ye do in word or deed, do all in the name of the Lord Jesus, giving thanks to God and the Father by him.

Before becoming specific about the things the Colossians should prioritize, the Apostle gives the reason for not only eliminating the negative, but for accentuating the positive (9*b*-10*a*). They *have put off the old man with his deeds; and have put on the new man* (self). The old manner of life is out of place in the new sphere of Christian living, just as dirty, tattered clothing is out of place in a first-class dining room. The old priorities don't fit; they are inappropriate for the new life in Christ. New and fresh priorities must in fact replace the old, outmoded ones. Paul's rationale for this change seems to be a paradox. Put off the old vices and habits and sins of the old sinful nature precisely because you have put off the old sinful nature with its vices and habits and sins. Simultaneously put on the virtues of the new nature because you have put on the new nature with its virtues (McDonald).

1. *Continue to Renew the New Man* (10). At conversion one puts on the new man in Christ, formed after Christ. He is a new creature in Christ (2 Cor. 5:17), given a new nature. This new nature or life is "being [present tense] continually renewed" (10, lit. trans.). One's conversion or transformation into a new creature occurs in the moment of faith, but it initiates a process that is "always going on toward the full or perfect knowledge which is the goal of God's purpose in creating us in his image" (Robertson; see Eph. 4:24). This constant renewal, however, is not man's work or through his feverish activity, since Paul's word *(anakainoō)* is in the passive voice (see Eph. 2:10; Titus 3:5). Rather, it is the "renewing by the Holy Spirit" (Titus 3:5, NASB) who renovates the inner man day by day.

a. This renewal *in knowledge,* contrary to that offered by the Gnostics, is the illumination of the Holy Spirit, an increasing knowledge of the things of God, a deepening communion with God, a fuller understanding of His will. It is *knowledge after the image of him that created him.* This, of course, is a reminder of Gen. 1:27, where God is denoted as the Creator. But it fits the Christological theme of the whole passage to assert that Christ is the image into whose likeness the believer is being transformed (cf. Rom. 8:29; 2 Cor. 3:18; 4:16). In 1:15 Paul refers to Christ as "the image of the invisible God." But in Paul's thought Christ is also the "image of true manhood," the "second Adam" (cf. Rom. 5:12-21; 1 Cor. 15:44-49). To be renewed after His image—continuous and increasing likeness—is the grand aim of His work for us and in us.

b. Paul Rees has suggested that "the whole dialectic of New Testament sanctification is involved" here. *Provisionally,* when Christ died, and *positionally,* when the Colossians believed on Christ, they *put off the old man* (self) and *put on the new.* Christ became their "righteousness, and sanctification" (1 Cor. 1:30). But to these believers Paul is saying: You are not yet in fact, in experience, what you are in spiritual position and privilege. And you cannot be until you see what your union with Christ really means—until you cease your struggling or even asking for Christ's assistance. You must understand that spiritual victory and holy living are not the result of your own efforts, "but rather the consequences of your letting Christ take over, letting him be in fact Christ in you living out his life in your always impotent and unworthy, but unreservedly yielded being."[59]

The Colossians had put on the new man as a matter of *position* and *possession.* But "there must also be the 'putting on' of *realization* and of *use,* and *manifestation;* or the blessed means will miss its end" (Moule). This realization can be an epochal day in the life of the believer, without in any way minimizing the ongoing process of sanctification which Paul so clearly recognized.

2. *Acknowledge the Unity of Believers* (11)

a. The new man may be thought of in one or more of three senses, all of which the Apostle probably has in mind: (1) The new man is Christ, who is "made unto us wisdom, and righteousness, and sanctification, and redemption" (1 Cor. 1:30). (2) The new man is individually the "new creature" (2 Cor. 5:17), the believer. (3) The new man is corporately the new community, the Church (Eph. 2:15). The believer not only becomes a new *individual* in Christ, he also becomes a part of a new *family.*

b. In this spiritual region, at the level of the new man, where the regenerate man finds himself, class distinctions— including race, religion, culture, social status—mean nothing. Paul insisted in Galatians that the traditional barriers between male and female also were abolished by Christ (3:28). This is not to say that these distinctions cease to exist in the Christian community—Jews are Jews, Greeks (Gentiles) are Gentiles; men remain men, women remain women; and so on. But in the Christian community they are viewed as being inconsequential and provide no grounds for a spirit either of superiority or inferiority.

In Paul's day the Greeks looked down on the barbarians; and to the Greeks any man who did not speak Greek was a barbarian, which literally means a man who says, "bar-bar." The Jews looked down on every other nation. They belonged to God's chosen people, and the other nations were fit only to be fuel for the fires of hell. But in Christ all such barriers are broken down: racial *(Greek nor Jew)*, ceremonial *(circumcision nor uncircumcision)*, lingual-cultural *(Barbarian, Scythian)*, social *(bond nor free)*.

Max Muller, an expert in the science of language, has indicated that it was Christianity which drew men together sufficiently to wish to know each other's languages. He said, "I therefore date the real beginning of the science of language from the first Day of Pentecost."

Christ as the Head of a new humanity has broken down every "wall of partition" (Eph. 2:14) which would separate man from man as well as man from God. Racial prejudices, nationalistic idolatries, class distinctions, religious bigotry, and social complexes (either superior or inferior) have been abolished and welded together into one Body. H. Dermot McDonald has stated this truth beautifully: "There is no special class in grace. Sin levels all men to the same low position; grace lifts all men to the same high privilege. Sin puts us under the table as slaves; grace puts us at the table as sons. And all seats are of equal status."[60]

These distinctions which men exalt are now insignificant in the light of Christ who *is all, and in all* (11*b*), or as Phillips paraphrases: "Christ is all that matters for Christ lives in all." The key to unity lies not in the believers, except secondarily; it lies in Christ who is their common Lord. He is the Supreme One *(all)*, and by His interpenetrating presence *(in all)* true unity is realized.

3. *Put on the Virtues of Christ* (12-14). Having *put on the new man* (10), the Colossians are admonished to *put on* (12)

the virtues and graces that belong to the new man, just as they had *put off the old man with his deeds* (9). Because *Christ is all, and in all, therefore* they are to demonstrate and model in their individual lives the spirit and virtues of Christ.

The distinctive community aspect of Paul's meaning can be seen in the way he addresses his readers: *The elect of God, holy and beloved.* These terms originally described the Jews who were "God's chosen people," separated and "dearly loved" (NIV). Now, however, these belong to all who are in Christ, including the Gentiles. All who possess the "new self" are "God's picked representatives" of the new humanity (Phillips). Because the Colossians are God's chosen ones, *holy* and *beloved,* does not exempt them from right living. The implication is: You *are* holy, so *be* holy; you *are* loved, so *live* as sons who also love.

This understanding of the Christian community is seen also in the phrase *one another,* used twice in verse 13 and once in verse 16, and in the fact that the virtues listed all have to do with personal relationships between man and man.

Paul proceeds to list some positive qualities of the Christian life (12-14), items of the Christian's wardrobe which are to be *put on.* They stand in sharp contrast, even opposition, to the vices mentioned in verses 8-9. Alexander Maclaren refers to these virtues as "the garments of the renewed soul." The Apostle is saying, Since you are God's people, set apart for His service, therefore "clothe yourselves" (NIV) with:

a. bowels of mercies—better, "heart of compassion" (ASV), since the word *splanchna (bowels)* is used metaphorically for the seat of the affections and emotions. Jesus was often moved with compassion (Matt. 9:36; Mark 1:41). Tenderness and empathy characterize one in Christ, enabling him to share and help heal the hurts of others.

Barclay has observed that in Paul's time little was being done for the aged, the handicapped, the retarded. It was largely through the inspiration of Christianity that compassion was generated for these, as well as for women and children.

b. kindness—that goodness of heart which enables one to deal justly with other persons. It is love in action, genuine care for another. Paul refers to it as a part of the fruit of the Spirit (Gal. 5:22-23). The word *chrēstotēs* was sometimes used of wine which has lost its harshness and grown mellow. Jesus described His yoke with the word, saying, "My yoke is easy" *(chrēstos),* or gentle (Matt. 11:30).

c. humbleness of mind, or "humility"—a genuine acceptance of one's creatureliness which makes one dependent on God, and an acknowledgment that whatever one possesses —talents, skills, and so on—is divinely bestowed. True "lowliness" (ASV) is based on a proper self-love, whereas false humility masks its desire for recognition (see 2:18).

d. meekness—quiet strength, or strength restrained to gentleness. Harshness has no place in the Christian's wardrobe. *Meekness* is the opposite of rudeness but possesses a courage to defend the rights of others even when it requires waiving one's own.

e. longsuffering, or "patience"—the endurance of wrong (insults, ill treatment, and so on) without demanding vengeance or revenge. It is the opposite of malice, resentment, bitterness, or wrath. Yet it is not passive, but quietly and fairly works for change with sensitivity to the needs of others.

In order that these virtues not seem abstract, Paul adds two vivid illustrations of them, specifically patience: (1) *Forbearing one another* (13*a*), or more simply, "Bear with each other" (NIV). The verb means holding yourselves back from one another when tempted to hurt others, verbally or otherwise. (2) *And forgiving one another . . . even as Christ forgave you* (13*b*). The forgiven man who is a new creature forgives others (see Matt. 6:11-15), whether or not there is ground for the "faultfinding" or "complaint" (ASV) or "grievances" (NIV; cf. Weymouth, NBV; KJV uses the archaic word *quar-*

rel). The only way to overcome the faultfinding is to forgive the fault and forget it.

The verb translated *forgiving (charizomai)* comes from *charis,* which means "grace." Thus one is to forgive graciously and wholeheartedly, or as Weymouth translates it, "readily forgiving."

f. charity (14)—the NIV reads: "And over all these virtues put on love, which binds them all together in perfect unity" (or "completeness").

Since Paul is using the metaphor of clothing, he may be thinking of the girdle frequently worn by the ancients to hold in place and in proper relation other garments. If so, the Apostle is suggesting that love is the outer garment to be put over and around all the rest. Love is the bond which holds persons together in unbreakable fellowship. Referring to this list of the believer's garments, Lightfoot has said that love is "the power which unites and holds together all those graces and virtues, which together make up perfection."

4. *Let Christ's Peace Rule You* (15). Because of strong manuscript authority, most translators say this verse should be rendered "the peace of Christ." Keep in mind that peace is Christ's legacy. To His troubled disciples just prior to His crucifixion, He said: "Peace I leave with you, my peace I give unto you: not as the world giveth, give I unto you. Let not your heart be troubled, neither let it be afraid" (John 14:27). Speaking of the Comforter, the Holy Spirit, He promised: "I will not leave you comfortless [orphans]: I will come to you" (John 14:18). To have Christ is to have peace, "for he is our peace" (Eph. 2:14). By "the blood of his cross" (Col. 1:20) He has reconciled us to himself in order that we might "have peace with God" (Rom. 5:1).

a. Paul's appeal is to allow the peace of Christ to *rule* the hearts of his readers. (See discussion at 2:18.) The imperative *let rule (brabeuetō),* which occurs only here in the New Testament, comes from a term meaning "umpire." Clearly the Apostle has in mind here the total Christian community by his words *in one body.* Christ's peace is to be the "arbiter" (NEB), not only in the believer's heart, but also in the total life of the community. Within the church the peace of Christ must settle every dispute, resolve every conflict, and cast the decisive vote in every deadlock—for "God hath called us to peace" (1 Cor. 7:15).

The call is for unity of spirit, not necessarily for organic unity. In the local church at Colossae the Apostle wants the peace of Christ to act as umpire. "Disunion in the body is incompatible with the peace of individual members" (Peake). It is a contradiction for individuals to claim to share the *peace of Christ* while at the same time not allowing Him to bind the community of believers into a fellowship of love.

b. And be ye thankful, literally, "keep on being thankful." Gratitude must be a habit of the soul, a quality of spirit even when blessings do not come in the form or measure we would choose. The Colossians were thankful in some measure (1:12), but the ideal is not yet reached. Paul wants them to keep on being more thankful, to grow in gratitude. Lightfoot captures the meaning: "Forget yourselves in thanksgiving toward God."

5. *Make Your Heart the Home for Christ's Word* (16). One of the best ways to manifest continuous thanksgiving is by appropriating *the word of Christ,* which parallels "the peace of Christ" (ASV) in the previous verse. "The peace of Christ will rule in hearts as the word of Christ overrules in lives" (McDonald). Thus the Apostle admonishes: "Let the word of Christ dwell in you richly as you teach and admonish one another with all wisdom" (NIV). Only here in the New Testament is the expression "the word of Christ" found. Normally "the word of God" or "the word of the Lord" is used, and refers to the gospel—not only to Christ's teachings, but also to His saving deeds. Some interpreters think "the word of Christ" here means the presence of Christ in the heart "as our inward monitor" (Lightfoot) or strength. This latter idea is consonant with 1 John 2:14: "Ye are strong, and the word

of God abideth in you, and ye have overcome the wicked one."

Whatever the precise meaning, Paul desires that this Word might have a continual home, or *dwell* "as a permanent part, always present" (Moule) in the hearts of the Colossians—not just *among* them, but *in* them. And *richly* as well, "not with a scanty foothold, but with a large and liberal occupancy" (Eadie).

Further, this Word of Christ is to be present "as you sing psalms, hymns and spiritual songs with gratitude in your hearts to God" (NIV). The Jews had developed psalmnody and hymnody for their religious services, and the early believers followed this pattern in public worship.

It has been suggested that "the leading idea in 'psalm' is the musical instrument, and in 'hymn' it is praise to God, while 'spiritual songs' is the general expression for song, whether accompanied or unaccompanied."[61] This may seem arbitrary, but these words do denote the rich diversity of our musical heritage.

While the Holy Spirit is mentioned directly only in 1:8, it is noteworthy that there are two passages in which the word "spiritual" occurs (1:9 and here). *Spiritual songs* may suggest songs inspired by the Spirit (see 1 Cor. 14:15). In addition to the Psalms, no doubt new compositions which included the newer elements of the Christian revelation were framed. The gratitude of the Church has always gone up to God in praise and Christian song. Paul's exhortation to sing *with grace in your hearts to the Lord* suggests that Christian hymns and music must express the devotion and gratitude of the heart, and should offer worship and adoration to the Lord in a style that is worthy of our Savior God.

6. *Do Everything in Jesus' Name* (17). At the close of this section on the superior quality of the Christian's life, Paul gives an all-inclusive principle for Christian living. From the more narrow range of Christian hymnody, the Apostle moves to every part of our common life. Everything the Christian does, and not merely the smaller circle of religious

worship, is to be done *in the name of the Lord Jesus.* This public worship must harmonize with one's everyday life and activities. Every aspect of our mundane and sometimes monotonous existence is to be brought under the Lordship of Christ. Every task, if truly performed in the name of Jesus and for the purpose of bringing Him glory, is hallowed.

It is instructive to observe that in each of the three injunctions in verses 15, 16, and 17 relating to the believer's well-being, the Apostle speaks of the virtue of gratitude. He refers to the attitude of being *thankful* (15); *singing with grace* (16)—the word can mean "thankfulness" or "thanks" (see 2 Tim. 1:3); and *giving thanks.* Thanksgiving, then, is a dominant characteristic and necessary note of the Christian's life. Praise and thanksgiving to God and one another are to be in our hearts, on our minds, and expressed with our lips and actions. If every word and deed are tested by the presence of Jesus Christ, our life will demonstrate the superior quality of Christ's life in us.

The Superior Quality of the Christian's Relationships

Colossians 3:18—4:18

The Christian faith has always taught that we have social obligations to our neighbors and to all men everywhere. The caricature that Christians are interested only in "pie in the sky by and by" is unjust. While Jesus and Paul (and the prophets before them) could not use modern technical terms in teaching social responsibilities, they made clear the duties of everyday life on the part of Christians in the family, the marketplace, the political and international arenas, as well as in the worshiping community.

It must be admitted, however, that in certain periods of Christian history these practical responsibilities have been minimized or overlooked. It was such neglect which occasioned the formation of William Booth's Salvation Army and the rescue missions in large urban centers. Attempts in recent years to do work left undone by the churches is nonetheless largely in response to, and an expression of, the Christian spirit.

To Paul, Christianity's ethical concern finds its basis and motivation in its relation to Christ, the Source of its love and power. Any tendency to put social activity in the place of a transforming faith in Christ is a perversion of Paul's position. True humanitarianism is the fruit of Christianity, not a substitute for it. The service of humanity properly grows out of the worship of Christ. If the root of worship is removed, the branch of effective service soon withers or becomes idolatry. But Jesus himself made our relationships toward those in need an indication of our attitude toward Him and an evidence of our new life in Him (see Matthew 7 and 25). "By their fruits ye shall know them" (Matt. 7:20).

At this point the ethical part of Paul's letter becomes intensely relevant and specific. The Apostle turns to the practical outworking of Christian faith in the ordinary relationships of life and living—in the home, the world of work, in difficult circumstances, in an unbelieving world, and in the circle of believers.

In the Family

Colossians 3:18-21

> 18 Wives, submit yourselves unto your own husbands, as it is fit in the Lord.
> 19 Husbands, love your wives, and be not bitter against them.
> 20 Children, obey your parents in all things: for this is well pleasing unto the Lord.
> 21 Fathers, provoke not your children to anger, lest they be discouraged.

As in the Ephesian letter (5:22-33), so here the Apostle

shows how Christ transforms the home. Wives, husbands, children, fathers are all brought under a new obligation. Christ must dominate the relationship. Paul recognizes the home and family as the citadel of contentment and moral instruction, a profound source of personal security and development, and as the "seed-plots of the Christian Church" (Jones). The asceticism and license advocated by the Gnostics undercut this foundation of civilization.

Paul is describing the ideal home and his instructions are to be understood in the context of the Christian community, *in the Lord.*

1. The Apostle's first injunction is to the *wives,* perhaps because the wife is the key person in the home (18). All of the family relationships tend to revolve around her, and for this reason her relationship to the husband and to the children is crucial. The word translated *submit (hypotassesthe),* literally, "be subject to," was originally a military metaphor denoting organizational structure. Its use points up the need for order and stability in the home but in no way indicates that the wife is the slave of the husband.

To permit this verse to raise the question about authority in marriage, or stimulate discussion about who is to be "in charge"—husband or wife—is to miss the point. Clearly the "submission" spoken of is not that of a blind or arbitrary obedience, nor does it allow for a claim of superiority over the other marriage partner. Rather, as Eph. 5:21-22 shows, this is a particular instance of a general principle which is to govern all believers. We are to submit ourselves "one to another in the fear of God." In Christian marriage, mutual deference, cooperation, and partnership must characterize the relationship of the spouses. This "subjection" as is "fitting in the Lord" (NIV) is one of those "whatsoevers" which are to be done *in the name of the Lord Jesus* (17). In the Colossians' culture where almost all the rights and privileges belonged to the man with virtually none for the woman, this teaching that the obligations and duties of husband and wife are reciprocal was revolutionary.

2. The word Paul uses in exhorting husbands to love their wives is *agapate,* love, or "keep on loving" them (19). This is the highest love of all, the kind of love with which God has loved unworthy sinners. It far exceeds mere erotic love *(eraō)* which may be expressed in sexual passion, or even the love *(phileō)* which is affection with friends or within a family. It is that love which in every circumstance seeks the other's welfare above one's own. This is the love that is to govern all relationships of the Christian (see 1:4, 8; 2:2; 3:14, all of which use *agapē*) and which therefore is to be expressed in the home, especially between husband and wife.

Anything less than this can lead to bitterness and harshness (most versions). Too often coldness or neglect replaces warm affection in the marital relation. A harshness of temper, being *bitter* or cross toward one's partner, or even becoming habitually thoughtless or insensitive to the other's needs, is incompatible with Christian faith.

3. Children are to keep on obeying parents *in all things* (20). The obedience of the child is not the same as the submission appropriate for the wife. The latter is "tempered by equality." The child is to give obedience *in all things*. No doubt Paul is thinking of the ideal Christian family and therefore is not addressing the situation where parental orders might be contrary to the law of Christ. Jesus, however, seems to have implied that if father or mother is hostile to Christ and seeks to keep the child from coming to Christ, the child must obey God (Luke 14:26). But nonetheless, the principle of obedience holds, and normally there should be no limitation given to obedience on the part of the child. For such obedience in Eph. 6:1-3, Paul adds the special promise of long life from the fifth commandment.

4. The demand for obedience to parents was nothing new, but the idea that parents have an obligation to treat their children with love and care was bold and startling (21; see Eph. 6:4). The word *pateres (fathers)* is thought by some commentators to include both parents. Certainly neither fa-

ther nor mother is to irritate their children. The reference here is to that irritation which results from an explosion of temper. It is not uncommon for the father to irritate by over-exacting or unreasonable demands and faultfinding. Often as a result, the child's spirit is broken *(discouraged)*—"the plague of youth" (Bengel). Constant nagging or overseverity, particularly when love is not evident or expressed, may induce in children excessive resistance to authority or an unhealthy regressiveness and dejection.

Parents have a responsibility to discipline but also to encourage. Martin Luther once said, "Spare the rod and spoil the child. It is true. But beside the rod keep an apple to give him when he does well." Children are not merely to be seen; they are to be heard at the appropriate times, treated as persons, and welcomed in home and heart.

5. The revolutionary character of these injunctions can be understood only in the light of the social situation in which Paul wrote them. Barclay describes the context sharply. For example, according to Jewish law a woman was a "thing," the husband's possession just like his house or flocks. She had no legal rights. The husband could divorce his wife for any cause, but the wife was not permitted to initiate divorce.

In Greek society a woman of repute lived in complete seclusion. She never appeared on the streets alone, never joined the menfolk even for meals. Complete servitude and chastity were required while the husband without stigma could enter as many extramarital relationships as he desired. In both Jewish and Greek societies "all privileges belonged to the husband and all the duties to the wife."

Children in the ancient world were completely dominated by the parents. The parent could sell the child into slavery, work him like a laborer, condemn him to death, and even carry out the execution. "Privileges and rights belonged to the parent, and all the duties to the child."[62]

Contrary to this kind of social practice, Paul wants the Colossian believers to know that the Christian ethic is one of mutual obligation. Every man has rights but also corresponding responsibilities. But privileges and rights are always secondary, and duty and obligation always primary. To the believer in Christ this order of things is not grievous, but fulfilling.

In the Working World

Colossians 3:22—4:1

> 22 Servants, obey in all things your masters according to the flesh; not with eyeservice, as menpleasers; but in singleness of heart, fearing God:
> 23 And whatsoever ye do, do it heartily, as to the Lord, and not unto men;
> 24 Knowing that of the Lord ye shall receive the reward of the inheritance: for ye serve the Lord Christ.
> 25 But he that doeth wrong shall receive for the wrong which he hath done: and there is no respect of persons.
>
> 1 Masters, give unto your servants that which is just and equal; knowing that ye also have a Master in heaven.

For Paul the gospel has direct implications for every segment of man's life. Consequently he expresses his concern for the quality of the believer's vocational life as strongly as he has done for the family. In fact, in his day many households included slaves so that the master/slave relationship was an extension of the family. They worked in the household, in the fields, and in the shop. The fact that Paul does not attack the system of slavery as such is not to give his approval to it. He seems to have in mind primarily the Christian master and Christian slave. Some of these had come into the community of faith. His concern at this point is to bring to bear upon the everyday lives of both master and slave the principles and spirit of the gospel. Every social relationship is to be brought within the circle of Christ's reigning Lordship.

It is noteworthy that the Apostle has more to say to slaves in this section than to husbands, wives, parents, children, or masters. This may be accounted for by the fact that, for Paul, in Christ there is no distinction between the Christian slave and Christian master. Also, we must keep in mind that at this time Paul is writing Philemon about his Christian responsibility to welcome back Onesimus, the slave who had deserted. It appears that Philemon was a part of the Christian community at Colossae, and Onesimus had just been converted to the faith. Clearly, Paul's words would have special meaning to the Colossians which would explain Paul's care in what and how much he said.

While our Western society is no longer bound by the terrible system of slavery, the principles advanced here are applicable to our world of employee/employer relations, with its labor/management disputes and collective bargaining maneuvers. The responsibilities enjoined are essentially obedience on the part of the slaves (*servants,* or employees) and justice on the part of the *masters* (employers and executives).

1. *Slaves to Masters* (22-25). In Paul's day the slaves had few privileges—as was the case with women and children. Before the law, a slave was property, an object, a thing. When he was no longer able to work and became useless to his owner, he could be discarded legally and left to die. Even before that time he had no right to marry, to cohabit, to have children. If he did have children, they became the property of the master. The master could scourge, brand, or kill his slave, and none could stop him. All rights belonged to the master and none to the slave.

a. It is significant that slaves who had become converted were allowed equal privileges in the Christian community. Some probably became pastors of churches and because of this spiritual role may have been inclined to despise their masters. Hence Paul exhorts them to give their masters proper regard (1 Tim. 6:2), even though the masters *according to the flesh* (22) are not their spiritual lords. In other words, the slaves' higher relationship to the Lord does not absolve them of their responsibilities in their outward relationship to their earthly masters. Equal status in Christ does not give the slave license to disregard the direction of his master. On the contrary, it should heighten one's sense of responsibility and underscore one's duty to be obedient and faithful.

b. Paul insists that the slave be conscientious in his work. He thinks that other things being equal, a Christian slave should be a better and more efficient slave than a non-Christian one. He will not be guilty of *eyeservice,* or "eye-bondage." The modern counterpart of this kind of bond servant is the office or factory employee who is a clock-watcher or one who works diligently only when the boss is watching. The Christian employee will not display a show of eagerness while allowing a grudge or bitter spirit to develop toward the company or employer. Rather, he will perform his work *heartily,* that is, cheerfully and with all his heart.

c. The motivation for this kind of attitude toward master and work grows out of one's relationship to the Lord—*fearing God;* and out of the fact that whatever one does is *as to the Lord, and not unto men* (23). This spirit is to prevail even if the master is not Christian. Should injustice occur, the Christian slave is to leave the question of reward to the Lord. While the slave was not allowed to possess property, Paul is promising nothing less than *the reward of the inheritance* (24) of God. That is, the time will come when the accounts will be adjusted. Ultimately evil will be punished and faithfulness rewarded—the faithful steward will be paid in full. In the meantime, the slave is to remember that his true Master whom he serves is *the Lord Christ.*

In short, the relationship of slave to master is to come under the Lordship of Christ. If the master is unjust, the slave must remember that with God there is no partiality and the Lord will repay. Whatever the workman does, he does for Christ. He does not work primarily for pay, for ambition or promotion, or even to satisfy an earthly employer. He works so as to take every task and responsibility so he can offer them up to God as a sacrifice. It is this motivation which alone gives meaning to the otherwise menial and mundane tasks of the working world.

2. *Masters to Slaves* (4:1). Here is a wrong chapter division. The new chapter should begin with 4:2, rather than 4:1. Paul's strong words condemn all disregard of human rights and an unmerciful exploitation of oppressed humanity for selfish purposes: "Masters, provide your slaves with what is right and fair, because you know that you also have a Master in heaven" (1, NIV). The word translated *equal (isotēta)* literally signifies "equality," but here it seems to mean "equity" or "fairness" (Earle).

a. As slaves are to give obedience to their masters, the masters are to return justice to the slaves. The word translated *give (parechesthe)* carries the idea of "reciprocation" and suggests a responsibility on the part of the masters. "Grant" (NASB), or perhaps "treat" (Moffatt, NBV, RSV) is more exact than *give*. This obligation involves not only fairness of treatment but also a just remuneration.

b. Paul states that the Christian master is to treat a slave as a brother in Christ, remembering that he himself has *a Master in heaven.* The masters, just like slaves, are answerable to God. Both have a "heavenly Employer" (Phillips). Therefore even the master acknowledges that the business belongs to God, though he has been charged to operate it. The master is a steward and is accountable to God for his stewardship in dealing fairly with slaves or employees. Both master and slave work for God and are His servants. Their duty is lifted into obedience to God, and "obedience to Him, utter and absolute, is dignity and freedom" (Maclaren).

In Difficult Circumstances

Colossians 4:2-4

2 Continue in prayer, and watch in the same with thanksgiving;
3 Withal praying also for us, that God would open unto us a door of utterance, to speak the mystery of Christ, for which I am also in bonds:
4 That I may make it manifest, as I ought to speak.

As he nears the close of his Epistle, Paul underscores several practices which are important for developing the life in Christ. Here, as in most every one of his Epistles, he admonishes his readers to pray. His exhortations deal with the inner attitudes of the believer in verses 2-4 before he moves on to the outward activities which are open to public view. He seems to assume that many things can be done after prayer, but nothing can be done until first one has prayed.

1. *Vigilance and Thanksgiving in Prayer* (2)

a. The Apostle urges his readers to *continue in prayer* (see Rom. 12:12; 1 Thess. 5:17). Perseverance, steadfastness, unweariness in prayer are virtues to be developed and cultivated. Perseverance in prayer saves from spiritual death and is the secret of spiritual power. But lest continuance in prayer produce "listlessness" (Lightfoot), Paul admonishes the Colossians to *watch,* to be alert, to bring wandering thoughts into captivity to Christ (2 Cor. 10:3-5). The mind must remain engaged in prayer lest it become a mere empty form. In Eph. 6:18-20 we are told that prayer is part of the armor supplied by God. Only steadfastness in prayer will ensure steadfastness in faith (2:4-5).

b. Further, thanksgiving permeates true prayer. Repeatedly in his Epistles the Apostle highlights the habit of giving thanks (see Phil. 4:6; Col. 1:3). Our prayers must be saturated by a spirit of gratitude. Clearly, thanksgiving is the proper spirit in which prayer is to be offered. As joy characterizes Philippians, thanksgiving is a hallmark of Colossians. This reference to thanksgiving is the second one in this letter and indicates the importance of gratitude. R. E. O. White has said: "Private prayer, however persevering, is impoverished if it descends to endless asking for things, forgetting *thanksgiving.*"

Paul seems never to have been without his "garment of praise" (Isa. 61:3). Colossians continuously expresses the music of gratitude—see 1:3, 12; 3:17; 4:2. The Apostle's imperative, *be ye thankful* (3:15), seems to indicate that gratitude is not a luxury of the Christian spirit but rather is a part of the Christian's obligation. True gratitude cannot be produced by man; it is more than a fleeting emotion occasioned by prosperity or favorable circumstance. Instead, it is "through Christ"—*by him* (3:17). Yet gratitude can be nurtured and cultivated by the believer. Verse 15 of chapter 3 may be translated, "Become ye thankful." In 2:7 Paul speaks of *abounding . . . with thanksgiving.* Phillips renders the verse like this: "Yes, be rooted in him and founded upon him, continually strengthened by the faith as you were taught it and your lives will overflow with joy and thankfulness." Clearly, gratitude is not dependent for its existence upon other circumstances; it is an "inner disposition towards life as a whole" (Rees).

2. *Unselfishness in Prayer* (3-4). Paul requests a special interest in the prayers of the Colossians. The phrase *for us* probably includes such companions as Timothy and Epaphras. The verse expresses the Apostle's belief in the efficacy of intercession. He knows prayer is the key to unlock closed doors (see Acts 14:27; 1 Cor. 16:9; 2 Cor. 2:12; Eph. 6:19-20).

One detects the restless spirit of Paul, much like an eagle in bondage. He is in prison. Though he had been given his own hired house and could welcome visits from his friends (Acts 28:30-31) and had used his bondage as an occasion for testimony and witness (Phil. 1:13), still he is a prisoner, unable to enter doors of opportunity as he once did (2 Cor. 2:13). Yet he does not ask the Colossians to pray for his release. He does not request prayer for his personal benefit, but for the advancement of the Kingdom—*that God would open unto us a door of utterance.*

Whatever the phrase may mean previously, Paul wants *to speak the mystery of Christ* (3). He wants to declare that the gospel is for all men everywhere, Jews and Gentiles alike. And for this burning desire and his view of the universality of the gospel, he is *in bonds.* It cost something for Paul to be the servant of Christ, but he found peace in being in the center of God's will. He is in prison for Christ's sake. As a consequence, though he is bound, he is nonetheless free—"chained, but . . . not contained" (McDonald). His only desire, which is the burden of every genuine preacher, is to be able to make the gospel *manifest,* completely clear. Release from prison, or a successful outcome to his coming trial, are not his top priorities. He wants prayer only that he might be given strength and opportunity to do the work God has called him to do.

Similarly, we should, as Phillips Brooks expressed it, pray not for tasks commensurate with our powers or abilities, but for powers commensurate with our tasks. Conquest, not release, is the keynote of the Christian life.

In an Unbelieving World

Colossians 4:5-6

> 5 Walk in wisdom toward them that are without, redeeming the time.
> 6 Let your speech be alway with grace, seasoned with salt, that ye may know how ye ought to answer every man.

These verses describe the ideal relationship of the believer to a secular and unbelieving society and to powers in that society. *Them that are without* refers to non-Christians, those outside the community of faith (see 1 Cor. 5:12-13; 1 Thess. 4:12; 1 Tim. 3:7). Believers, on the other hand, are "those within" (1 Cor. 5:12). The Colossians are reminded that they too were once on the outside. Those still "out there" are now watching the Colossians' lives—their walk and their talk. The idea is expressed by Paul graphically in 2 Cor. 3:2: "Ye are our epistle written in our hearts, known and read of all men." The daily life of Christians is the only Bible that some persons read.

1. One's conduct *(walk, peripateō)* is to be characterized by *wisdom,* common sense and practical insight. Further, the believer is to "buy up" the time (cf. Weymouth, ASV margin) and search for opportunities for doing good (see Gal. 6:10). Lightfoot puts it this way: "Letting no opportunity slip by

you, of saying and doing what may further the cause of God." The word translated *time (kairon)* means the "opportune time," the "appropriate time," or "the right moment." In most human needs there is a particular moment like no other moment when help is needed and will be received. Christians are to go into the marketplace and buy up the opportunities to minister to others. In Paul's day they had no church buildings, no New Testament as we have it, no gospel tracts or literature. The Christians had to commend their gospel by their lives. While we have these aids, we are still called upon to draw men to the gospel by the attraction of our conduct and the superior quality of our relationships.

2. The Christian's "talk" complements his "walk." Christian speech always is to display *grace (chariti).* Some have interpreted the term *grace* in the spiritual sense of an imparted gift. Eph. 4:29 refers to the Christian's talk which imparts "grace unto the hearers," that is, benefits the hearer. This may be the meaning here. Probably, however, Paul is suggesting that the Christian's conversation is to be gracious. Certainly, the Christian's talk even "about grace" is to be given "with grace."

Seasoned with salt further qualifies the believer's talk. It must be pleasing and winsome, but also courteous, wise, and with good sense. Charm and wit in speech can be achieved without resorting to off-color stories or suggestive innuendo. Jesus is our best example of commending His message with attraction. As salt is to preserve, flavor, and cleanse, so our speech should preserve the dignity and wonder of life; it should edify and build up rather than destroy; it should cleanse our environment and add a zest and flavor that brings out the best in people. The NEB gives the last of verse 6 strikingly: "Study how best to talk with each person you meet."

While more detailed exhortations might be given regarding our relation to the unbeliever, Paul has given sufficient examples to provide sound guidance for everyday Christian action.

In the Circle of Believers

Colossians 4:7-14

> 7 All my state shall Tychicus declare unto you, who is a beloved brother, and a faithful minister and fellowservant in the Lord:
> 8 Whom I have sent unto you for the same purpose, that he might know your estate, and comfort your hearts;
> 9 With Onesimus, a faithful and beloved brother, who is one of you. They shall make known unto you all things which are done here.
> 10 Aristarchus my fellowprisoner saluteth you, and Marcus, sister's son to Barnabas, (touching whom ye received commandments: if he come unto you, receive him;)
> 11 And Jesus, which is called Justus, who are of the circumcision. These only are my fellowworkers unto the kingdom of God, which have been a comfort unto me.
> 12 Epaphras, who is one of you, a servant of Christ, saluteth you, always labouring fervently for you in prayers, that ye may stand perfect and complete in all the will of God.
> 13 For I bear him record, that he hath a great zeal for you, and them that are in Laodicea, and them in Hierapolis.
> 14 Luke, the beloved physician, and Demas, greet you.

The remaining portion of the letter is concerned with personal matters of Paul. Where Paul is well known he seldom mentions individuals, possibly to avoid omitting anyone or of being accused of making invidious comparisons. Since he is unknown personally to the Colossians it is not inappropriate to acknowledge certain persons, heroes of the faith, with whom he has been working or had worked and who had contributed significantly to his ministry. With the possible exception of the last chapter of Romans, there is not a more fascinating galaxy of companions than this one in any of Paul's writings.

While the reader may be inclined to pass over these remarks as being less significant than the earlier teaching passages, there are valuable lessons here which may be seen only if we place ourselves in the position of the Colossians. In such a letter personal matters are not only fitting but would be eagerly received. The phrase *all my state* (7) must include such items of information as Paul's health, his general situation in prison, his hopes for a fair trial, and the prospects or lack of them for his soon acquittal and dismissal. Eph. 6:21 uses the same expression ("my affairs,"

ASV). In Paul's letter to the Philippians, he relates such matters for himself in the Epistle, whereas here he leaves those things to the bearer of the letter, Tychicus, to deliver orally. The Apostle was very close to the Philippians, however—unlike the Colossians; and further, his affairs in Philippi were directly related to the progress of the gospel in the Roman capital.

1. *Bearers of the Epistle* (7-9). If a man can be known by the friends he treasures, from those individuals we can learn a good deal about Paul. Tychicus and Onesimus were chosen to be the bearers of the letter to Colossae.

a. Tychicus hailed from the Roman province of Asia (Acts 20:4), possibly from Ephesus (2 Tim. 4:12). He was obviously a special friend whom the Apostle had come to trust over a period of time. He may have been the messenger who delivered the offering of the church to the fellow Christians of Jerusalem who were suffering from famine. Paul entrusted him with the responsibility of conveying the letter we know as the Epistle to the Ephesians to its various congregations and destinations (Eph. 6:21), including probably Laodicea. In addition, Tychicus was with Paul when the latter wrote to Titus in Crete before being sent to Crete (Titus 3:12); and evidently was with Paul again in Rome for the last time before being sent to Ephesus (2 Tim. 4:12).

Every reference to this friend seems to be that of a messenger. In this case Tychicus would provide additional information "that you may know how we are" (8, RSV—and not as the KJV has it). Paul describes him as *a beloved brother . . . a faithful minister and fellowservant in the Lord.* The Apostle's deep sense of calling attracted strong associates; and Tychicus' faithfulness indicates his willingness to stand in the background with little or no recognition. The term *minister (diakonos,* "deacon"), or "helper" (NEB) does not refer to the official office of deacon but to one who forwards the work. Tychicus seems to have been given the gift of helping. Therefore, says Paul, he will *comfort your hearts.* That is, he will "encourage" (many versions) the saints and instill within them courage to withstand the onslaught of the Gnostic heretics and to be faithful to the gospel of Christ. Paul uses here the verb form of the familiar word *paraklētos* (Paraclete), which in John's Gospel is used to refer to the Holy Spirit. As the Holy Spirit is the divine Comforter or Encourager, so Tychicus will be used of the Spirit to bring strength and encouragement from God to the Colossians. He would do the same for the Ephesians' church also which was in danger of losing its "first love" (Rev. 2:1, 4).

b. Onesimus accompanied Tychicus and delivered the Epistle to Philemon, who lived in Colossae and to whom Onesimus still belonged as a slave. Earlier, Onesimus, weary of his slave conditions, robbed his master and ran away from his owner. Through some providence he came to Rome and contacted Paul, who led him to Christ. Paul seizes this opportunity to send him back to his owner in Colossae.

However, the Apostle views him not merely as a slave, but as a brother in Christ. Onesimus means "useful," and in his letter to Philemon Paul makes a play on this name. Though he has become "useless" to Philemon, Onesimus has become "useful" to Paul, and can be useful again to Philemon (Philem. 11). Here Paul is not only revealing his own great spirit of forgiveness and acceptance, but is magnifying the grace of Christ which transforms individuals' lives and makes them new and fruitful.

Rather than referring to Onesimus as a "runaway slave," he calls him a *faithful and beloved brother* (9). Here is the Christian model of always putting others in the best light possible and highlighting the good things in their lives. To the Colossians Paul is commending Onesimus on a par with Tychicus—together they will bring reliable information concerning Paul's situation.

c. Thus these two messengers—Tychicus and Onesimus—are linked together with Paul's love as they travel across land and sea to Colossae with this bundle of letters—to the Colossians, to the Ephesians (circular letter), and to Philemon.

2. *Greetings for Other Believers* (10-14). Being a man of action, Paul drew others to himself and they became his co-laborers. Seldom was he alone as he was at Athens (Acts 17:15-16). Even in prison he seems always to have one or more of his associates with him. He enjoyed a circle of choice friends, and several of them are at his side as he writes Colossians. They wish him to send their greetings to the saints in Colossae.

a. Aristarchus had been with Paul in a variety of experiences. Acts indicates that he was a Macedonian (19:29; 27:2) from Thessalonica (20:4). He was with Paul in Ephesus and was captured by the mob when the people of Ephesus rioted in the Temple of Diana (19:29). He was present when Paul set sail from Caesarea as a prisoner for Rome (27:2), and may have volunteered to become a slave of the Apostle so he could make this last journey with him. If Aristarchus left Paul at Myra and went back home to Thessalonica (as Lightfoot thinks), nonetheless he came on later to Caesarea and to Rome when the Apostle needed him.

Paul refers to him as *my fellowprisoner* (10). The language probably is to be taken literally. It may be that after reaching Rome, Aristarchus was accounted guilty by association with the Apostle and was forced to share Paul's imprisonment. Or it may be that he volunteered to become a prisoner with Paul as a source of strength to his friend. From Philem. 23 which speaks of Epaphras as a "fellowprisoner" it has been inferred that Aristarchus and Epaphras may have alternated sharing quarters with the Apostle.[63] Whatever the case, Aristarchus clearly was one who had taken his stand with Paul for the sake of the gospel.

b. The mention of *Mark* would have been surprising to some. He is evidently the "John Mark" whose mother's house the Christians used in Jerusalem in the early days of the church (Acts 12:12, 25). The KJV refers to him as *sister's son to Barnabas* (i.e., nephew), but this reflects a later usage of the word after Paul's time. The term used *(anepsios)* probably should be translated "cousin."

Mark had accompanied Paul and Barnabas on their first missionary journey from Antioch but had deserted them at Perga and returned home (Acts 13:5, 13). When Barnabas wanted to take Mark again on their second missionary venture, Paul steadfastly refused. The dispute may have been heightened because of the blood relationship of Barnabas and Mark. Tension became so great that Paul and Barnabas separated, and thereafter there were two missionary teams instead of one—Paul and Silas, and Barnabas and John Mark.

Barnabas was one of the early converts to Christianity and even championed Paul in the Apostle's early career (Acts 9:27). He opened the door for Paul's ministry in the church at Antioch (11:22-26), and was with Paul on the journey to Jerusalem to relieve the fellow Christians who were suffering in Judea (29-30). In the debate about Gentile Christians in Galatia, Paul indicates that even Barnabas was "hypocritical" (Gal. 2:13, cf. NBV), although Barnabas had stood firmly with Paul at the Council of Jerusalem (Acts 15). Whether any of this colored Paul's views concerning John Mark is mere conjecture.

Whatever the tensions may have been, warm relations with Barnabas were restored (1 Cor. 9:6), and as time passed Mark redeemed himself. By the time of Paul's last imprisonment in Rome, Mark has become so useful for his ministry that the Apostle longs for him and Timothy to be with him (2 Tim. 4:11). Already Paul graciously commends Mark to the Colossians who evidently had come to think of him as one who had put his hand to the plow and turned back. He requests that the Colossians "make him welcome" (Phillips).

c. *Jesus, which is called Justus,* along with Aristarchus and Mark, had broken away from their adherence to the law, or the ceremonialism of the Judaizers, and insisted that the gospel was for Gentiles as well as Jews. Thus they are described by Paul as *my fellowworkers . . . which have been a comfort unto me* (11). From Philippians (1:15-20) we learn that later there were Jewish Christians in Rome who were not sympathetic to Paul and his views on the universality of the gospel. Opposition may have been developing at the time he is writing the Colossians. These three loyal figures gave strength and courage to the Apostle.

d. In addition to these three Jews, there were also several Gentiles by birth who were faithful to the imprisoned Apostle. Three of them send greetings to the Colossian church.

(1) *Epaphras* was the better known, for he was a Colossian. In fact, he was the founder of the church there, and probably established the Christian communities and was their overseer in the neighboring cities of Hierapolis and Laodicea. Now, years later, he has brought to Paul disturbing news from Colossae, which formed the burden of Paul's letter. Though he is not ready to leave Paul to return home, he is anxious to forward greetings.

Paul calls him a *servant of Christ* (12). His particular ministry was that of intercessory prayer. The term translated *labouring fervently* (the verb is *agōnizomai,* from which is derived *agonize*) is rendered "fight" in John 18:36, and describes an athlete who contends with others for the prize ("striveth," 1 Cor. 9:25). Epaphras is thus viewed as one who is "wrestling" in prayer (Weymouth) for the Colossians that they may not fall for the false teachings of the Gnostics.

The purpose of his prayer is that they may *stand perfect and complete in all the will of God. Perfect* (12) is rendered "mature" in several modern versions. This does not, however, lessen the need for precision of definition. The question still must be faced, In what sense is one to be mature? Paul Rees has an illuminating discussion of this issue. If all perfection, excepting God's, is relative, then it is possible that, for Paul, Christian maturity or perfection is a "stage on the way, an enterable and verifiable stage, in the same sense as puberty is a stage on the way to adulthood." The paradox —of perfection, yet not perfect; maturity, yet not mature; realized, yet not realized (seen in Phil. 3:12-14)—is confirmed in Eph. 4:12-15, "where the 'mature man,' he who has become the receiver of the 'fullness of Christ' is not the finished man, the end-product in character of all God's chastening and ripening." Rather, he is the believer "who is no longer among the 'children, tossed to and fro and carried about with every wind of doctrine.' It is after this, and beyond this, that the 'growing up' (v. 15) process goes on and on."

Clearly, Paul and Epaphras want the Colossians to be mature and *complete,* that is, "fully persuaded," or "fully assured" (many versions) in all the will of God. Any congregation is rich which has within it an intercessor like Epaphras.

(2) *Luke, the beloved physician,* was with Paul to the end (2 Tim. 4:11). It is interesting that both Mark and Luke, writers of two of the Gospels, are here with Paul at the same time. Perhaps both had already written their Gospels. Luke was a Greek, a man of refinement and culture. Greatly devoted to Paul, he was with the Apostle on parts of his second and third missionary journeys, on his perilous journey to Rome, and now is sharing Paul's imprisonment. He is the embodiment of fidelity.

(3) *Demas* is the only one mentioned for whom there is no word of commendation. In Philem. 24 he is classed with men who were Paul's "fellowlabourers." Here is simply Demas's name with no comment. Finally, in 2 Tim. 4:10 he is Demas who has "forsaken" Paul, "having loved this present world." Barclay has commented that here we have the "outlines of a study in degeneration, of the loss of enthusiasm and ideals, of failure in the faith." In contrast to Luke, Demas has become a synonym for disloyalty and moral breakdown.

Final Instructions
Colossians 4:15-17

15 Salute the brethren which are in Laodicea, and Nymphas, and the church which is in his house.
16 And when this epistle is read among you, cause that it be read also in the church of the Laodiceans; and that ye likewise read the epistle from Laodicea.
17 And say to Archippus, Take heed to the ministry which thou hast received in the Lord, that thou fulfil it.

The text is difficult, and it is not certain whether *Nymphas* is male or female, though probably the latter. Whichever, this person's home was the center of worship as was the custom until approximately the third century (see Acts 12:12; 16:40; Rom. 16:5; 1 Cor. 16:19; Philem. 2). Until that time church and home were virtually the same.

The letter to the Colossians evidently was meant to be read in the public assembly. Then it was to be sent, or probably a copy of it made and sent, to the church in Laodicea. We do not know what the "letter from Laodicea" was, but it did not originate from the congregation there. It may be a lost letter from Paul. There is an extant "Epistle to the Laodiceans," but Jerome called it a forgery in the fourth century. It is possible that the reference is to the letter to Philemon. The best assumption is that it was the letter we know as Ephesians. The phrase "in Ephesus" does not appear in Eph. 1:1 in some manuscripts, suggesting that it was an encyclical meant to be circulated among all the churches of Asia. It may have been that this encyclical had reached Laodicea and was now on the way to Colossae.

A special communication is reserved for Archippus. His name is linked with Philemon and Apphia (Philem. 2), leading some to speculate that he was their son. Since Paul does not address him directly, however, it may be that he was associated with the church at Laodicea, which from a later reference we know to be a lukewarm, complacent church (Rev. 3:14-17). If he lived at Laodicea, the church there evidently had given him some special task—perhaps a charge to the ministry. Thus Paul admonishes: "Keep your eye on your ministry, and keep filling it full." He reminds Archippus that the source of his effectiveness is God from whom his ministry has been *received.* Paul later gave a similar charge to Timothy: "Fulfil thy ministry" (2 Tim. 4:5, ASV).

Grace: The Last Word

Colossians 4:18

18 The salutation by the hand of me Paul. Remember my bonds. Grace be with you. Amen.

Paul ceases dictating words and takes the pen in his own hand, asking his friends to remember his *bonds*. Alford's comments are moving: "When we read of 'his chains' we should not forget that they moved over the paper as he wrote [his signature]. His hand was chained to the soldier that kept him." His chains "are his claims to authority; . . . the guarantees of his right to speak" (Barclay).

The wounds he bore for Christ's sake. Like Mr. Valiant-for-Truth, Paul is saying: "My marks and scars I carry with me to be my witness to Him who will soon be my Rewarder."

Amy Carmichael has captured the thought in verse:

> *No wound? No scar?*
> *Yet, as the Master, shall the servant be,*
> *And pierced are the feet that follow Me;*
> *But thine are whole! Can he have followed far*
> *Who has no wound, nor scar?*

"Oh, to be like Thee"—scars and all.

Grace. The letter started with grace and ends there. Paul has moved full circle. Only grace can bring us into captivity to the gospel and make Jesus truly Lord of all.

The Epistle to
PHILEMON

Introduction

Authorship and Date

That Paul is the author of Philemon is virtually unquestioned. Belonging to the collected Epistles of Paul from the time the collection was first made and published, it has early attestation. It was unanimously accepted as Paul's in ancient times, and no reputable modern scholar doubts its authenticity.

The internal evidence also is overwhelming. The vocabulary and style are consistent with those of Romans, Corinthians, Galatians, and Philippians. There can be little, if any, doubt that Philemon and Colossians were written by the same author. If the latter is by Paul, as we believe (see Colossians), then the authenticity of Philemon necessarily follows. Most would agree with Ernest Renan's comment that "few pages have so clear an accent of truth; Paul alone, it would seem, could have written this little masterpiece." John Knox, in *The Interpreter's Bible,* has said, "The letter [to Philemon] brings us a dramatic moment in the life of Paul which no later writer would have had either the skill or the motive to invent."

In the introductions to Philippians and Colossians in this volume, it is stated that Paul was most probably in Rome when he wrote these Prison Epistles. There are evidences that Philemon was written at approximately the same time as Colossians. For example, since Onesimus returned to Colossae with Tychicus, the bearer of Colossians (Col. 4:7-9), and since the same associates are mentioned in both Colossians and Philemon, we may assume that Philemon is to be dated like Colossians. If so, this little letter is one of the Apostle's last Epistles, and may be dated in the summer of A.D. 62, or perhaps earlier.

Occasion and Purposes of the Letter

The letter is addressed to Philemon, who was a wealthy householder and apparently a respected member of the church at Colossae. He appears to have been led to Christ through the influence of Paul, and came to use his wealth to advance the Christian cause. Onesimus, one of his slaves, illegally absconded and in time came in contact with Paul, who directed him to faith and new life in Christ. The Apostle and he formed a warm friendship, and the latter ministered to Paul in fruitful ways. However, Paul could not, and would not, indefinitely harbor a fugitive slave. The issue could have been brought to a climax by some event, possibly the coming of Epaphras from Colossae. Epaphras may have recognized Onesimus or persuaded him to tell the full story. For the Apostle the only right course was for Onesimus to give himself up to his master. Thus Paul writes his friend, Philemon, to receive back the slave who had betrayed him, not as a slave, but as a Christian brother.

Onesimus was returning to his Christian master under the protective care of Tychicus, whom Paul was sending to Colossae with the Epistle to that church. The letter to Philemon was sent with Tychicus and Onesimus on their joint journey to Colossae. Whether one or both delivered the letter is not indicated. It is probable that Tychicus, in personally delivering Onesimus to Philemon, would also present Philemon with this appeal from the apostle Paul.

The purpose of the letter is not only to assure a favorable reception for Onesimus; it is also to urge Philemon to return Onesimus to the Apostle that he may give himself to ministry. The first purpose is prominent; the second is a veiled suggestion.[1] The *more* spoken of in verse 21 may be that Philemon would return Onesimus to Paul. However, though Paul would like to have Onesimus back, he acknowledges Philemon's claim of ownership. Paul makes clear that he is aware of Roman and Greek law, which makes the father the financial guarantor for the debts of his child, and states that he will assume responsibility for Onesimus' debts to Philemon (cf. 18-19).

Characteristics and Significance of the Epistle

Philemon may be "the first anti-slavery petition ever penned"[2] and is certainly one of the most skillful letters ever written. In addition to these considerations, several factors make this letter distinctive, if not unique, among all the letters of the Apostle.

1. It is the only one of Paul's letters which is addressed to a particular person. The Apostle may have written numerous such memos, but this is the only one which has been preserved. The letter contains no statement of Christian doctrine and no general exhortation regarding Christian conduct. Because of this, some early writers objected to its canonicity on the ground of its subject being beneath an apostle to write about. Jerome argued for it against them. His position is sound, for the brief letter is an invaluable object lesson in applied Christianity.

2. Philemon possesses an unparalleled beauty of expression and is a classic example of Christian courtesy. It has been called the "polite Epistle." Speaking of "the incomparable delicacy of this letter," Alexander Maclaren remarks, "I do not know that anywhere else in literature one can find such a gem, so admirably adapted for the purpose in hand."[3] In style the Epistle to Philemon is simple and charming. It is characterized by directness, yet reveals a rare sensitivity. A purely personal letter, it breathes the spirit of love and brotherhood. Of it Erasmus said: "Cicero never wrote with greater elegance."

3. The Epistle is an incomparable model of spiritual counsel, tact, and love. It is Paul's briefest and most personal letter, concerned solely with a specific problem in personal relationships. Nonetheless, it is not a private communication. It is distinctly a church Epistle as seen in the opening paragraph (1-3), and the church is still in view at the close of the letter where the final benediction uses the plural form of the personal pronoun. In the Body of Christ, there may be personal matters, but not private or individual ones. New life in Christ is both personal and communal.

What affects one member affects the whole body (cf. 1 Cor. 12:12-27). Thus Paul sandwiches personal address between greetings to the congregation.

4. Philemon is the only Epistle in which Paul describes himself as a *prisoner* (1, 9, 23). This reference to himself, in lieu of the designation "Apostle," avoids calling attention to his apostolic authority to which he refuses to appeal because of the personal character of the letter.

5. "The importance of this brief letter to Philemon lies in the fundamental principle it enunciates concerning the rights and relationships between one man and another. And it raises the inevitable question of the New Testament attitude to slavery" (H. Dermot McDonald). Philemon gives a practical illustration of Paul's view on slavery as expressed in 1 Cor. 7:20-24 and Col. 3:22—4:1. Paul did not challenge the social and legal order. He knew that the Christian faith binds men together as brothers across barriers of class. He expected the runaway slave to return to his master, and expected the master to extend a forgiving reception to the *brother beloved* (16).

The Apostle has been criticized for not attacking the institution of slavery itself. However, he exercises great wisdom in approaching pervasive social evil. To have attacked the institution of slavery itself would have been useless. Paul knows that bringing slavery into contact with Christian faith ultimately is to kill slavery. "History vindicated this approach in the Roman Empire, for under Constantine the effects of Christian teaching and ethics appeared in the church and in legislation concerning slaves" (Vincent). "This letter is a seed that finally split the rock of slavery" (Geo. Buttrick, *The Interpreter's Bible*).

In order to appreciate the strategy of the Apostle, one must understand the social situation of his time. The economy of the Roman Empire was sustained on slavery. All forms of manual labor were viewed as inappropriate for a citizen and were performed by slaves. Tasks ranged from work in the mines, the galleys, and the cattle sheds, to artisans, bookkeepers, and even doctors, teachers, musicians, and artists. The social and economic structure of the city of Rome required that one-third (approximately 600,000 persons) of its population be enslaved. "These hundreds of thousands of persons were subject not only to social barriers but to severe legal limitations: by Roman law, and in the common view, slaves were accorded no recognized existence in Roman society. They were not persons but chattels, possessing neither rights nor legal recourse against harsh and brutal treatment."[4]

Obviously, many of the early Christian converts were slaves, as was Onesimus; and others owned slaves, as did Philemon. Thus Paul was compelled to give the Christian position on slavery. Two important passages aside from Philemon summarize what he says on this issue:

a. 1 Cor. 7:20-24 (written about A.D. 55). Here Paul does not challenge the institution of slavery but deals with the situation as it then existed. Every Christian can and must serve God in his or her social setting or circumstance. External circumstances are secondary, though not unimportant.

b. Col. 3:22—4:1 (written several years after Corinthians and approximately the same time as Philemon). A contrast is drawn between earthly masters whom slaves must obey and Jesus Christ, the Divine Master of both slaves and their owners. Slaves are admonished to obey their masters, and masters are reminded of their accountability to a higher authority for treatment of their slaves. Nearly twice the amount of space (74 words) is given to the relationship of masters and slaves than to that of free members of the household (42 words). When Paul wrote Colossians, including this passage, he also was dealing with the question of how to handle the runaway slave, Onesimus, and his master, Philemon.

The legal questions Paul was struggling with are not totally clear, but we know penalties for civil transgressions were severe. Tracking fugitive slaves was a trade, and if a runaway slave were captured, the master could inflict almost any punishment he chose. Frequently, the recovered slave would be branded on the forehead, and sometimes was put to death by crucifixion. If Philemon were a Roman citizen, the *lex Fabia* provided a penalty of 50,000 sesterces to be paid to him, the owner, by anyone who concealed the runaway slave. Further, wages or services owed for the period of the slave's absence could also be demanded.

Whatever the circumstances, Paul decided to send Onesimus home, in spite of the fact that Onesimus, having become a Christian, had become quite useful to him. Thus in the company of Tychicus, who bore the letters to the churches at Colossae and Laodicea and to Philemon, Onesimus returned to the Lycus Valley (Col. 4:8-10).

6. Philemon is significant because of what it reveals about the great Apostle. It indicates Paul's willingness to become involved in the lives of individuals as well as churches. The fact that Onesimus had a Christian master raised the larger issue of the proper Christian response to the question of slavery and life in Christ. For Paul, whatever happens to Onesimus is to be decided *in the Lord* (15-16, 20). The new relationship with Christ shatters all traditional understandings of the relationship between master and slave. Because Onesimus is now a Christian, Philemon is to recognize him as a brother in his own family, the family of Christ. Thus Paul challenges the master's right of ownership over his slave (14). Here is a subtle, but pointed, condemnation of slavery itself. Consequently, Paul, believing regeneration to be better than revolution, cut deeply into the social fabric which depended largely upon slavery.[5]

7. Finally, the Epistle to Philemon is significant because it testifies to the transforming grace of Jesus Christ. There is a divine power in the gospel to redeem wasted lives and to bring rebellious persons under the dominance of unselfish love. That Onesimus' conversion was genuine may be assumed from the fact that he voluntarily faced the fate of a runaway slave.

Whether Paul's requests were complied with we cannot be certain. However, the fact that the letter has been preserved provides strong reason to believe they were. It is fascinating to observe that one of the Epistles of Ignatius, written near the beginning of the second century, says that the bishop of the church at Ephesus at the time was one named Onesimus. Ignatius, bishop of Antioch in Syria, had been arrested and was being taken to Rome for execution. On their journey he and those with him stopped in Smyrna, a city of Asia, and were visited by Onesimus, the bishop of Ephesus (cf. Ignatius' *Letter to the Ephesians*, 1:3; 2:1; 6:1). In this letter there are numerous reminiscences of Philemon. Ignatius seems to be thinking about Paul's letter to Philemon as he writes to Bishop Onesimus and the Ephesian church. Paul's Onesimus would not have been too old to be bishop of Ephesus when Ignatius passed through Asia.

If Onesimus were bishop of Ephesus about A.D. 110, there is no reason to suppose that he did not hold the same office a score of years earlier, when a collection of Paul's letters was published there. Indeed, the publication was probably done with his oversight. With the publication of these Pauline letters, the history of the New Testament as a fixed collection of books properly begins, for a half century later Marcion appropriated this corpus. It was this move which gave the impulse toward the formation of the New Testament as a second and formalized canon.

We cannot be certain if Paul's Onesimus is the same mentioned by Ignatius, but if so, "then here is one of the great romances of grace of the early Church" (Barclay). If they are the same, then this brief and sometimes ignored Epistle "may well be from the standpoint of the history of the canon the most significant single book in the New Testament—the living link between the Pauline career and the Pauline tradition, between the letters of Paul and the New Testament of the church" (John Knox). Paul insisted that Onesimus had become "useful" to him (many versions). He could not have dreamed how much so!

And who can begin to imagine the overwhelming power of the gospel of Christ to transform human personality, and through it society itself.

Topical Outline of Philemon

Salutation (vv. 1-3)

The Past: Thanksgiving (vv. 4-7)

The Purpose: A Far-reaching Request (vv. 8-14)

The Prospect: A Hopeful Expectation (vv. 15-21)

Closing Words and Benediction (vv. 22-25)

Salutation

Philemon 1-3

PHILEMON

Philemon 1-3

> 1 Paul, a prisoner of Jesus Christ, and Timothy our brother, unto Philemon
> our dearly beloved, and fellowlabourer,
> 2 And to our beloved Apphia, and Archippus our fellowsoldier, and to the
> church in thy house:
> 3 Grace to you, and peace, from God our Father and the Lord Jesus Christ.

The Writer: Paul (1)

1. Following the custom of his day, Paul begins with his own name. His salutation here is the same as in Gal. 1:3; Eph. 1:2; and Col. 4:17 except for one significant difference. Normally he describes himself as "an apostle of Christ Jesus," indicating his position and authority. On occasion he refers to himself as a "servant of Jesus Christ." However, in this very personal letter, he painstakingly avoids any allusion to his official authority and speaks of himself as *a prisoner of Jesus Christ.*

In pleading for mercy for the bondsman Onesimus, he points to his own bonds. At least six times in this short memo Paul speaks of his imprisonment (1, 9, 10, 13, 22, 23). Paul does not want Philemon to obey slavishly a command, but rather to follow the dictates of Christian brotherhood. Reference to his own imprisonment should motivate Philemon to the proper Christian action. "How could Philemon resist an appeal which was penned within prison walls and by a manacled hand?" (Lightfoot).

Yet Paul is not seeking to arouse sympathy; he is describing his relationship to Jesus Christ. He is not simply a prisoner of the Roman Emperor Nero. His imprisonment is not because of some inadvertent action or crime against the state, but because of his loyalty and service to "Christ Jesus" (the best manuscripts give this order). The Apostle is clearly acknowledging the divine activity even in the unpleasant circumstances of life. His eyes of faith enable him to see beyond his bound wrists to a higher authority who will use these conditions for the accomplishing of His purposes. Ralph Earle puts it graphically: "Paul was bound to Christ as His prisoner. That made him actually a free man in the Roman prison" *(Word Meanings in the New Testament)*. Though he is Christ's imprisoned man, he knows himself to be free (cf. Rom. 6:18; 8:2; Gal. 5:1).

2. The reference to *Timothy our brother* (lit., "the brother") suggests that Timothy stands in agreement with Paul on the question which occasioned the letter. Certainly he was a great comfort to Paul in his late years of suffering. Being with Paul during a large part of his three years' residence at Ephesus, Timothy probably became acquainted with Philemon at that time. Following this reference to him, Timothy disappears from the letter, and Paul speaks only in the first person singular. Thus it is Paul himself who is making the appeal to Philemon.

The Persons Addressed (2)

1. Though several persons are mentioned, the letter is directed primarily to Philemon. The second person plural pronoun, used in the greeting (3), does not occur again until the conclusion (22, 25). The second person singular pronoun, referring directly to Philemon, occurs no less than 20 times in this brief letter. Twice Paul addresses him as *brother* (7, 20). John Knox recently has claimed that Archippus is the

master who owned Onesimus and that Philemon resided in Laodicea; but the traditional view is more convincing. Col. 4:9 states that Onesimus belongs to Colossae and is returning there. In Philemon (12) Paul informs Philemon that he is sending Onesimus back to him. Thus it seems clear that Philemon made his home in Colossae.

Verse 19 suggests that Philemon was a convert of Paul. Since Paul had not labored at Colossae, it is likely that Philemon was converted during the Apostle's protracted stay at Ephesus (Acts 19:10). It appears that Philemon was a man of some financial means since he provided a home for Christian worship and had generously contributed to the needs of others even at a distance (5-7). Paul refers to him as *fellowlabourer,* not necessarily meaning he was an official in the church at Colossae, but rather had worked in the same cause so dear to Paul.

2. It is not known who Apphia and Archippus were, though it is usually surmised without evidence that they are Philemon's wife and son. The position of Apphia's name between that of two active Christians does suggest a close relation to Philemon; otherwise her name would have been placed after that of Archippus. "Our sister Apphia," rather than *our beloved Apphia,* is supported by a majority of ancient authorities and suits the context best. It has been suggested that Apphia is Philemon's sister. More likely she was "our sister" in the same sense that Timothy was "our brother" in the family of faith.

Whether Archippus was a friend, or teacher in the household, a brother or son of Philemon, all of which have been suggested, he evidently was involved in some kind of ministry. From Col. 4:17 it has been assumed that he ministered at Laodicea. However, the reference here places him in Colossae. The proximity of the cities would make it possible for him to minister at both places. It may be that the departure of Epaphras to Rome may have left Archippus in charge of the work in the Lycus Valley. As a *fellowsoldier* and follower of Christ he was under orders and under discipline.

This designation is given to only one other person in the New Testament, Epaphroditus (Phil. 2:25). It has been suggested that Archippus took the lead against the Judaizers in Colossae during the absence of Epaphras and was the overseer of the church there (Col. 4:16-17).

3. The address, *to the church in thy house,* may have saved this letter from the fate of most personal notes and led to its being kept by the Christian community. It was not until the third century that there were church buildings. Prior to that time the congregation met in some large room in the house of a wealthy member. Assuming that Philemon and Apphia were husband and wife and that the home belonged to them, we have a beautiful view of what a Christian home should be—totally consecrated to the Lordship and service of Christ.

It is this appeal to the church which keeps this letter from being purely a private letter. Since it is addressed to a church as well as to several individuals (only one of whom owned the slave), it is in a real sense a church letter, as already suggested. The indication is that the request is to be considered not only by an individual, but by the entire Christian community. Paul's appeal was not made in secret. From this we may infer that there is value in the corporate judgment of the body of believers, and that individual judgment must be subject to that of the whole body.

The Spiritual Greeting (3)

This is the normal Pauline greeting found in his other writings and has been discussed earlier (see Philippians and Colossians). It may be viewed as a prayer or as a promise. In either case it applies to all who have been mentioned, for the *you* is in the plural. Paul's words are far more than a mere conventional greeting. They embody a spiritual quality, for they refer to God's *grace,* God's unmerited favor, and to the resulting *peace* which follows. The significance of this greeting is that it "lifts at once this whole affair [of the relation of Philemon and Onesimus] into the very presence of God and sanctifies it with the name of the Lord."[6] Thus the sacramental character of daily, moral decision making is underscored. The Source of *grace* and *peace—God our Father and the Lord Jesus Christ*—would be available to Philemon and the church at Colossae in dealing justly and lovingly with the problem surrounding the runaway, but now reborn, Onesimus.

The Past: Thanksgiving

Philemon 4-7

Philemon 4-7

4 I thank my God, making mention of thee always in my prayers,
5 Hearing of thy love and faith, which thou hast toward the Lord Jesus, and toward all saints;
6 That the communication of thy faith may become effectual by the acknowledging of every good thing which is in you in Christ Jesus.
7 For we have great joy and consolation in thy love, because the bowels of the saints are refreshed by thee, brother.

Paul shows considerable tact in not immediately forming the request which is the occasion for the letter. Rather, he begins the core of his communication with a genuine expression of his high esteem for Philemon. However, this is not merely a calculated strategy. In almost all of his letters following the greeting he includes a paragraph of thanksgiving and prayer. The exceptions to this rule are 2 Corinthians and Galatians, in both of which he deals with severe problems in the churches. Clearly his normal practice suggests a habitual devoutness of spirit. Gratitude and praise should be standard qualities of every Christian.

1. Specifically, Paul is grateful for Philemon (4). The Greek makes clear that one person is meant. *Thee* ("you") points back to Philemon. Paul cannot lay his needs before God without also expressing gratitude and thanksgiving for his friend. The Apostle seems to have lifted everything which came into his life up to God in thanksgiving and prayer. His words *I thank my God* reflect the vital personal relationship he maintains with his Heavenly Father. God was the most significant reality in his life, and to Him he turned in both good times and bad. Paul's thanksgiving was not a one-time affair but a continuous attitude, as indicated by the use of the present tense of the verb and by the word *always*.

2. The cause of Paul's thanksgiving is the good reports he has heard concerning Philemon (5-6). These may have been received from Epaphras, now with Paul at Rome (23; Col. 1:7-8). Paul expresses appreciation for his fellow believer's positive influence before stating his request. In speaking of Philemon's *love and faith* (5), Paul is preparing to appeal to that same love in interceding for Onesimus. Likewise the phrase *the communication of thy faith* (6), that is, the active sympathy and charity growing out of your faith, serves the same purpose. This idea recognizes that the theological order is first faith, then love, the fruit of faith. The word *communication (koinōnia)* may be rendered "sharing" (many versions) or "partnership" and anticipates the request that Paul may be treated as a *partner (koinōnon,* 17).

The Greek text of verse 6 is difficult and the meaning is obscure. Whether Paul wrote *in you* or "in us" is debated, but the latter is supported by the oldest manuscripts and is preferred. While fine points may be debated, the RSV helps clarify the meaning with the translation: "I pray that the sharing of your faith may promote the knowledge of all the good that is ours in Christ." Paul is sensitive and responsive to the love and brotherhood of Christians. He receives comfort in witnessing and experiencing this fellowship.

Effectual (energēs) is used only in the New Testament of superhuman powers, good and evil (see Eph. 1:19; Matt. 14:2;

Phil. 2:13; 1 Cor. 12:10; Heb. 4:12). Thus Paul has in mind a divine work or result of sharing. *The acknowledging* means "through the recognition of" or "through coming to know," leading Vincent to give the meaning of verse 6 thus: "He that gives for Christ's sake becomes enriched in the knowledge of Christ."

Verse 7 expresses Paul's joy because of Philemon's ministry to the saints who have been refreshed in their "hearts" (cf. Phil. 1:8 for a discussion of *splanchnois, bowels*) because he has opened his home to them and in other ways served them. Clearly Philemon was generous in his help to the poor saints. Philemon's love was not directed to Paul personally but to others. But Paul rejoices that others, rather than himself, are the recipients (cf. 2 Cor. 7:4, 7).

3. It is noteworthy that Paul, still preparing for his request regarding Onesimus, ends verse 7 with the emphatic word *brother* ("my brother," many versions) in order to evoke favorable attention to the request which will follow. Philemon is a brother to Paul as is Timothy (1). Later Paul will say that Onesimus is now to the Apostle *a brother beloved* (16). Paul hopes and believes that Philemon will follow this connection and also will accept Onesimus as a "brother" in Christ.

Frequently it is observed that verses 4-7 include a number of words which reappear with effect in verses which follow (cf. RSV): *love (agapē)* in verse 5, which is also in verse 9 *(for love's sake)* and in verse 16 *(a brother beloved); prayers (proseuchōn)* in verse 4 and again in verse 22; *fellowship* or "partnership" *(koinōnia)* in verses 6 and 17; *the good,* verses 6 and 14; *heart(s)* in verses 7, 12, and 20; and *brother,* verses 7 and 20.

This expression of thanksgiving and prayer occasioned by the reported kindness of Philemon forms a warm atmosphere in which to bring the request which immediately follows and which forms the main body of the letter. However, as George Buttrick reminds us, "The thanksgiving does not become insincere because Paul uses it as entrance for the request he is about to make. Common thanksgiving is the proper climate for any worthy plea." Since Philemon is and has been so kind and generous, surely he will show one further deed of Christian love by receiving Onesimus as a "brother."

The Purpose: A Far-reaching Request

Philemon 8-14

Philemon 8-14

> 8 Wherefore, though I might be much bold in Christ to enjoin thee that which is convenient,
> 9 Yet for love's sake I rather beseech thee, being such an one as Paul the aged, and now also a prisoner of Jesus Christ.
> 10 I beseech thee for my son Onesimus, whom I have begotten in my bonds:
> 11 Which in time past was to thee unprofitable, but now profitable to thee and to me:
> 12 Whom I have sent again: thou therefore receive him, that is, mine own bowels:
> 13 Whom I would have retained with me, that in thy stead he might have ministered unto me in the bonds of the gospel:
> 14 But without thy mind would I do nothing; that thy benefit should not be as it were of necessity, but willingly.

Though Paul has arrived at the main purpose for his writing, he even yet approaches his request with delicacy and tact. He does not pointedly state his desire all at once, but weighs every word and gradually makes his plea for the runaway slave. He carefully prepares the ground to assure a favorable response to his appeal.

1. His method is to beseech, rather than to command (8-9). He will not appeal on the basis of his apostolic authority or as an ambassador for Christ, but will adopt the way of persuasion. The word *enjoin* translates too weakly the word *epitassō*, which means "order, command"; the verb *anēkō*,

translated *is convenient,* means "be fitting, or proper." Thus Paul is saying that though he has authority to order that which should be done, he pleads as the prisoner of Jesus Christ that *for love's sake* the right or appropriate action will be taken. The warm reception of Onesimus will be a "becoming" thing to grant. *Wherefore* (8) refers back to verse 7 and suggests that Philemon's active love assures Paul that his appeal will receive a favorable response. The Apostle and Philemon were bound by a common relationship to Christ, and evidently also enjoyed an intimate friendship with each other.

2. Adopting the position of the intercessor, Paul first pleads his own condition and makes two points: his age and his imprisonment (9). The word translated *aged* is *presbutēs.* By the addition of one letter, *presbeutēs,* the word becomes "ambassador." Because of this and also Paul's actual age, which by today's standards is not old, some prefer the latter translation. However, this does not seem appropriate to a private letter and does not fit Paul's attitude of entreaty. Further, as Barclay points out, Hippocrates, the Greek medical writer, says that a man is *presbutēs* (that is, "senior"), from the age of 49 to the age of 56. Thereafter one becomes an "old man" *(gerōn).* The years 56-60 would fit this period in Paul's life. Thus *aged* is preferred. This appeal to his age is not inconsistent with the fact that Philemon, if he were the father of Archippus, could himself not be much younger. Paul must have been around 60 years old at this time, but prematurely aged by labor, hardship, and physical privations.

The further description of himself as *now also a prisoner of Jesus Christ* would make an even stronger appeal to Philemon. The man who had led Philemon to Christ was now in bondage because of his faith. Here was a reminder of the fact that "the weakness of age was aggravated by the helplessness of bonds" (Moule).

3. Whether Paul is pleading "for the sake of" Onesimus or "in the place of" Onesimus is unclear. Both meanings may

well be intended. In any case, Paul describes Onesimus as his own son, suggesting that while in prison, Paul was the means of leading him to Christ (10). As a result of his conversion, the formerly *unprofitable* slave (cf. Matt. 25:30, "unprofitable servant") has become true to his own name, which means "profitable" or "useful" (11, many versions). Paul obviously is making a play on words. Onesimus will be a better slave because he is a better man, a Christian. He is now more than a slave; he is a brother because of his union with the Lord, the Master in heaven. The Apostle is not affirming the universal brotherhood of man, regardless of one's relationship to Christ; but the universal brotherhood of Christians. Social differences must not separate Christians into distinct classes (Col. 3:11). Alexander Maclaren comments beautifully on the transforming power of the gospel: "Christianity knows nothing of hopeless cases. It professes its ability to take the most crooked stick and bring it straight, to flash a new power into the blackest carbon, which will turn it into a diamond" *(Expositor's Bible).*

4. Paul's next argument is filled with emotion, for he asserts that in sending Onesimus back he is sending a part of himself. Goodspeed renders verse 12 thus: "Now that I send him back to you, it is like sending my very heart." The Greek verb translated *sent again* means "sent up," and was used to indicate the reference of a case from a lower to a higher court. In four other times used in the New Testament it has this meaning (Luke 23:7, 11, 15; Acts 25:21). The inference is that now the request is for Philemon to resolve. Paul is referring the issue to the man legally qualified and responsible to settle it.

5. Paul acknowledges that he had desired to keep Onesimus with him (13). The use of the imperfect tense suggests that Paul not only wanted to retain Onesimus but had actually considered doing so. For a period he was torn between desire and duty. However, he thrust the temptation aside, refusing to tantalize his conscience, and chose not to have Onesimus'

assistance without Philemon's consent. He wants the decision to be the voluntary choice of the owner, and in accord with his own judgment (14). "Coercion does not validate, but violates the gospel."[7] Only Philemon could decide what love required of him regarding Onesimus and Paul. Furthermore, Paul does not want to violate Roman law by harboring a fugitive slave, and thereby possibly scandalize or reproach the Christian faith. Also he recognizes the importance of Onesimus returning to his master and making restitution for the wrong done to him.

The Prospect: A Hopeful Expectation

Philemon 15-21

Philemon 15-21

> 15 For perhaps he therefore departed for a season, that thou shouldest receive him for ever;
> 16 Not now as a servant, but above a servant, a brother beloved, specially to me, but how much more unto thee, both in the flesh, and in the Lord?
> 17 If thou count me therefore a partner, receive him as myself.
> 18 If he hath wronged thee, or oweth thee aught, put that on mine account;
> 19 I Paul have written it with mine own hand, I will repay it: albeit I do not say to thee how thou owest unto me even thine own self besides.
> 20 Yea, brother, let me have joy of thee in the Lord: refresh my bowels in the Lord.
> 21 Having confidence in thy obedience I wrote unto thee, knowing that thou wilt also do more than I say.

With his mind turned expectantly to Philemon's response, Paul even suggests that Onesimus' defection may have been providentially turned to something good, since he now returns as a brother instead of a slave (15-16). This was a daring argument, but was put with such grace that Philemon could hardly have resisted the idea. In fact, Paul introduces the suggestion of divine providence with a modest *perhaps.* The Apostle was aware that the providential purposes of God are veiled to men. All believers must be careful about claiming to know with certainty what God intends by such and such a thing. It is inappropriate to claim to have the "key to the cabinet of God's purposes" (Maclaren).

However, we may be certain that God does bring good out of evil. And in the case of Philemon and Onesimus, Christianity was transforming slave relationships from within. The separation was *for a season* (lit., "for an hour"). We do not know how long Onesimus had been gone, but in the light of eternity it was only briefly. And now Philemon can have him *for ever* as a brother. "The bond between the master and the slave would no longer be that of ownership by purchase which death would dissolve, but their common relation to Christ which made them brethren, now and evermore" (Vincent).

While Paul does not speak against the institution of slavery as such, he does deal radically with the moral and spiritual relationships. He does not say, "no longer a servant," but "no longer *as* a servant" (16, ASV). D. Edmond Hiebert has put it well: "He does not make a frontal attack on the human institution; rather he injects the dynamic of Christian love and allows it to transform the conditions of temporal servitude into a holy brotherhood. It was this principle which effected the eventual abolition of slavery as a legal institution."[8] Maxie D. Dunnam's comment is perceptive: "If this is not the outward and complete destruction of an oppressive order, the dynamite is planted, the fuse ignited, and the coming demolition sure. When slaves become brothers, the system has lost its control."[9]

2. Paul now is ready to formulate the request which was begun in verse 12, but was disrupted by other preparatory thoughts. Verse 17 completes the broken structure, but with one more powerful argument, namely, Philemon's regard for Paul himself. "So if you consider me your partner, receive him as you would receive me" (RSV). Paul is not thinking merely of their friendship, their common interests, or common work. He is referring to their "fellowship" *(koinōnia)* which is grounded in their belonging to the Lord, their com-

mon Master. It is upon Philemon's acceptance of this fellowship that Paul bases his appeal. Philemon's refusal of Paul's
request would be inconsistent with his acknowledgment of
this partnership.

3. So solicitous is Paul that Philemon will give a warm reception to Onesimus that he takes care to remove a last
hindrance by promising to assume any obligations which
Onesimus has to Philemon (18-19). Whether Onesimus was
guilty of theft, as well as flight from his master, is not
known. But if one or both, Paul will stand good for any
damage or loss entailed by Onesimus' absence of service. *I
Paul have written it with mine own hand* (19) may suggest
that Paul is writing the entire Epistle without dictation, or
that he takes pen in hand at this point of promise rather
than at the end of his writings as was his custom.

In verse 19 Paul deliberately protests against saying
anything about the debt which Philemon owes him while at
the same time mentioning it (a construction called a "para-
leipsis"). He implies that Philemon's debt to Paul might ex-
ceed that of Onesimus' debt to him. "To say nothing of your
owing me even your own self" (RSV) probably means that
Philemon was brought to Christ through the Apostle's
agency and thus was greatly indebted to the Apostle. Paul
assumes Onesimus' obligation in order to avoid bringing up
the large debt which Philemon owes him. It has been suggested that Paul's assuming the obligations of this slave, is
an appropriate picture of what Christ, on a higher plane, has
done for the entire human race. Thus Martin Luther in his
preface to this Epistle wrote: "What Christ has done for us
with God the Father, that St. Paul does for Onesimus with
Philemon. . . . For we are all his Onesimi, if we believe." For
Philemon to receive Onesimus would be, then, a godlike
deed.

4. The word *onaimēn (have joy)* in verse 20 is the verbal
form of "Onesimus" and evidently is a play on words. Thus
it has been rendered: "Yes, brother, I would like to make a

profit off thee in the Lord" (Lenski). Paul is not talking about material or personal gain for himself, but rather about the spiritual "benefit" accruing from it for the gospel. An act of forgiveness on Philemon's part will make the nature of the gospel better understood, all of which will *refresh* Paul's "heart" (ASV) *in the Lord* (20). The failure of Philemon to respond appropriately will add to Paul's burdens, seriously misrepresent Christianity, and discredit the gospel before unbelievers.

However, the Apostle's confidence seems to have grown as he has built his appeal, and he feels sure that Philemon will do *more* than he has actually asked (21). What this *more than I say* means is unclear. Some think it suggests the emancipation of Onesimus (cf. Introduction); others think it is a veiled compliment to Philemon's goodwill and character. Whatever Paul may have in mind, he is asking Philemon to receive and love Onesimus as a brother in the same way that he loves Paul and other brothers in Christ. *Obedience* may be a veiled reference to Paul's "apostolic authority." Paul is not asking Philemon to be obedient to him, however, but rather to the gospel.

Though we do not know for certain just what Philemon's response was in detail, we may be confident it was a positive one. As observed earlier, the fact that this Epistle has been preserved for us is strong evidence that Paul's delicate and beautiful appeal was heeded and Onesimus was accorded an appropriately Christian reception.

Closing Words and Benediction
Philemon 22-25

Philemon 22-25

> 22 But withal prepare me also a lodging: for I trust that through your prayers I shall be given unto you.
> 23 There salute thee Epaphras, my fellowprisoner in Christ Jesus;
> 24 Marcus, Aristarchus, Demas, Lucas, my fellowlabourers.
> 25 The grace of our Lord Jesus Christ be with your spirit. Amen.

The final words of this intriguing Epistle indicate the optimism which was fostered by the faith of the Apostle. He seems to be expecting a speedy release from imprisonment and purposes to sojourn with Philemon. If Paul visited Philemon he would see how Onesimus had been received, a possibility which should motivate Philemon to grant Paul's request. The *lodging* he desires may be either quarters in an inn or a room in a private house. Philemon would no doubt arrange to entertain the Apostle in his own home. The request for a room may have been a spontaneous word of encouragement to the saints at Colossae praying for him, as if to say, "Before you know it I may be needing your guest chamber" (E. F. Scott).

Your prayers (22) is plural and marks a return to the plural of the salutation. The word *trust* is literally "hope" in the Greek. Paul hopes to be able to visit them but does not presume to receive special favors from the Divine. Nonetheless, whatever the outcome, he is confident of the effectiveness of the prayers of all the Colossian saints on his behalf. He may have received information that his case will soon receive a hearing by the imperial court. When writing to the Philippians, probably shortly after, he implies that the trial is already in progress and that a verdict is expected soon. He also promised the Philippians a visit before very long (Phil. 2:23-24). Evidently his earlier plans to go to Spain directly from Rome (Rom. 15:22-24) had been altered during the intervening years.

It is surprising that in this brief letter Paul refers to 10 other persons. Five were mentioned earlier: Timothy, Philemon, Apphia, Archippus, and Onesimus. Verses 23 and 24 list five others. Epaphras is described as *my fellowprisoner,* [10] suggesting that he also is in prison, though we have no details. He had a part in founding the church at Colossae (Col. 1:7-8) and was much trusted by Paul. His name is a contraction for Epaphroditus, but he is not to be confused with the person from Philippi bearing that name and spoken of in the Philippian letter (2:25). The other four—Marcus (Mark), Aristarchus, Demas, and Lucas (Luke)—also greet the church at Colossae, and all we know about them is mentioned in comments on Colossians. They are designated, with Philemon himself (1), as Paul's *fellowlabourers* (24). It has been observed that the list of names runs "the gamut from wealth to poverty, educated to uneducated."

The concluding benediction is similar in form and content to that used in Paul's other Epistles. However, there is an interesting divergence at its close, found only here and in the Epistles to the Galatians and the Philippians. Paul says *with your spirit,* instead of the usual "with you" or "with you all." While the meaning is not different, the words underscore the fact that *the grace of our Lord Jesus Christ* has as its sphere of operation the spirit of man. "*Grace* is thus Paul's final benediction for his readers; in that one word there is included all that is good and true for them in the household of Philemon, all that can ever surpass their desirings and their deservings."[11]

Reference Notes

THE EPISTLE TO THE PHILIPPIANS

Abbreviations:
DSBS *Daily Study Bible Series*
EGT   *Expositor's Greek Testament*
IB   *Interpreter's Bible*
NBC   *New Bible Commentary*

1. *Clement's First Letter,* 47:1-2; Ignatius' *Letter to the Smyrneans,* 4:2; 11:3; Polycarp's *Letter to the Philippians,* 3:1-5; *Letter to Diognetus,* 5:1-9.

2. J. B. Lightfoot, *St. Paul's Epistle to the Philippians,* 8th ed. (London: Macmillan Co., 1888), 30-46. Such an argument is tenuous and at most only indicates that one can continue to maintain style and convictions arrived at much earlier.

3. H. A. A. Kennedy, "The Epistle to the Philippians," *Expositor's Greek Testament* (EGT), ed. W. Robertson Nicoll (Grand Rapids: Wm. B. Eerdmans Publishing Co., n.d.), 3:400. Cf. also M. R. Vincent, *Word Studies in the New Testament* (New York: Charles Scribner's Sons, 1914), 3:414.

4. Lightfoot, *Philippians,* 53-54. For a summary of the character of all the Macedonian churches, cf. J. B. Lightfoot, *Biblical Essays* (New York: Macmillan Co., 1904), 235-50.

5. Paul's first visit to Philippi after Acts 16 and 17 was while he was on his way from Ephesus to Corinth ca. A.D. 56 (1 Cor. 16:5). His second occurred on leaving Corinth the following spring, A.D. 57, when he observed Easter at Philippi (Acts 20:1-6). On the first of these visits Paul was suffering bodily illness and apparently anxiety over the Corinthian or Galatian trouble. Philippi (2 Cor. 1:8-11; 2:12-13; 7:4-12) may have served as a place of respite for him, thereby deepening his tender relationship to this congregation.

6. H. C. G. Moule, *Philippian Studies* (New York: A. C. Armstrong and Son, 1897), 5.

7. J. Hugh Michael, *The Epistle of Paul to the Philippians,* in

The Moffatt New Testament Commentary (New York: Harper and Bros., 1927), 2.

8. Robert R. Wicks, "The Epistle to the Philippians" (Exposition), *The Interpreter's Bible* (IB), ed. George A. Buttrick et al. (New York: Abingdon-Cokesbury Press, 1955), 11:16.

9. B. C. Caffin, "Letter to the Philippians" (Exposition), *The Pulpit Commentary,* ed. H. D. M. Spence and Joseph S. Exell (Grand Rapids: Wm. B. Eerdmans Publishing Co., 1950), 20:2.

10. Francis Davidson, "Letter to the Philippians," *The New Bible Commentary* (NBC), ed. F. Davidson (Grand Rapids: Wm. B. Eerdmans Publishing Co., 1960), 1034.

11. "Letter to the Philippians," *Matthew Henry Commentary* (New York: Fleming H. Revell Co., n.d.), 6:723-24.

12. E. F. Scott, "The Epistle to the Philippians" (Exegesis), IB, 11:20; also see Davidson, NBC, 1034.

13. Chrysostom, "Homilies on the Epistle of St. Paul to the Philippians" (Homily 1, Phil. 1:1-2), *Nicene and Post-Nicene Fathers,* ed. Philip Schaff (Grand Rapids: Wm. B. Eerdmans Publishing Co., 1956), 13:185.

14. William Barclay, *The Letter to the Philippians, Colossians, and Thessalonians,* 2nd ed., in *Daily Study Bible Series* (DSBS) (Philadelphia: Westminster Press, 1959), 14. For a slightly varying enumeration cf. Charles R. Erdman, *Commentaries on the New Testament: The Epistle of Paul to the Philippians* (Philadelphia: Westminster Press, 1932), 35.

15. Lightfoot, *Philippians,* 84.

16. R. P. Martin, *The Epistle of Paul to the Philippians,* in *The Tyndale New Testament Commentaries* (Grand Rapids: Wm. B. Eerdmans Publishing Co., 1959), 62-64.

17. EGT, 3:420.

18. Paul Rees, *The Adequate Man* (Westwood, N.J.: Fleming H. Revell Co., 1959), 21.

19. "The Epistle of Paul the Apostle to the Philippians," *Adam Clarke's Commentary* (New York: Abingdon Press, n.d.), 6:490.

20. A. T. Robertson, *Word Pictures in the New Testament* (New York: Harper and Bros., 1931), 4:437.

21. EGT, 3:423.

22. Vincent, *Word Studies,* 3:419.

23. EGT, 3:423.

24. Vincent, *Word Studies,* 3:421.

25. D. D. Whedon, *Commentary on the New Testament* (New York: Nelson and Phillips, 1875), 4:318.

26. Barclay, DSBS, 38.

27. Bernhard Weiss, "The Present Status of the Inquiry Concerning the Genuineness of the Pauline Epistles," *American Journal of Theology* 1, no. 2 (April 1897): 388-89.

28. Verses 16 and 17 are reversed in the best manuscripts, with the exception of the opening words of each: *hoi men* (16) and *hoi de* (17).

29. Michael, *Philippians,* 48.

30. Vincent, *Word Studies,* 3:679; Rees, *Adequate Man,* 27.

31. H. A. W. Meyer, *Critical and Exegetical Handbook to the Epistles to the Philippians and Colossians and to Philemon* (New York: Funk and Wagnalls, 1889), 31.

32. Quoted by Barclay, DSBS, 32.

33. John Eadie, *A Commentary on the Greek Text of the Epistle of Paul to the Philippians* (New York: Robert Carter and Bros., 1859), 51.

34. A. T. Robertson, *Word Pictures,* 4:440.

35. J. W. C. Wand, *The New Testament Letters* (London: Oxford University Press, 1946), 129.

36. *The Great Texts of the Bible,* ed. James Hastings (New York: Charles Scribner's Sons, 1913), 17:272.

37. Robert Rainy, "Epistle to the Philippians," *An Exposition of the Bible* (Hartford, Conn.: S. S. Scranton and Co., 1903), 6:127.

38. Alexander Maclaren, *Exposition of Holy Scripture* (Grand Rapids: Wm. B. Eerdmans Publishing Co., 1952), 14:204.

39. *A Commentary, Critical and Explanatory, on the Old and New Testaments,* Robert Jamieson, A. R. Fausset, and David Brown (Hartford, Conn.: S. S. Scranton and Co., n.d.): A. R. Fausset, "The Epistle of Paul the Apostle to the Philippians," 2:362.

40. Chrysostom, "Homilies" (Homily 4, 1:22-26), 13:199.

41. Michael, *Philippians,* 65.

42. Ibid., 70.

43. Vincent, *Word Studies,* 3:427-28.

44. Michael, *Philippians,* 76.

45. EGT, 3:28.

46. Cf. James Alexander Robertson, "The Epistle to the Philippians," *The Abingdon Bible Commentary,* ed. Carl Eiselen et al. (New York: Abingdon-Cokesbury Press, 1929), 1244; also John Peter Lange, *Commentary on the Holy Scriptures,* trans. and ed. Philip Schaff (1870; reprint, Grand Rapids: Zondervan Publishing House, n.d.), Phil. 2:1.

47. Albert Barnes, *Notes on the New Testament, Explanatory and Practical: Philippians,* ed. Robert Frew (Grand Rapids: Baker Book House, 1950), 165.

48. Fausset, "Philippians," 2:363.

49. H. C. G. Moule, *Cambridge Bible on Philippians* (Cambridge: University Press, 1895), 63.

50. F. W. Beare, *A Commentary on the Epistle to the Philippians,* Harper Torchbook Commentaries (New York: Harper and Brothers, 1959), 73.

51. IB (Exegesis), 11:48.

52. John F. Walvoord, *To Live Is Christ: An Exposition of the Epistle of Paul to the Philippians* (Findlay, Ohio: Dunham Publishing Co., 1961), 43.

53. A. T. Robertson, *Paul's Joy in Christ: Studies in Philippians,* rev. ed. (Nashville: Broadman Press, 1959), 72.

54. Beare, *Philippians,* 84.

55. A. T. Robertson, *Paul's Joy in Christ,* 75.

56. IB (Exegesis), 11:50-51.

57. Walvoord, *To Live Is Christ,* 47.

58. A. T. Robertson, *Paul's Joy in Christ,* 83.

59. Michael, *Philippians,* 108-9.

60. Barnes, *Notes,* 181.

61. Philip Doddridge, *The Family Expositor,* 8th London ed. (Charleston, Mass.: S. Etheridges, 1808), 5:213.

62. IB (Exegesis), 11:68.

63. A. T. Robertson, *Paul's Joy in Christ,* 95.

64. J. A. Robertson, "Philippians," 1246.

65. Fausett, "Philippians," 2:366.

66. Karl Barth, *The Epistle to the Philippians* (Richmond, Va.: John Knox Press, 1962), 26.

67. Walvoord, *To Live Is Christ,* 63-64.

68. EGT, 3:450.

69. Michael, *Philippians,* 148.

70. J. N. Darby, *Synopsis of the Books of the Bible* (New York: Loizeaux Brothers, n.d.), 4:490.

71. Quoted in J. A. Robertson, "Philippians," 1247.

72. *Holiness the Finished Foundation* (Winona Lake, Ind.: Light and Life Press, 1963), 94.

73. Ralph A. Guinn, *The Biblical Expositor,* ed. C. F. H. Henry (Philadelphia: A. J. Holman Co., 1960), 3:318.

74. A. T. Robertson, *Word Pictures,* 4:456.

75. Meyer, *Exegetical Handbook,* 146.

76. C. Latley, *A Catholic Commentary on Holy Scripture,* ed. Dom. Bernard Orchard (New York: Thomas Nelson and Sons, 1953), 1130.

77. Thomas Manton (d. 1667), "Lectures on James," *The Bible-Work: The New Testament,* ed. J. Glentworth Butler (New York: Funk and Wagnalls Publishers, 1883), 2:461.

78. IB (Exegesis), 11:103.

79. J. R. Dummelow, ed., *A Commentary on the Holy Bible* (New York: Macmillan Co., 1943), 977.

80. Cf. Michael, *Philippians,* 196; Fausset, "Philippians," 2:368.

81. George Williams, *The Student's Commentary on the Holy Scriptures,* 5th ed. (Grand Rapids: Kregel Publications, 1953), 964.

82. Henry Alford, *The Greek Testament,* 3rd ed. (London: Revingtons, Waterloo Place, 1862), 3:192.

83. James C. Gray and George M. Adams, *Gray and Adams Bible Commentary* (Grand Rapids: Zondervan Publishing Co., n.d.), 312.

84. Cf. A. T. Robertson, *Word Pictures,* 461.

85. Dummelow, ed., *Commentary,* 978.

86. Michael, *Philippians,* 226.

Abbreviations:

    BBC   *Beacon Bible Commentary*
    CBC   *Cambridge Bible Commentary*
    DSBS *Daily Study Bible Series*
    EGT   *Expositor's Greek Testament*
    IB   *Interpreter's Bible*
    NICNT *New International Commentary on the New Testament*
    PNTS *Proclaiming the New Testament Series*

1. John Eadie, *Commentary on the Epistle of Paul to the Colossians* (1856; reprint, Grand Rapids: Zondervan Publishing House, 1957), xxii.

2. Ibid., xxix.

3. H. Dermot McDonald, *Commentary on Colossians and Philemon* (Waco, Tex.: Word Books, 1980), 18.

4. G. H. P. Thompson, *The Letters of Paul to the Ephesians, to the Colossians, and to Philemon,* in *The Cambridge Bible Commentary* (CBC), ed. P. R. Ackroyd et al. (Cambridge: University Press, 1967), 107.

5. Francis W. Beare, "The Epistle to the Colossians," *The Interpreter's Bible* (IB), ed. George A. Buttrick et al. (New York: Abingdon Press, 1955), 11:134.

6. Paul S. Rees, *The Epistles to the Philippians, Colossians, and Philemon,* in *Proclaiming the New Testament Series* (PNTS) (Grand Rapids: Baker Book House, 1964), 81.

7. John B. Nielson, "Colossians," *Beacon Bible Commentary* (BBC), ed. A. F. Harper et al. (Kansas City: Beacon Hill Press, 1965), 9:364.

8. Robert Rainy, "Epistle to the Philippians," *An Exposition of the Bible* (Hartford, Conn.: S. S. Scranton and Co., 1903), 6:116.

9. William Barclay, *The Letters to the Philippians, Colossians, and Thessalonians,* 2nd ed., in *The Daily Study Bible Series* (DSBS) (Philadelphia: Westminster Press, 1959), 8.

10. Alexander Maclaren, *The Epistles of St. Paul to the Colossians and Philemon,* in *The Expositor's Bible,* ed. W. Robertson Nicoll (New York: Eaton and Mains, n.d.), 27.

11. Barclay, *Colossians,* DSBS, 127.

12. A. S. Peake, "The Epistle to the Colossians," *The Expositor's Greek Testament* (EGT) (Grand Rapids: Wm. B. Eerdmans Publishing Co., n.d.), 3:499.

13. Ibid., 500.

14. Joseph Henry Thayer, ed. and trans., *Greek-English Lexicon of the New Testament,* rev. ed. (New York: Harper and Bros., 1889), 175.

15. Hermann Kleinknecht in Gerhardt Kittel, ed., *Theological Dictionary of the New Testament,* trans. and ed. Geoffrey W. Bromiley (Grand Rapids: Wm. B. Eerdmans Publishing Co., 1964), 2:389.

16. J. B. Lightfoot, *St. Paul's Epistles to the Colossians and to Philemon* (London: Macmillan Co., 1884), 146-47.

17. A. T. Robertson, *Paul and the Intellectuals: The Epistle to the Colossians,* rev. ed. (Nashville: Broadman Press, 1959), 45.

18. T. K. Abbott, *The Epistles to the Ephesians and to the Colossians,* in *The International Critical Commentary* (Edinburgh: T. and T. Clark, 1897), 216.

19. E. K. Simpson and F. F. Bruce, *Commentary on the Epistles to the Ephesians and the Colossians,* in *New International Commentary on the New Testament* (NICNT), ed. F. F. Bruce (Grand Rapids: Wm. B. Eerdmans Publishing Co., 1957), 197-98.

20. Herbert M. Carson, *Commentary on the Epistles of Paul to the Colossians and Philemon* (Grand Rapids: Wm. B. Eerdmans Publishing Co., 1960), 44.

21. William Hendriksen, *Epistles to the Colossians and Philemon* (Grand Rapids: Baker Book House, 1964).

22. Thompson, "Ephesians, Colossians, Philemon," CBC, 136.

23. Charles R. Erdman, *The Epistles of Paul to the Colossians and to Philemon* (Philadelphia: Westminster Press, 1933), 52.

24. McDonald, *Colossians and Philemon,* 55.

25. Rees, *Philippians, Colossians, Philemon,* PNTS, 79.

26. Robertson, *Paul and the Intellectuals,* 55-56.

27. C. J. Ellicott, *A Critical and Grammatical Commentary on Philippians, Colossians, and Philemon* (Andover, Mass.: Warren F. Draper, 1884), 145.

28. Simpson and Bruce, *Ephesians and Colossians,* NICNT, 213.

29. A. T. Robertson, *Word Pictures in the New Testament* (New York: Harper and Bros., 1931), 4:482-83.

30. Maclaren, *Colossians and Philemon,* 102.

31. G. Preston MacLeod, "Colossians," IB, 11:175.

32. Robertson, *Paul and the Intellectuals,* 64.

33. Ralph Earle, *Word Meanings in the New Testament* (Kansas City: Beacon Hill Press of Kansas City, 1977), 5:78.

34. MacLeod, "Colossians," IB, 11:180.

35. Maclaren, *Colossians and Philemon,* loc. cit.

36. Everett F. Harrison, *Colossians: Christ All Sufficient* (Chicago: Moody Press, 1971), 46.

37. Rees, *Philippians, Colossians, Philemon,* PNTS, 92.

38. Ibid., 93-94.

39. Robertson, *Paul and the Intellectuals,* 73.

40. Beare, "Colossians," IB, 11:187.

41. Barclay, *Colossians,* DSBS, 166.

42. McDonald, *Colossians and Philemon,* 78.

43. Harrison, *Colossians,* 58.

44. Thompson, *Ephesians, Colossians, Philemon,* CBC, 144.

45. Peake, "Colossians," EGT, 3:524.

46. Robertson, *Paul and the Intellectuals,* 82.

47. Thompson, *Ephesians, Colossians, Philemon,* CBC, 147.

48. Eadie, *Colossians,* 172.

49. McDonald, *Colossians and Philemon,* 87-88.

50. Gary Demarest, *Colossians: The Mystery of God in Us* (Waco, Tex.: Word Books, 1979), 116.

51. Eadie, *Colossians,* 180.

52. Demarest, *Colossians,* 134.

53. Eadie, *Colossians,* 206.

54. Maclaren, *Colossians and Philemon,* loc. cit.

55. Rees, *Philippians, Colossians, Philemon,* PNTS, 99.

56. Eadie, *Colossians,* 215.

57. Rees, *Philippians, Colossians, Philemon,* PNTS, 100.

58. Ibid., 101.

59. Ibid., 102.

60. McDonald, *Colossians and Philemon*, 111.

61. Robertson, *Paul and the Intellectuals*, 112.

62. Barclay, *Colossians*, DSBS, 192-93.

63. Harrison, *Colossians*, 122 (citing L. B. Radford, *The Epistle to the Colossians*, 308).

The Epistle to Philemon

1. John Knox, along with others, thinks the "deeper purpose" of the letter is to secure Onesimus' return to Paul. This view is based on such considerations as the fact that Paul does not mention anything about repentance on the part of the slave, and makes no explicit appeal for forgiveness on the part of the master. Further, Paul distinctly says he wants more than he requests (21), meaning Onesimus' return. Also, Paul's use of terms with a certain legal or commercial connotation gives the letter a "quasi-business character." (See *Interpreter's Bible*.)

2. P. B. Fitzwater, *Preaching and Teaching in the New Testament* (Chicago: Moody Press, 1957), 531.

3. Alexander Maclaren, *Expositions of Holy Scripture*, vol. 10 (Grand Rapids: Wm. B. Eerdmans Publishing Co., 1952), loc. cit.

4. Glenn W. Barker, Wm. L. Lane, and J. Ramsey Michaels, *The New Testament Speaks* (New York: Harper and Row Publishers, 1969), 211.

5. See ibid., 212.

6. D. Edmond Hiebert, *Titus and Philemon* (Chicago: Moody Press, 1957), 94.

7. Maxie D. Dunnam, *Communicator's Commentary: Galatians, Ephesians, Philippians, Colossians, and Philemon*, ed. Lloyd J. Ogilvie (Waco, Tex.: Word Books Publishers, 1982), loc. cit.

8. Hiebert, *Titus and Philemon*, 116.

9. Dunnam, *Communicator's Commentary*, 413.

10. The word Paul uses to describe Epaphras is *sunaichmalotos*, which denotes a "prisoner of war." In verse 2 he speaks of Archippus as *desmios* ("our fellow soldier") which means locked in a cell or dungeon. The Apostle may be viewing himself as

being engaged in a war for Christ's sake and as being a battle casualty.

11. H. Dermot McDonald, *Commentary on Colossians and Philemon* (Waco, Tex.: Word Books Publishers, 1980), 193.

Bibliography

THE EPISTLE TO THE PHILIPPIANS

Alford, Henry. *The Greek Testament.* Vol. 3. 3rd ed. London: Revingtons, Waterloo Place, 1862.

Baillie, D. M. *God Was in Christ.* New York: Charles Scribner's Sons, 1948.

Barclay, William. *The Letters to the Philippians, Colossians, and Thessalonians.* 2nd ed. *The Daily Study Bible Series.* Philadelphia: Westminster Press, 1959.

Barnes, Albert. *Notes on the New Testament, Explanatory and Practical: Philippians.* Edited by Robert Frew. Grand Rapids: Baker Book House, 1950.

Barth, Karl. *The Epistle to the Philippians.* Richmond, Va.: John Knox Press, 1962.

Beare, F. W. *A Commentary on the Epistle to the Philippians.* Harper Torchbook Commentaries. New York: Harper and Bros., 1959.

Bruce, A. B. *The Humiliation of Christ.* New York: A. C. Armstrong and Son, 1907.

Caffin, B. C. "Letter to the Philippians" (Exposition). *The Pulpit Commentary.* Edited by H. D. M. Spence and Joseph S. Exell. Vol. 20. Grand Rapids: Wm. B. Eerdmans Publishing Co., 1950.

Chrysostom. "Homilies on the Epistle of St. Paul to the Philippians." *Nicene and Post-Nicene Fathers of the Christian Church.* Edited by Philip Schaff. Vol. 13. Grand Rapids: Wm. B. Eerdmans Publishing Co., 1956.

Clarke, Adam. *The New Testament of Our Lord and Saviour Jesus Christ.* Vol. 2. New York: Abingdon-Cokesbury Press, n.d.

Darby, J. N. *Synopsis of the Books of the Bible.* Vol. 4. New York: Loizeaux Brothers, n.d.

Davidson, Francis. "Letter to the Philippians." *The New Bible

Commentary. Edited by F. Davidson. Grand Rapids: Wm. B. Eerdmans Publishing Co., 1960.

Doddridge, Philip. *The Family Expositor.* Vol. 5. 8th London ed. Charleston, Mass.: S. Etheridges, 1808.

Dummelow, J. R., ed. *A Commentary on the Holy Bible.* New York: Macmillan Co., 1943.

Eadie, John. *A Commentary on the Greek Text of the Epistle of Paul to the Philippians.* New York: Robert Carter and Bros., 1859.

Earle, Ralph. *Word Meanings in the New Testament.* 6 vols. Kansas City: Beacon Hill Press of Kansas City, 1974-84.

Erdman, Charles. *The Epistle of Paul to the Philippians.* In *Commentaries on the New Testament.* Philadelphia: Westminster Press, 1932.

Fausset, A. R. "The Epistle of Paul the Apostle to the Philippians." *A Commentary . . . on the Old and New Testaments,* by Robert Jamieson, A. R. Fausset, and David Brown. Vol. 2. Hartford, Conn.: S. S. Scranton and Co., n.d.

Finlayson, R. "Letter to the Philippians" (Homilies). *The Pulpit Commentary.* Edited by H. D. M. Spence and Joseph S. Exell. Vol. 20. Grand Rapids: Wm. B. Eerdmans Publishing Co., 1950.

Fletcher, John W. *The Works of the Rev. John William Fletcher.* Vol. 1. New York: Waugh and Mason, 1833.

Gray, James C., and Adams, George M. *Gray and Adams Bible Commentary.* Grand Rapids: Zondervan Publishing Co., n.d.

Guinn, Ralph A. *The Biblical Expositor.* Edited by C. F. H. Henry. Philadelphia: A. J. Holman Co., 1960.

Hastings, James, ed. *The Great Texts of the Bible.* New York: Charles Scribner's Sons, 1913.

Henry, Matthew. *Commentary on the Whole Bible.* Vol. 6. New York: Fleming H. Revell Co., n.d.

Kennedy, H. A. A. "The Epistle to the Philippians." *Expositor's Greek Testament.* Edited by W. Robertson Nicoll. Vol. 3. Grand Rapids: Wm. B. Eerdmans Publishing Co., n.d.

Lange, John Peter. *Commentary on the Holy Scriptures.* Translated and edited by Philip Schaff. 1870. Reprint. Grand Rapids: Zondervan Publishing House, n.d.

Latley, C. *A Catholic Commentary on Holy Scripture.* Edited by Dom. Bernard Orchard. New York: Thomas Nelson and Sons, 1953.

Lightfoot, J. B. *St. Paul's Epistle to the Philippians.* 8th ed. London: Macmillan Co., 1888.

―――. *Biblical Essays.* New York: Macmillan Co., 1904.

Maclaren, Alexander. *Expositions of Holy Scripture.* Vol. 14. Reprint. Grand Rapids: Wm. B. Eerdmans Publishing Co., 1952.

Meyer, H. A. W. *Critical and Exegetical Handbook to the Epistles to the Philippians and Colossians and to Philemon.* New York: Funk and Wagnalls, 1889.

Michael, J. Hugh. *The Epistle of Paul to the Philippians. The Moffatt New Testament Commentary.* New York: Harper and Bros., 1927.

Morgan, G. Campbell. *The Unfolding Message of the Bible.* Westwood, N.J.: Fleming H. Revell Co., 1961.

Moule, H. C. G. *Cambridge Bible on Philippians.* Cambridge: University Press, 1895.

―――. *Philippian Studies.* New York: A. C. Armstrong and Son, 1897.

Rainy, Robert. "Epistle to the Philippians." *An Exposition of the Bible.* Vol. 6. Hartford, Conn.: S. S. Scranton and Co., 1903.

Rees, Paul. *The Adequate Man.* Westwood, N.J.: Fleming H. Revell Co., 1959.

Robertson, A. T. *Paul's Joy in Christ: Studies in Philippians.* Rev. ed. Nashville: Broadman Press, 1959.

―――. *Word Pictures in the New Testament.* Vol. 4. New York: Harper and Bros., 1931.

Robertson, J. A. "The Epistle to the Philippians." *The Abingdon Bible Commentary.* Edited by Carl Eiselen et al. New York: Abingdon-Cokesbury Press, 1929.

Scott, E. F. "The Epistle to the Philippians" (Exegesis). *Interpreter's Bible.* Edited by George A. Buttrick et al. Vol. 11. New York: Abingdon-Cokesbury Press, 1951.

Vincent, M. R. *Word Studies in the New Testament.* Vol. 3. New York: Charles Scribner's Sons, 1914.

Walvoord, John F. *To Live Is Christ: An Exposition of the Epistle of*

Paul to the Philippians. Findlay, Ohio: Dunham Publishing Co., 1961.

Wand, J. W. C. *The New Testament Letters.* London: Oxford University Press, 1946.

Whedon, D. D. *Commentary on the New Testament.* Vol. 4. New York: Nelson and Phillips, 1875.

Wicks, Robert R. "The Epistle to the Philippians" (Exposition). *The Interpreter's Bible.* Edited by George A. Buttrick et al. Vol. 11. New York: Abingdon-Cokesbury Press, 1955.

Williams, George. *The Student's Commentary on the Holy Scriptures.* 5th ed. Grand Rapids: Kregel Publications, 1953.

Articles

Weiss, Bernhard. "The Present Status of the Inquiry Concerning the Genuineness of the Pauline Epistles." *American Journal of Theology* 1, no. 2 (April 1897): 388-89.

THE EPISTLE TO THE COLOSSIANS

Abbott, T. K. *The Epistles to the Ephesians and to the Colossians. The International Critical Commentary.* Edinburgh: T. and T. Clark, 1897.

Barclay, William. *The Letters to the Philippians, Colossians, and Thessalonians.* 2nd ed. In *The Daily Study Bible Series.* Philadelphia: Westminster Press, 1959.

Beare, Francis W. "The Epistle to the Colossians." *The Interpreter's Bible.* Edited by George A. Buttrick et al. New York: Abingdon-Cokesbury Press, 1955.

Carson, Herbert M. *Commentary on the Epistles of Paul to the Colossians and Philemon.* Grand Rapids: Wm. B. Eerdmans Publishing Co., 1960.

Demarest, Gary. *Colossians: The Mystery of God in Us.* Waco, Tex.: Word Books, 1979.

Eadie, John. *Commentary on the Epistle of Paul to the Colossians.* 1856. Reprint. Grand Rapids: Zondervan Publishing House, 1957.

Ellicott, C. J. *A Critical and Grammatical Commentary on Philippians, Colossians, and Philemon.* Andover, Mass.: Warren F. Draper, 1884.

Erdman, Charles R. *The Epistles of Paul to the Colossians and to Philemon*. Philadelphia: Westminster Press, 1933.

Harrison, Everett F. *Colossians: Christ All Sufficient*. Chicago: Moody Press, 1971.

Hendriksen, William. *Epistles to the Colossians and Philemon*. Grand Rapids: Baker Book House, 1964.

Kittel, Gerhardt, ed. *Theological Dictionary of the New Testament*. Translated and edited by Geoffrey W. Bromiley. Grand Rapids: Wm. B. Eerdmans Publishing Co., 1964.

Lightfoot, J. B. *St. Paul's Epistles to the Colossians and to Philemon*. London: Macmillan Co., 1884.

Lohse, Eduard. *A Commentary on the Epistles to the Colossians and Philemon*. Edited by Helmut Koester. Philadelphia: Fortress Press, 1971.

McDonald, H. Dermot. *Commentary on Colossians and Philemon*. Waco, Tex.: Word Books, 1980.

Maclaren, Alexander. *The Epistles of St. Paul to the Colossians and Philemon*. In *The Expositor's Bible*. Edited by W. Robertson Nicoll. New York: Eaton and Mains, n.d.

MacLeod, G. Preston. "Colossians." *The Interpreter's Bible*. Edited by George A. Buttrick et al. New York: Abingdon-Cokesbury Press, 1955.

Nielson, John B. "Colossians." *Beacon Bible Commentary*. Edited by A. F. Harper et al. Vol. 9. Kansas City: Beacon Hill Press, 1965.

Peake, A. S. "The Epistle to the Colossians." *The Expositor's Greek Testament*. Vol. 3. Grand Rapids: Wm. B. Eerdmans Publishing Co., n.d.

Rainy, Robert. "Epistle to the Philippians." *An Exposition of the Bible*. Vol. 6. Hartford, Conn.: S. S. Scranton and Co., 1903.

Rees, Paul S. *The Epistles to the Philippians, Colossians, and Philemon*. In *Proclaiming the New Testament Series*. Grand Rapids: Baker Book House, 1964.

Robertson, A. T. *Paul and the Intellectuals: The Epistle to the Colossians*. Rev. ed. Nashville: Broadman Press, 1959.

———. *Word Pictures in the New Testament*. New York: Harper and Bros., 1931.

Simpson, E. K., and Bruce, F. F. *Commentary on the Epistles to the*

Ephesians and the Colossians. In *New International Commentary on the New Testament.* Edited by F. F. Bruce. Grand Rapids: Wm. B. Eerdmans Publishing Co., 1957.

Thayer, Joseph Henry, ed. and trans. *Greek-English Lexicon of the New Testament.* Rev. ed. New York: Harper and Bros., 1889.

Thompson, G. H. P. *The Letters of Paul to the Ephesians, to the Colossians, and to Philemon.* In *The Cambridge Bible Commentary.* Edited by P. R. Ackroyd et al. Cambridge: University Press, 1967.

THE EPISTLE TO PHILEMON

Barker, Glenn W.; Lane, Wm. L.; and Michaels, J. Ramsey. *The New Testament Speaks.* New York: Harper and Row Publishers, 1969.

Dunnam, Maxie D. *Communicator's Commentary: Galatians, Ephesians, Philippians, Colossians, and Philemon.* Edited by Lloyd J. Ogilvie. Waco, Tex.: Word Books Publishers, 1982.

Fitzwater, P. B. *Preaching and Teaching in the New Testament.* Chicago: Moody Press, 1957.

Hiebert, D. Edmond. *Titus and Philemon.* Chicago: Moody Press, 1957.

Knox, John. "The Epistle to Philemon." *The Interpreter's Bible.* Edited by George A. Buttrick et al. Vol. 11. New York: Abingdon-Cokesbury Press, 1955.

McDonald, H. Dermot. *Commentary on Colossians and Philemon.* Waco, Tex.: Word Books Publishers, 1980.

Maclaren, Alexander. *Expositions of Holy Scripture.* Vol. 10. Grand Rapids: Wm. B. Eerdmans Publishing Co., 1952.